Terrorism

Terrorism

The Self-Fulfilling Prophecy

JOSEBA ZULAIKA

THE UNIVERSITY OF CHICAGO PRESS   CHICAGO AND LONDON

JOSEBA ZULAIKA is professor at the Center for Basque Studies at the University of Nevada, Reno. He is the author of fourteen previous books, including *Basque Violence* and *Terror and Taboo.*

The University of Chicago Press, Chicago 60637
The University of Chicago Press, Ltd., London
© 2009 by The University of Chicago
All rights reserved. Published 2009
Printed in the United States of America
18 17 16 15 14 13 12 11 10 09   1 2 3 4 5

ISBN-13: 978-0-226-99415-4 (cloth)
ISBN-13: 978-0-226-99416-1 (paper)
ISBN-10: 0-226-99415-5 (cloth)
ISBN-10: 0-226-99416-3 (paper)

Library of Congress Cataloging-in-Publication Data

Zulaika, Joseba.
  Terrorism : the self-fulfilling prophecy / Joseba Zulaika.
    p. cm.
  Includes bibliographical references and index.
  ISBN-13: 978-0-226-99415-4 (cloth : alk. paper)
  ISBN-13: 978-0-226-99416-1 (pbk. : alk. paper)
  ISBN-10: 0-226-99415-5 (cloth : alk. paper)
  ISBN-10: 0-226-99416-3 (pbk. : alk. paper) 1. Terrorism–Prevention. 2. Terrorism—
Government policy. 3. War on Terrorism, 2001– 4. Discourse analysis. I. Title.
  HV6431 .Z853   2010
  363.325—dc22

                                                                        2009010358

♾ The paper used in this publication meets the minimum requirements of the American
National Standard for Information Sciences—Permanence of Paper for Printed Library
Materials, ANSI Z39.48-1992.

FOR MARITXU ERLANZ DE GULLER
FOR HER PROPHECIES

Contents

Acknowledgments

I owe Richard Jackson the original impetus for this book. Following his invitation to speak at Manchester University, he asked me to turn my paper "Read My Terrorist Desire" into a monograph. I wrote this book to keep my word to him.

The text owes the most to my colleague and friend William Douglass. He has edited practically every page I have written in English and his contribution is by now constitutive of my very style. He has no time to spare but spent many weeks editing this work—caring for the writing and the thinking, thus extending our long collaboration in articulating a critical view of terrorism discourse. I stopped thanking him long ago, for this is no longer a matter of collegial duty, but the gratuitous excess of the gift of friendship. Only nonnative writers can fully appreciate how lucky I am.

An initial conversation with Leonard Weinberg was most helpful. My colleagues Richard Siegel and Robert Winzeler read the manuscript and made extensive and sharp comments; I am grateful to them although I did not adequately respond to all of their concerns. Andreas Hess, Robert English, and Cameron Watson read the text and challenged me to clarify some of my positions; I am much indebted to them. Two anonymous reviewers from the University of Chicago Press asked relevant questions that led to significant revisions. My gratitude to the editor, David Brent, for believing in the manuscript is everlasting.

I owe a debt of gratitude to Elixabete Garmendia and Juanjo Dorronsoro for the background they provided for my chapter on Yoyes. In the final stretch, I was greatly helped by Garazi Zulaika, who read parts of the manuscript and made valuable corrections; and in particular by Mariann Vaczi, who incisively edited the entire text, solving many issues of form and content. John Raymond did a superb job in copyediting it.

The Center for Basque Studies at the University of Nevada, Reno's Getchell Library has provided me a perfect setting for scholarly work. I could not have been more fortunate. I am deeply thankful to the library staff who attended me over the years. I am most grateful to my colleagues at the Center—Carmelo Urza, Sandra Ott, Xabier Irujo, Mari Jose Olaziregi, and Eric Herzik—for their many forms of intellectual feedback and professional assistance. I cannot thank enough the Center's office manager, Kate Camino, publication editor, Jill Berner, and librarian, Marimar Ubeda, who have helped me unfailingly in so many ways. Finally, I could not have written this book without the personal and intellectual company of Goretti Etxaniz and the guitar music of Joannes Zulaika—I owe them the deepest gratitude.

An early version of chapter 5 was first published as "Retorno y profecía de Yoyes," in *Polvo de ETA*, Joseba Zulaika (Irun: Alberdania, 2007). Small parts of chapter 1 appeared as "From Dictatorship to Empire" in *Wildness and Sensation*, ed. Rob van Ginkel and Alex Strating (Antwerp: Het Spinhuis, 2007) and "Intellectuals among Terrorists: Experts vs. Witnesses," in *Intellectuals and Their Publics: Perspectives from the Social Sciences*, ed. Christian Fleck, Andreas Hess, and E. Stina Lyon (Burlington, Vt.: Ashgate, 2008). A section of chapter 7 appeared as "The War on Terror and the Paradox of Sovereignty: Declining States and the States of Exception," in *Politics, Publics, Personhood: Ethnography at the Limits of Neoliberalism*, ed. Carol J. Greenhouse (Philadelphia: University of Pennsylvania Press, forthcoming). They are reproduced here with permission.

Rethinking the War on Terror

Counterterrorism has become self-fulfilling and it is now pivotal in *promoting* terrorism. This book is an attempt to prove it.

There is now near consensus, on both the Left and the Right, that the war in Iraq has been a catastrophe and that the War on Terror has made the United States far less secure than before. Yet we barely understand the thinking that, with the generalized approval of the public, led us to this situation. Why the sense of missed opportunities and failure of George W. Bush's presidency? A response requires understanding the role of counterterrorism in designing public policy.

In order to think and write terrorism without thereby further constituting it, the preliminary task at hand is conceptual: What are the impasses and blind spots in counterterrorist thinking that led us to the self-fulfilling nature of the War on Terror?

The first part of the book is devoted to the ways in which discourse creates and perpetuates the very thing it abominates. It repeats the call in my book *Terror and Taboo* (coauthored with William Douglass) for an exorcism against such culture—"Terrorism discourse must be disenchanted if it is to lose its efficacy for all concerned,"[1] terrorists and counterterrorists alike. I fully agree with Richard Jackson's conclusion that "resisting the discourse is not an act of disloyalty; it is an act of political self-determination; and it is absolutely necessary if we are to avoid another stupefying period of fear and violence like the cold war."[2]

There is little doubt by now that terrorism discourse *creates* its own reality.

My arguments here go beyond discourse analysis. Terrorism is premised on the *will* of insurgents, rebels, fighters, terrorists. Terrorism studies are about tactics, financial networks, organizational structures, ideologies, psychological types—the observable expressions of the terrorist agenda. But first we must reckon with the terrorist as an individual subject. We are baffled by his or her seeming madness, the horrific freedom of his *amor fati*, the willing acceptance of death and killing as one's mission, the embrace of a truth that can only be expressed in the form of terroristic massacre. And it is a madness that is all the more disconcerting because we know it is strategically willed and aimed directly at us for reasons that we cannot clearly see nor accept. These issues cannot be properly addressed without the awareness that the terrorist subject is deeply engaged in the politics of the unconscious, including the Freudian "death drive" expressed in willfully embracing suicide.

Counterterrorism's ignorance of the languages, cultures, and histories of the people it purports to monitor is proverbial. The crisis of knowledge begins with the quality of the intelligence when the analysts are not able to look into their own ideological investments. What is one to make of the fact that scores of people in the intelligence community had known for months that two of the people who were going to take part in 9/11 were living in the United States, yet nothing was done about it? According to the findings of the 9/11 Commission (officially, the National Commission on Terrorists Attacks upon the United States), "evidence gathered by the panel showed that the attacks could probably have been prevented."[3] Why such blindness? What needs to be established is that the system had sufficient evidence to know about the upcoming plot yet it *preferred not to know that it knew*. These are problems that derive directly from a faulty epistemology—beginning with the placement of the entire phenomenon in a context of taboo and the willful ignorance of the political subjectivities of the terrorists. They have to do with what counts as a standard of evidence, what is valuable information, what type of experience should be respected, what sort of associative logic links together various kinds of events, and other various contexts and mind-sets.

One only has to compare Paul Bremer's and David Petraeus's policies in Iraq to become aware of the disastrous self-generating logic of counterterrorism. The ecounterterrorist Bremer acted as if anything touched by Saddam Hussein was contaminated with evil and drove tens of thousands of former soldiers and officers into the insurgency; the military man Petraeus studied the culture and ended up negotiating with and partially dissolving the enemy. The counterterrorist is typically like the proverbial dumb policeman who, by ignoring the actor's subjectivity in its complex interaction of cultural background, social motivation, and unconscious desire, is unable to read the evidence in front of his eyes while taking seriously "evidence" deliberately planted by the criminal to fool him. What is required is to make the sweeping change from the policeman's to the detective's mind frame. We went to war against Hussein because we did not figure out that he was *bluffing*.

What kind of writing can do justice to the terrorists' suicidal madness? Since at least the Old Testament, writers have dealt with murder; far from utterly alien human beings, murderers have been depicted by writers as all-too-human members of ordinary communities; at times heroicized, at other times their actions are deplored as tragic, they are always the objects of intense curiosity and study. Before he wrote his "nonfiction novel" *In Cold Blood*, Truman Capote spent hundreds of hours with the multiple murderers Perry Smith and Dick Hickock. They became for him anything but tabooed people. In fact, he projected himself into Perry's life and concluded that he was too much like himself. The final result is that Capote *knew* his murderers thoroughly and intimately—they could not lie to him, nor would he underestimate their human potential. Counterterrorism thinking precludes in principle the subjective knowledge of a Truman Capote or a detective or an ethnographer. Hence, I argue in this book, the categorical blunders and the systemic blindness.

A Self-Fulfilling Temporality: Waiting for Terror

"It is not *if*, but *when*"—how many times have we heard this mantra of every expert turned prophet warning the viewer of the impending catastrophe of nuclear terrorism? The seemingly wise caution assumes that, by ruling out the conditional "if" from terrorists' evil minds, we are reaffirming our own unconditional certainty. The assertion of "when" invokes some real time rather than the Beckettian type of waiting that characterizes terrorism.

On the one hand, the real success of counterterrorism is when a foreseeable attack does *not* happen. Thus counterterrorists can legitimately claim each day in which another 9/11 does not take place as a success; these non-events prove they are right in their premises. Yet, on the other hand, if and when an attack does occur, then counterterrorist thinking can also say "we told you so" and argue that they were *always* right in their predictions. In short, whether there are terrorist attacks or not, counterterrorist knowledge pretends to be always right. Such imperviousness to historical events points to a time warp that goes to the heart of counterterrorist mythology. The waiting implies in fact that historical time has surrendered itself to a fateful future. The strategy of the terrorists consists of creating terror by acting randomly and against innocent bystanders—the actions are thus perceived as if they were utterly unpredictable instances, beyond any actual temporal process, almost unplanned sudden outbursts that are outside of historical time. Such instantaneous *atemporality* finds its true counterpart in the counterterrorists' fatalism of "not if, but when"—a surrender to a passive temporality that is simply inevitable Fate, rather than an active temporality emerging from a new political will to determine the actual reasons, sources, and solutions to the sudden violence. If the terrorists are acting and planning against us in an inevitable and nonhypothetical manner, there is nothing we can do to prevent their course of action. A next step in such fateful thinking is that the terrorists' actions are not based on hypotheses and premises either—they are born out of hatred and arbitrary blame. The result is the same: there is nothing we can possibly do to restrain them. The consequence of this mind-set is that the counterterrorist loses interest in the intellectual premises, subjective motivations, and political goals that underlie and guide terrorist actions; his only concern is how to react against utterly dangerous, secretively sinister actors that he does not know.

Sociologist Robert Merton defined and formalized the consequences of the self-fulfilling prophecy: "The self-fulfilling prophecy is, in the beginning, a *false* definition of the situation evoking a new behavior which makes the original false conception come *true.* This specious validity of the self-fulfilling prophecy perpetuates a reign of error. For the prophet will cite the actual course of events as proof that he was right from the very beginning. . . . Such are the perversities of social logic."[4] It was false that al Qaeda was in Iraq before March 2003 (the excuse to go to war) but it is true that there is al Qaeda in Iraq now—which serves as justification for Bush to continue the war.

Historical events, large and small, are affected by such self-fulfilling prophecies. One can hardly assess the cold war without taking into account the predictive logic by which the perceived threat of annihilation forced an armaments race. Or can we understand the behavior of the financial markets during the last decade without such a hypothesis? In the field of education, the ways in which the attitudes and expectations of teachers will influence students' performance can be tested and measured. Symbolic interactionists have elaborated on the idea of the self as an inherently self-fulfilling prophecy. [5] Current counterterrorism is another prime example of that most classic of sociological truisms that Merton labeled "the Thomas theorem": "If men define situations as real, they are real in their consequences."[6] Once the situation is defined as one of inevitable terrorism and endless waiting, what *could* happen weighs as much as what is actually the case. The primary definition of our political reality as dependent on controlling the future becomes in itself the terrorists' fundamental victory *now*. One example of such radical subversion of temporality is the adoption by the Bush administration of the doctrine of *preventive war* in a nuclear era. Only the figure of the Terrorist and its potential for a nuclear attack can justify it. This is in keeping with the assumption of nuclear monopoly by the United States inherent in its promise to disarm *after,* and not before, the rest of the world eschews nuclear arms.[7] Such a time warp ensures that the very building and possession of nuclear arsenals is no longer the real issue; rather, it is the future possibility that potential terrorists might one day obtain the remnants of ours. The Evil is not the reality that we now have nuclear arms, rather it is the *desire* of others to have them in the future.

During the decade of the 1980s, when almost no one can remember a single terrorist fatality in the United States, terrorism was still frequently hailed as the country's number-one threat—it was the fantasized enemy of the waiting for terror. How did President Ronald Reagan's terrorism sideshow become the overwhelming discourse in U.S. politics, media, and everyday life after 9/11? Already with President Bill Clinton, particularly after his improved standing in public opinion polls in the aftermath of the Oklahoma City massacre, "terrorism" became a dominant frame through which American politics had to be interpreted. Far from remaining a discourse in which the boundaries between the real and the fictional were never clear, terrorism became a functional reality of American politics that could be deployed in the midst of any political crisis. If, with Clinton, terrorism turned into an autonomous prime mover of enormous consequences, effecting national policy and legislation, with President George W. Bush the War on Terror has become the sole mission of American politics. If with Reagan and Clinton terrorism had been "naturalized" into a constant risk that is omnipresent, a sort of chaotic principle always ready to strike and create havoc, with Bush it became the prime raison d'état, the one enemy against which society must now marshal all its resources in an unending struggle.

What is remarkable in the use of the "war" rhetoric is the confusion of the various *types of warfare*—from a conventional military invasion of Iraq, to the proclamation of this being a battle in the worldwide War on Terror, to the nuclear danger posed by combining the desires of "rogue regimes" with terrorists, to the denials of an insurgency in Iraq. The most deceptive premise about the War on Terror is that *it is war* understood literally in conventional terms. Previous to all these types of warfare, there is the "religiously sanctioned moral duty"[8] to fight the evil of terrorism, a war that is rooted as much in morality as it is based on military technology. Only this religious apocalyptic frame can explain how President Bush could turn "the axis of evil" into the cornerstone of U.S. international politics. "Terrorism" is the catalyst for confusing all these levels of warfare. One obvious result of such confusion was that soon after the occupation of Iraq U.S. soldiers were confronted with a humiliated Iraqi population that consisted of millions of potential "terrorists."

After 9/11 there was a clear displacement of the taboo concerning weapons of mass destruction into the taboo of terrorism. Saddam Hussein represented the master Terrorist because not only had he manifested an undisguised appetite for nuclear might, he had also used chemical weapons against his own people (with U.S. help and silence). More than ever the issue became *who* would be allowed to possess the bomb. Even if the probability that terrorists will develop or acquire a nuclear device is shown by the experts to be extremely low,[9] the very possibility materializes in apocalyptic alarm once the situation is one of waiting for terror. What matters is the prophecy that Saddam Hussein or a terrorist group might one day have them. Since "the greatest failure of the new approach [by the Bush administration] was its belief that it could indefinitely maintain a global double standard,"[10] the figure of the Terrorist serves to displace and obfuscate the dangers coming from the difficulties of controlling the spread of nuclearism. Similarly, the moral bankrupcy of a war premised on plain falsehoods is too much to bear—unless we are fighting a crusade against the demonic figure of the Terrorist.

In the end, as stated by Begoña Aretxaga, the terrorist and the counter-terrorist interface within "a structure and modus operandi which produce both the state and terrorism as fetishes of each other, constructing reality as an endless play of mirror images. This play of terrorism is what makes the State (with a capital S) and Terrorism (with a capital T) so real, organizing political life as a phantasmatic universe where the 'really real' is always somewhere else, always eluding us."[11] Thus we get the Catch-22 of a labyrinthine, self-fulfilling repetition.

The analytic challenge is to show the time loop by which Empire and Terrorism produce each other simultaneously. What do Ayatollah Ruholla Khomeini, Saddam Hussein, Muammar Qaddafi, Manuel Noriega, Sheikh Omar Abdel Rahman, and Osama bin Laden have in common? Their careers are intimately tied to U.S. counterinsurgency. Khomeini appeared on the political stage during the 1953 Iranian coup engineered by the Central Intelligence Agency; Hussein came to power "on a CIA train"[12] in the early 1960s; Qaddafi had extensive dealings with former CIA arms dealers; Noriega, Rahman, and bin Laden worked side by side with the CIA. They all were close allies of the United States only to later become its nemeses—the archterrorists. The same schizophrenic dynamic can be seen in the ease with which counterterrorism has forced the United States to switch sides regarding those countries accused of sponsoring terrorism: Iran, Iraq, Libya, Afghanistan, and Pakistan have all switched back and forth from being friends to becoming the sponsors of terrorism. Both plots, the one of the ally and the one of the terrorist, are generated *by the same self-fulfilling process*.

One time loop that we should be particularly concerned with has to do with the constitution of terrorist subjectivities. We must pay attention not only to the militant as the author of the act but also to the subject's anticipated *passage à l'acte*, a terrorist subject that is itself displayed as the ultimate "work of art" and weapon of the dispossessed. The terrorist subject is inaugurated by the event of such *passage*, "the event is precisely the 'crystal' of the duality; it is the moment when the subject, encountering herself, splits. In other words, the event exists only in this montage of these two subjects."[13] If we want to understand 9/11 we must also see it as the montage by which the subjects who perpetrated it had been "inaugurated" to it for years previously. To see how the prediction of the terrorist subject becomes self-fulfilling, all we need is look at the case of Timothy McVeigh whose plot was scripted to the last detail by the dominant terrorism discourse.[14]

The War on Terror, by legitimizing preventive wars, by passing into law the Patriot Act, by normalizing torture, by turning neoconservative fantasies into policy priorities, has become the last ideological refuge for an imperial military. The 9/11 attacks turned the United States into a victim and justified self-defense, but it did something else as well: it provided the perfect excuse for the *just war* and for implementing an agenda that includes advancing further weapons of mass destruction while displacing their overwhelming threat onto the terrorists.

The crucial issue is how to conceptualize this dynamic of mutual denial and mutual constitution between the couple terrorist/counterterrorist. It displays the qualities of "the edge" as a feature intrinsic to the Lacanian Real, "a duality that has nothing to do with the dichotomies between complementary oppositional terms (which are ultimately always two sides of the One) . . . the edge as the thing whose sole substantiality consists in its simultaneously separating and linking two surfaces. This specific duality aims at the Real, and makes it take place through the very split that gives structure to this duality. It is a duality that simultaneously constitutes the cause, the advent, and the consequence of the Real—but also a duality that thereby captures or expresses the Real."[15] It is the duality of such an edge that must be grasped regarding the duality terrorism/counterterrorism as well—despite their intimate linkage, the relationship is a "nonrelationship" in the Lacanian sense that the very impossibility is what *constitutes* it.

But How Can That Be?

Since terrorism is so tabooed, the reader can legitimately ask what my subjective position is regarding the terrorist. Since my youth I have been confronted in the Basque Country with the existence of militants in the underground armed group ETA (Euskadi and Freedom). My own response to ETA's violence was to write an ethnography around the perplexing realities of murder justified as a political necessity by the nationalists. "But how can that be?"—that was the question thrown at me by my neighbors when the village informer and bus driver of my own village was murdered by the ETA one Saturday morning. My mother was on the bus among the housewives who had gone shopping. During their ride back home she saw the two young men, pistols in hand, advance toward the driver, shouting at him, "You are a dog!" before killing him. The hysterical housewives fled the bus and were brought to the village by passing drivers. I found my mother in shock, sitting on the doorstep, unable to climb the stairs to our home. Other women who had witnessed the crime were on the street, still sobbing. "But how can that be?" is all they could say, their faces twisted in horror.

I composed an ethnography trying to make sense of that "But how can that be?"[16] I provided historical, sociological, and cultural models of performance that could help contextualize, albeit never *explain*, the bewildering phenomenon of murder. But are you allowed to attempt an ethnography of murder? Is it morally and politically correct to keep ethnographic detachment when murder is at stake? Nobody in the discipline would question that you could write of infanticide, regicide, or headhunting, and produce a valuable monograph without anyone assuming that you favored killing infants or kings or decapitation. But can you employ the anthropological perspective as a distancing device to study "terrorism"? This book is grounded on the radical ethnographic legacy of modern anthropology, one that was summarized by Clifford Geertz as "looking into dragons, not domesticating or abominating them, nor drowning them in vats of theory."[17] Affirming a common humanity with savages and terrorists is not only the inaugural premise of such tradition but also an epistemological necessity.

Anthropologists of my generation, informed mostly by the works of Karl Marx, Émile Durkheim, and Max Weber, have taken for granted the profound interaction between individuality and collectivity. This perspective sympathizes with Antonio Gramsci when he wrote in his essay "What Is Man?" that "it is essential to conceive of man as a series of active relationships (a process) in which individuality, while of the greatest importance, is not the sole element to be considered." Gramsci's view was that "the individual does not enter into relations with other men in opposition to them but through an organic unity with them, because he becomes part of social organisms of all kinds from the simplest to the most complex."[18] This might be reasonable for ordinary social relations, but when you are dealing with the taboo of terrorism, can you postulate that the terrorist has some ties and dependencies with his or her community, his or her culture? Still, the interdependence between the individual and the collective does not deny agency. The subject can in fact change those relations. An ethnographic approach to the phenomenon of political terrorism will in fact place emphasis on both sides of the equation: on the structure that conditions the militant's actions, and on the purposes that both guide and fool the actor. Both moves are unwelcome for the counterterrorist who would not grant the terrorist any leeway as a subject.

A central theme to the entire terrorism/counterterrorism dynamics is *innocence*. Terrorists by definition kill innocent victims chosen randomly— hence their aberration in every military, legal, or moral sense. There is no middle ground between the killer and the victim. And yet, remember the biblical allegory of Abraham's willingness to sacrifice his innocent son for the sake of a higher calling. Søren Kierkegaard called this the "teleological suspension of the ethical"—the ethical is overridden altogether by a higher telos. For Abraham, despairing yet obedient to superior orders, and with knife in hand poised over his son, the ethical is that which might prevent him from fulfilling God's will—ethics itself becomes a *temptation*. Abraham's aberration testifies both to the existence of an ethical norm and the need to transgress it for the sake of any transcendence. "Abraham is therefore at no instant a tragic hero but something quite different, either a murderer or a believer."[19] It is by resisting the "temptation" of being moral (that is, preserving his son's life) that he reaches the "suspension" of ethics in order to become the monstrosity of an absolute murderer/believer.

What can you do as a writer when your primary community of family, friends, village, or country produces "terrorists"? Is it your intellectual challenge to define them, diagnose them, condemn them, persuade them, understand them, exorcise them? Whether in the Basque Country or the United States, intellectual approaches to "terrorism" are of necessity enmeshed in the writer's self-definitions and ideological predilections.[20] There is the danger of a double moral and political blackmail of either blaming everything on the terrorist Evil (and Westerners are unconditionally innocent victims) or blaming the Western victims (and the Islamist extremists are innocent of their atrocities). Each of the two positions is one-sided and false. Against these two positions Slavoj Zizek resorts to the dialectical category of totality to argue that "from the moral standpoint, the victims are innocent, the act was an abominable crime; however, this very innocence is not innocent—to adopt such an 'innocent' position in today's global capitalist universe is in itself a false abstraction."[21] Jacques Derrida similarly wrote: "My unconditional compassion, addressed to the victims of September 11th, does not prevent me from saying it loudly: with regard to this crime, I do not believe that anyone is politically guiltless."[22] This does not entail a compromised notion of shared guilt by terrorists and victims; "the point is, rather, that the two sides are not really opposed, that they belong to the same field. In short, the position to adopt is to accept the necessity of the fight against terrorism, BUT to redefine and expand its terms so that it will include also (some) American and other Western powers' acts."[23] The dichotomy "us" versus "them" leads us into the bind of being incapable of true solidarity with all the victims. The responsibility toward those who suffer should transform the writer of terrorism into a witness but, as I found myself among my countrymen, a witness à la Abraham—horrified not primarily by some evil out there in the world but rather by the abyss of one's own participation in the murder.

Thirty years after I heard it in my own Basque village, the "But how can that be?" still reverberates. But now, as an American citizen teaching at a U.S. university for two decades, the question has been displaced to the perplexing follies of the War on Terror. For someone who lived his youth under General Francisco Franco's regime, his dictatorship justified as a "crusade" against the evils of communism and atheism, this new U.S. war against terrorism defined likewise as a "crusade," it is all like having a sense of déjà vu. Remember that historic photograph of President George Bush and prime ministers Tony Blair and José María Aznar standing side by side in the Azores before going to Iraq. And look at the results for the protagonists themselves: the presidency of Bush was destroyed by the War on Terror and its sequel the Iraqi War; Aznar's party lost the elections in Spain and had to relinquish power for his support of the Iraq War and his handling of Madrid's March 11, 2004, terrorist attack; Blair's reputation was shredded for siding with Bush. Previously, the Iran-contra affair had seriously endangered the reputation of President Reagan and Vice President George H. W. Bush. The life of most Israeli governments has been made unworkable because of their counterterrorist policies: it is known that Hamas was initially supported by Israel as a counterpart to the PLO (Palestine Liberation Organization), thus, typically, first promoting as an ally the same group that will later become your terrorist enemy; most commentators share the view that Israel's incursions into Lebanon and Gaza have decisively strengthened the positions of Hezbollah and Hamas vis-à-vis their societies. And one can safely predict that future U.S., Israeli, British, Spanish, and other governments will be undone because of counterterrorism. Why such self-defeating myopia regarding the terrorist nemesis?

This book attempts to unlock the conceptual impasses that lead to such counterterrorist dead ends. It is a sequel to a 1996 book that concluded with an "Epilogue as Prologue: The Apotheosis of Terrorism Foretold."[24] There, William Douglass and I stated what was obvious at the time: the old generation of the terrorist cast of characters and movements seemed all but moribund and perhaps we should be prepared to pronounce "terrorism" itself dead. Carlos the Jackal, Abimael Guzmán of Peru's "Shining Path," the blind Egyptian sheikh Omar Abdel Rahman, and others all languished in prison; previous bogeymen Saddam Hussein and Muammar

Qaddafi were by then international pariahs; the African National Congress was the ruling party in South Africa; the Red Brigades and the Baader-Meinhof group were but faded memories; the Irish Republican Army had agreed to a cease-fire; and so on. And yet something else was obvious at the time. By then, American public discourse was dominated by terrorism news and fears; waiting for terror had become the dominant political certainty. So we added: "Yet there is suddenly a new promised land for terrorism—the United States."[25] And we surmised that "the apotheosis of terrorism foretold" was around the corner. In short, this new culture of the apotheosis of *terrorism as mythology*, far from preventing its actual danger, would result in masking it in apocalyptic overtones and further contributing to it. This book attempts to show how this has been the case.

It is time for the War on Terror to be added to the list of perplexing historical phenomena that, on close inspection, are semantic and political aberrations that derive to a crucial extent from imaginary constructs embedded in the culture of the times. European witchcraft was one such grotesque construct that revealed the Janus face of progress—the age of the Renaissance, the Reformation, and the Scientific Revolution was also the age of the witch-craze and the most superstitious credulity, to the point that "the Dark Age [of the Middle Ages] was more civilized."[26] The paradox of knowledge was that the more learned a scholar was, the more he was ready to believe in the powers of witchcraft. Dissolving such phenomenon required undoing an entire worldview; its analysis should be guided by Giambattista Vico's canon that the first science is the study of mythology or the interpretation of fables.

The War on Terror, as a pivotal part of U.S. global politics, is not unrelated to the current crisis of global capitalism; it has been recognized that the lax oversight of Wall Street that led to the crisis was in good part due to the loosening of enforcement measures that were shifted to counterterrorism.[27] Whether in the case of capitalism or counterterrorism, the ideology of the moment will look for explanations that do not touch the core of the problem but attribute its crisis to some secondary distortion ("corruption of the markets," "the axis of evil") and thus the public can continue dreaming. The mythology of the War on Terror monopolizes the American Dream by lulling Americans into the belief that their Way of Life, with all its corollary liberties, is seriously jeopardized by some unknown and unknowable evil lurking out there and not because something might be wrong with that lifestyle.

"If there is anyone out there who still doubts that America is a place where all things are possible," began the newly elected President Barack Obama in his victory speech in Chicago on November 4, 2008, "who still wonders if the dream of our founders is alive in our time, who still questions the power of our democracy, tonight is your answer." That November night—not the eve of the invasion of Iraq. Obama's victory was contingent on his original opposition to that war. His words during the campaign could not have been more resonant: "I don't want to just end the war, but I want to end the mind-set that got us into war in the first place." But now, as the Iraq War is dropping out of sight, the question is whether a transformational president will keep his vision or whether he will let counterterrorist doctrine regain new life in the battleground of Afghanistan and doom his presidency. Reclaiming the promise dreamed by the founders now requires a radical rethinking of the doctrine that sustains the War on Terror; the first task is to show that counterterrorism has become terrorism's best ally and the dream's worst enemy. It also requires a new will to restore eroded constitutional rights, amend the Patriot Act, and bring the U.S. government fully under the rule of law. We should not be asking ourselves whether this is the end of the American Dream; it is time to decide that, if the dream is to survive, the War on Terror, as framed by Bush and Cheney, must come to an end.

PART I

The Rhetorics of Terrorism

CHAPTER ONE

Writing Counterterrorism

The Betrayal of the Public Intellectual

"President Abraham Lincoln was shot dead in 1865. President John F. Kennedy fell victim to an assassination in 1963. A terrorist shot and wounded President Ronald Reagan in 1981." This report from *Pravda* on January 19, 2007, typifies the transition: the assassinations of Lincoln and Kennedy were "assassinations;" the failed assassination attempt on Reagan was "terrorism." Why was the third attack more "terroristic" than the first two? Because during the 1970s a new discourse had taken hold of international politics. Until that decade newspapers had no entries for the statistical indices of "terrorism" and therefore there were no "terrorist acts" (only kidnappings, assassinations, bomb explosions, threats, and the like). Since then terrorism has turned into a news staple. This is a simple example of how counting and writing constitutes the thing itself.

Consider another notorious case that underlines the link between terrorism events and statistics: while a 1979 CIA report on terrorism claimed that there had been 3,336 terrorist incidents since 1968, the 1980 report claimed that there were 6,714 incidents *over the same period*. The doubling of terrorism was the result of including "threats" and "hoaxes" in the statistics. This is reminiscent of the paradox studied by Gottlob Frege regarding set theory: his numbers assume that the categories of counting *create* the objects that fall under those categories. This is also what power does in using statistics: by counting varieties of people, it not only accounts for but constitutes them. It can be said that modern nations are thus the product of counting, of collecting diverse peoples basically as citizens, that is, as members of an identical set after having discounted all their particularities. Terrorism is another instance in which the powers that be create, by numbering and writing, the objects described as "terrorist." In short, if there was no statistical category of terrorism, no terrorist incident would be possible—only murders, assassinations, kidnappings, and so forth. In *Terror and Taboo*,[1] William Douglass and I came close to this position in which the category subsumes the essence. In part II I will argue that one has to go beyond discourse to grasp the particular nature of terrorism.

Hayden White called this inaugural aspect of language "tropic," namely, it relies on the presence of tropes (metaphor,[2] metonym, synecdoche, irony) used in "the process by which all discourse *constitutes* the objects which it pretends only to describe realistically and to analyze objectively."[3] "Terrorism" has become the dominant tropic space in contemporary political and journalistic discourse. Such tropics of terror, by which attention is paid to the conceptual premises, emplotted stories, and the very "illusion of sequence" of terrorist narrativity, should be of primary concern to any study of terrorism—in particular to one that seeks to unveil how terrorism discourse further creates the very thing it abominates.

One decisive question that emerges from this perspective is: Does the new discourse of "terrorism" really add something—in terms of reporting, knowledge, or political will—to what we already know about the facts? There is a radical difference at the level of discourse, rhetorically as well as legally and morally, between calling an event, say, a "threat" and calling it "terrorism." The hypothesis of this chapter is that, not only do we not contribute anything substantive whether cognitive or political by labeling as "terrorism" acts that until the 1970s were described as "assassinations," "kidnappings," "attacks," "threats," and so on, but that the new overweening discourse, with its implications of essential Evil, taboo, and a logic of contagion, is a return to a form of thinking that is closer to the mental world of medieval witchcraft and inquisitorial nonsense. It is the type of discourse that becomes a self-fulfilling prophecy.

This raises the issue of the writer's betrayal (i.e., the journalist, the scholar, the politician, the expert, the intellectual). When examining how the United States made the blunder of going to war in Iraq, the easy answer is to point fingers at the Bush administration. What needs to be explained is how the large majority of Americans identified with Bush's conflation of weapons of mass destruction (WMD) and terrorism. The difficult task is accounting for the ways counterterrorism culture has taken root at the core of American thinking and politics—a culture that, from a skeptical perspective, is plagued by spectacular semantic errors combined with a flawed self-fulfilling prophecy. How? Clearly, the constitutive power of discourse is germane to any understanding of such an outcome. But then, again, how could so many well-informed politicians, journalists, and writers fall for a blindly self-righteous discourse? "Terrorism" rhetoric can so easily become a massively self-serving discourse because, at the core, we still hold on to the perspectival dichotomy between *their* "barbarism" and *our* "civilization," while believing that they are prone to mad, murderous inhumanity in ways that we don't recognize in ourselves—despite, of course, the historical evidence. Such blindness begins by tabooing their voices and desires, by categorizing their madness, suicides, and killings as qualitatively distinct from ours—in short, by denying "them" a complex subjectivity like ours.

Should our writing help to further constitute or, on the contrary, undermine the entire terrorism discourse? Following the lead of a distinguished list of anthropologists and social theorists,[4] *Terror and Taboo* clearly took the latter stance; our arguments, based on the ethnographic proximity we had enjoyed as anthropologists among "terrorists," centered on the rhetorical nature of counterterrorism and, more significantly, on the convulsive reality-making power of a discourse that played on the fears of taboo and imaginary apocalypse. If the book predicted 9/11 in its "Epilogue as Prologue: The Apotheosis of Terrorism Foretold," post-9/11 counterterrorism discourse has fulfilled our worst predictions. Richard Jackson's study examines in depth the massive discursive investment in the new "war on terrorism" and how it hinders rather than helps the search for solutions. A crucial requirement of the discourse is the creation of the "myth of exceptional grievance" by which the United States should be seen as the primary victim of terrorism. Public officials, such as Undersecretary of Defense Paul Wolfowitz, considered that "[t]his threat is as great as any we faced during the Cold War," national security adviser Condoleezza Rice spoke of "that mushroom cloud," and Vice President Dick Cheney made specific references to terrorists who may "detonate a nuclear weapon in one of our cities" and "who are willing to sacrifice their own lives in order to kill millions of others."[5] But, for our purposes of examining counterterrorist discourse and its new full-blown "war," the complete subservience of the media and the scholarly community is just as crucial. Every TV network, through story after story, proclaims the "War against Terrorism" and "America's New War"—in just the first month following the 9/11 attacks, ABC, CBS, NBC, CNN, and NPR had a total of 797 such stories. Similarly, there were 5,814 printed articles, employing both "war" and "terrorism." Up to October 23, 2001, 754 articles were published by the *New York Times*, the *Washington Post*, the *Chicago Tribune*, and the *Los Angeles Times* with references to World War II or Nazi Germany.[6] Jackson concludes: "The 'war on terrorism' was, in one sense, 'written' by the networks as a Hollywood blockbuster—an immediate sequel to 2001's widely anticipated *Pearl Harbor*."[7] Did the main TV channels challenge, say, the dangers of the Patriot Act for civil liberties? NBC and CBS did not have a single story on it during the process leading to its adoption.[8] This was a period when a bastion of liberalism such as the *New York Times* had columnists writing that the new war on terrorism was the beginning of World War III and printed on the front page false news about Saddam Hussein possessing weapons of mass destruction. Not surprisingly, by early March 2003, according to a Gallup poll, 88 percent of Americans believed that 9/11 was the product of terrorists supported by Saddam Hussein, or that 79 percent believed him to either possess or to be close to possessing nuclear weapons.

Counterterrorist thinking is so haunted by the phantoms of the Terrorist monster that there is no other alternative than a crusade against the "forces of Evil." The ultimate outcome of such discourse is the justification as inevitable of the *just war* against the phantom of terrorism, presumably the only just war in the nuclear era. It therefore becomes an intellectual and political imperative to resist counterterrorist discourse and practice. Chapter 7 will dwell on the deceptive rhetorics of "war" and the all too obvious displacements of our own military's nuclear fears to the threat of nuclear terrorism. This first chapter will focus on terrorism discourse and rhetorics per se.

Terrorism Studies: How Do You Define the Thing?

Let us invoke pornography. As a new disciplinary field of knowledge, terrorism studies typically begins by discussing "the definitional quagmire" before offering some new variant of it. Frequently, in a Solomonic resolution, the author will conclude by admitting the difficulties yet proclaiming solemnly an analogy that establishes the final proof of the existence of the thing itself: "like pornography, we know terrorism when we see it."[9]

In the most comprehensive research guide to concepts, theories, and literature on terrorism studies ever written, Alex Schmid complained in 1988 that the field did not only suffer from conceptual disarray—that is, there was no agreement regarding the basic concepts of "violence," "political," "aggression," and so on, concepts that are used to define "terrorism"—but it was the very "general framework [that] is chosen for definition"[10] that was the primary issue. More recently, in 2004, Andrew Silke summarized trends in terrorism research during the 1990s and came to the conclusion that "the situation . . . is even worse today" despite the fact that the published literature continues to expand impressively. Silke sees a literature that is still young (about 99% of it has been written since 1968), which remains plagued by a number of problems (such as the fact that as much as 80 percent is narrative, condemnatory, and prescriptive), which relies on the work of too few researchers, which is rarely carried out by teams of researchers, and which is dominated by political scientists.[11] In the ten-year period of the 1990s only one article was dedicated to al Qaeda, whereas nationalist/separatist groups such as the IRA or ETA received most of the research effort. As a final consideration, Silke looks at the conceptual issues in the discipline to state the obvious: "It is generally agreed that terrorism lacks an agreed on conceptual framework."[12] John Horgan sums up the literature on the psychology of terrorism and the search for a "terrorist personality" with the observation that "its presuppositions are built on unsteady empirical, theoretical and conceptual foundations"[13] and wonders whether "a fresh start" is not needed. After examining terrorist networks, Marc Sageman remarked likewise that "the findings seem to reject much of the conventional wisdom about terrorists."[14] Silke went on to observe that, even if such conceptual disarray might have presented a massive obstacle in other fields, in terrorism studies we seem to have reached "something of a war-wariness among established researchers over the definitional quagmire," adding that "researchers seem to have resigned themselves to accepting the current state of uncertainty" rather than engaging in "the somewhat wasteful definitional debate."[15] Silke's somber afterthought is that, at some point, "such conceptual confusion in the area must begin to severely hamper progress."[16]

This does not mean that there are not renewed efforts to summarize the scholarship and redefine the field. Louise Richardson's work is a case in point. "Terrorism simply means deliberately and violently targeting civilians for political purposes,"[17] she states, and adds seven defining characteristics: it is politically inspired; involves violence or the threat of violence; the point is not to defeat the enemy but to send a message; acts and victims are chosen for their symbolic significance; it is not perpetrated by states, but by substate entities; the victim and the target of the violence are not the same; civilians are deliberately targeted. These points serve well to typify what is understood as "terrorism" in public discourse, but each one of them can be, and has frequently been, contested by various authors.[18]

Richardson cites ETA as a prime example supporting her main contention that "a terrorist is a terrorist, no matter whether or not you like the goal s/he is trying to achieve, no matter whether or not you like the government s/he is trying to change."[19] But this is a simplicity that empties "terrorism" of any content. In ETA's case, it forces the author to not only fabricate facts, such as her contention that ETA "murdered tourists under the Franco regime"[20] (it wasn't until the 1980s that ETA began planting bombs in tourist spots, but first informing the police before they went off), but also, more relevantly, to rewrite a revisionist history in which the crucial difference between using violence against Franco's dictatorship and against democracy is erased. In the judgment of Basques and the international community, there was indeed a qualitative difference in the ethical and political meaning of ETA's actions against Franco and against the post-Franco democracy.[21] By categorically erasing all ambiguity between the freedom fighter and the terrorist, the priest and the assassin, or the hero and the murderer, and by linking one polar opposite with "good" and the other with "evil," while providing the blank tools of "The Three Rs: Revenge, Renown, Reaction" as the analytical framework for understanding the phenomenon, academic terrorism discourse adopts a position of intellectual and moral retreat from everything we have learned from anthropology, history, and psychoanalysis.

The problem with the so-called definitional quagmire does not have to do primarily with the definition of terrorism. Most disciplines debate furiously and endlessly their defining conceptual paradigm, whether it be "aggression" in sociobiology, the nature of "the market" or "money" in economics, "society" in sociology, "the unconscious" in psychoanalysis, or "culture" in anthropology. The problem with terrorism has more to do with how to diagnose the very nature of the *thing itself*—both in the starkly concrete "reality" of the event and the starkly abstract "unreality" of its premises and consequences. If those indictments by Schmid and Silke refer to the state of affairs in terrorism studies in the 1980s and 1990s, imagine the situation after 9/11. How do we *name* 9/11? Under what premises are we allowed to even speak about it? What is the "really real" of suicidal terror? Who is this terrorist subject? How do we study it?

Even those of us critical of the terrorism typologies of the 1970s and '80s still had a sense that, either as a form of warfare, ritual action, or sheer pathology, so-called terrorist groups had obvious ideological traits, followed concrete strategies for obtaining their nationalist or otherwise revolutionary strategies, and even had some definable structural and historical features that could be described and catalogued. The attacks on New York, Madrid, and London by Islamists seem to have made almost obsolete much of that literature that examined what now might be deemed the "old terrorism" of groups such as the IRA or ETA. In fact, if ETA can be taken as an example, a noticeable consequence of this "new type of terrorism" is that it has made the very existence of these former armed groups seem obsolete. Suddenly, by comparison, all their actions and goals seem so dwarfed and inadequate as to lose the threat or glamour of true insurgency to the wider world. If, in the past, the militants had taken Israel, Cuba, and Algeria as models of liberationist violence, now their only valid standard in the forum of international opinion and attention is al Qaeda. Some of the basic features of the old terrorism—nationalistic in the narrow sense of seeking a separate nation-state; against liberal states that represented historical oppression; left-leaning, secular, progressive; embedded in a larger social network—obviously do not apply to the new Islamist expression, which appears to transcend any concrete nation, history, ideology, or social organization. Mohammed Atta, the leader of the 9/11 attacks, did not consider himself to belong to any organization; besides bin Laden and his close confidantes, it has been written about al Qaeda that it has "no independent institutional anchor."[22] The very idea of "insurgency" and the tension between "terrorist/freedom fighter" have become obsolete. The classical distinctions and links between terrorist groups and political parties are unhelpful in understanding how al Qaeda operates.[23]

Terrorism is the Foucaltian *episteme* of our times, the epistemological space that acts as a gatekeeper of which ideas may appear and which sciences may be constituted. Excavating the genealogy of this worldview, investigating its conceptual premises and ritual strategies, delving into its political goals and rhetorical contexts, naming this new type of terrorism—these are the preliminary challenges of a critical analysis of the ubiquitous terrorism discourse. Hence the question about the thing itself—which are the categories and allegories, the actions and rhetorics that give shape to the beast? Analysts such as Bruce Hoffman have underscored the changing meaning of terrorism.[24] As pointed out above, we don't even have an adequate conceptual framework for it. Not surprisingly, as definitional dilemmas continue to be endemic to the entire field of counterterrorism, a new consensus seems to be emerging that it is better to leave the thing itself, the very object of study, undefined.

Counterterrorism in Action: The Ironic Figure of the Expert

The counterterrorist system includes a variety of intelligence agencies, police organizations, and public officials. Counterterrorist thinking is produced mostly in the writings of secret reports and academic research, later amplified by the pundits' ubiquitous commentaries and the media's coverage. The "terrorism expert" is, in the eyes of the general public, the most vocal and authorized spokesman of such knowledge. If we want to assess counterterrorist thinking in action, we must pay attention to the figure of the expert as "one who is supposed to know." The declaration of the War on Terror after 9/11 implied that counterterrorism had become the official policy of the administration. Various writers and officials might espouse the core doctrines of counterterrorism in various degrees and shift positions regarding their validity. But the terrorism expert shapes and anchors counterterrorist knowledge. Thus, when wondering what we mean by "counterterrorist" we cannot avoid a reference to the expert. So what does the expert know?

The terrorism expert is arguably the most ironic authority figure since the inquisitor of the European witch-craze of the sixteenth and seventeenth centuries. The role of the inquisitorial expert was to supply the mythology that fueled the witch-craze—a grotesque demonology based on the dualism of God and the Devil, and which rested on the confessions of witches obtained under torture. As the British historian Hugh Trevor-Roper put it, "Indeed, the more learned a man was in the traditional scholarship of the time, the more likely he was to support the witch-doctors."[25] Here is a similar commentary on experts predicting biological terrorism: "The less the commentator seems to know about biological warfare the easier he seems to think the task is."[26] The counterterrorism pundit is typically the authority figure who has never remotely met a terrorist.

Indeed, it would seem at times that cultivated ignorance of a terrorist's culture and subjectivity becomes a precondition for claiming expertise. I will illustrate this with an example from the Basque Country. In the summer of 1985 it was announced that an international panel of five terrorism experts had been commissioned by the autonomous Basque government to "find out the causes and consequences of Basque terrorism" and propose measures to contain it.[27] None of the experts—an Italian psychiatrist, a French criminologist, a German jurist, an English historian, and a British ambassador to NATO—knew much about Basque culture and history. Yet they were suddenly "terrorism experts" and could diagnose problems and propose solutions. After months of meetings held in a London hotel, the much anticipated report appeared. It provided a grand counterterrorist logistical strategy to eradicate the dreaded violence. Anthropologists like myself and other social scientists were exhorted to collaborate with the security and intelligence forces. "More information is needed about the aims, membership, personalities and methods of ETA," it stated. "This information should be sought in parallel with the implementation of the counter-measures recommended later in this report, which should not await the outcome of the research studies indicated below."[28] The well-intentioned purpose of it all was "implementing a politics of reinsertion and pacification," a key element at the time in the strategy of the Spanish Ministry of the Interior againt ETA.

The one thing that the experts knew about the ongoing Basque violence was that it *was* terrorism. Thus, two-thirds of the report is given to describing other terrorist groups, the assumption being that they are all the same thing—one should therefore look at the specifics of violence in Ireland, Germany, Italy, or South Tyrol (currently it would be al Qaeda) in order to know what is going on in the Basque Country. The Basque problem was that, whether it be directed against Franco or post-Franco Spain, the violence was terrorism. The remaining one-third of the report was devoted to what "ought to be": it proposed a crusade that included mobilizing the social sciences, legal dispositions, police provisions, intelligence recommendations, socioeconomic measures, and a "Plan for Consciousness-Raising." The last point requires a concerted use of the media, indoctrination against nationalist values at all levels from primary school to the universities, active opposition from the political parties, as well as clearly stated moral and ideological imperatives.

One problem the experts didn't even think worth considering was: How did they *know* what Basque politics ought to be, or what Basque children should be taught in school? Since Max Weber, the categorical distinction between factual and normative propositions has been standard in the social sciences;[29] this classic sociological position precludes the imposition of value judgments at all levels on a given society—the hallmak of a dictatorial regime—in the name of knowledge. So it is fair to ask: What kind of knowledge did the terrorism experts possess of the Basque case? It was not based on empirical research on the ground, as they were never seen in public in the Basque Country. They never gave interviews or talks. Neither did they consult a single Basque scholar, conduct any survey, or test any hypothesis. Such would, of course, be irrelevant for the experts. They "knew" in advance everything there is to know about terrorism: it is the epitome of evil.

In short, the ironic figure of the expert who presumes to know every-thing without knowing anything specific is deeply symptomatic of the problems of counterterrorism. It demonstrates how easily deceptive it is, given the horror of terrorist violence, to mask entrenched ignorance as moral and political imperative. In the case of the report at hand the experts, in what was touted as its greatest analytical insight, came to the conclusion that Basque violence is "ethnic terrorism:" "the basis of the Basque prob-lem is ethnicity which, in the case of the Basque country, means the feeling of shared identity and unity which comes from being Basque."[30] Ethnicity was thus singled out as the root of the matter. Thus, "ethnos" (a combination of "race and nationality") is "the basis" (root, source, cause) of "the Basque problem" (or terrorism), because, the experts added, "ethnocentrism" is endemic to terrorist groups. How did the Basques react to the report? Because of its irrelevance, it provoked a public storm. What had been hyped as a meaningful scientific overview of the problem came to be regarded as useless and subservient pandering to the local government that had commissioned it.

Expertise on any category of people would seem to require a certain acquaintance with the subjects themselves. Not so in terrorism discourse where the initial premise is that terrorists are tabooed and "untouchable"— people one should never see, talk to, hear from, or have any contact with of any sort. The experts, who of course never talked to the violent actors, not even to their affinal political groups, not only abided by their own taboo but turned it into their basic policy recommendation. Thus they insisted repeatedly that "television should not enjoy the same degree of latitude in reporting [terrorism] as is accorded to the press," the reason being that "people can see as well as hear the person being interviewed."[31] The general public was considered not sufficiently informed or capable of looking at or listening to the tabooed terrorists. A majority of Basques have a family member, or at least an acquaintance, who has been involved in the violent drama. Yet the expert solution is not only to ignore the plight of the thousands of families so affected but also to literally taboo their significant others: don't ever talk to them, don't ever see them, don't ever have anything to do with them—even if they are in your home, your peer group, your village, your school class. Seemingly, it is not the role of the expert to seek objective knowledge of the terrorist subject or the historical and political conditions that led to the violence (that would be too dangerously close to "justifying" it). Rather, the task is fundamentally to categorize and stigmatize the terrorist as the prior condition to the application of counterterrorism measures. Once the tabooed category of the terrorist is firmly established, such pariah status not only legitimates the extraordinary measures of counterterrorism, such as Guantánamo and Abu Ghraib, but also makes them almost a moral imperative.

Gary Sick documents how the Carter administration was fatefully influenced by a "terrorism expert." It was during the Iran crisis and the journalist Robert Moss, who lacked hard evidence and had no qualifications as a specialist on Iran, still had an enormous effect on top U.S. policymakers when he wrote a piece stating what many in the administration feared, namely, that the Soviets must have been guiding the events of the Iranian hostage crisis. Sick shows how allegedly expert advice based on plain ignorance was calamitous for U.S. policy.[32]

One of the experts working on the Basque report was the German jurist Hans Josef Horchem who had also become a consultant for Alexander Haig when, as the NATO commander in Germany, Haig was the target of a failed terrorist attack on his life. This was the period in which Horchem and other experts were convinced that the KGB (Russian acronym for the Committee for State Security) was behind international terrorism and that the Reagan administration linked terrorism with communism. At the time Claire Sterling's *The Terrorist Network* was for Reagan and Haig a key reference book before it was revealed that the book was CIA disinformation "blown back." In short, the same "international experts" were advising Washington and the Basques regarding allegedly the *same* enemy—the terrorist. The ongoing War on Terror is based on the premise that terrorism—either in Iraq or Afghanistan or a dozen other Muslim countries—is essentially *the same* phenomenon and even that its work is done by the *same* al Qaeda global organization.

The Realities and Gridlocks of Terrorism Discourse

The media confronts us daily with the realities of terrorism, as well as with the discursive nature of many of the "facts." As noted, far from being a mere mirror of the facts on the ground, discourse may create its own reality. The alleged plot uncovered by the British police in London in August 2006 to blow up as many as ten airplanes over the Atlantic with liquid explosives illustrates the point. Having arrested twenty-one people, the alarm could not have been more ominous. Paul Stephenson, the deputy chief of the Metropolitan Police in London, declared on August 10 that the plotters were intent on "mass murder on an unimaginable scale"; John Reid, the British home secretary, predicted that, as the result of the "highly likely" attacks, the loss of life would have been on an "unprecedented scale."

I had to fly from Spain to the United States with my family ten days after this front-page news; the anticipation became dreadful as daily reports detailed the hours of delay at the airports, the prohibition on carrying hand luggage, the repeated cases of flights aborted or returned to their point of departure because of the hysteria provoked by some unruly passenger. After we made it home safely, a report in the *New York Times* proclaimed that the plotters had left "a trove of evidence," thus fully vindicating the initial concern.[33] Yet, a careful reading of the report provided a very different picture of the events. It admitted that, according to five senior British officials, "the suspects were not prepared to strike immediately. Instead, the reactions of Britain and the United States in the wake of the arrests of 21 people on Aug. 10 were driven less by information about a specific, imminent attack than fear that other, unknown terrorists might strike." That is, fear of unspecified terrorists, not the ones arrested, had been the real reason for the apocalyptic alarm that turned the world's air traffic into chaos. In fact, "Despite the charges, officials said they were still unsure of one critical question: whether any of the suspects was technically capable of assembling and detonating liquid explosives while airborne." Some of the suspects had been under police surveillance for over a year and what had triggered the police action was that one of the key suspects, Rashid Rauf, who holds dual British and Pakistani citizenship, had been arrested in Pakistan. Initially, it was said by one official and later disclaimed by another that upon Rauf's arrest an explicit message to the plotters to "Go now" had been issued. This prompted the decision by Scotland Yard to proceed to arrest the entire group when, in fact, British investigators would have preferred to monitor the suspects longer. In short, the group was under close police surveillance; having installed video cameras and audio recordings in their "bomb factory," the police knew the group was not ready to attack (some of them did not even have passports yet, let alone tickets to fly) and, by the police's own admission, they even questioned the group's capacity to detonate a device. So we are left with the question: Was the threat, which must have cost the aviation industry billions, so credible as to create the air traffic chaos worldwide? The same senior official characterized the apocalyptic remarks of two weeks earlier as "unfortunate." After his dire predictions of August 10, Mr. Reid sought to calm the public by lowering the threat level from "critical" to "severe," and by acknowledging that "[t]hreat level assessments are intelligence-led. It is not a process where scientific precision is possible. They involve judgments." Here we have a typical case of terrorism's hyperreality in which the facts are there (the alleged plotters were clearly up to something) but they take shape against a background of threats and fears that then become constitutive of subsequent events themselves. That is, the scare was as much or more the product of the *interpretation* of messages as of the actual immediacy of the threat.

In short, we are confronted with a new epistemic space; a new act of naming was deemed to be necessary for a new historical reality. Awareness that reality is up for grabs, and that the U.S. administration's rationales for the war on terror have only the most tenuous connections to reality, has become a staple of the mainstream political debate as reflected in the daily media's coverage of the administration's political agenda. The big scare produced by the uncovered British plot ultimately had as much to do with the rhetorical dimension of terrorism as with the actual danger posed by those arrested on August 10, half of whom were later released without charges. Some evidence for the plot was there, but its apocalyptic nature became credible because of the rhetorical power of terrorism. To talk of its rhetorical dimension means that the link between actions and goals is mediated by perceptions and interpretations; that is, the primary persuasions that matter to the terrorist are the reactions themselves. Counterterrorism is equally rhetorical in that a primary concern for officials in their War on Terror is how the public perceives their actions.

There is a long history of politicians using terrorism to their advantage. The British terror case, for example, is credited with having improved President Bush's approval ratings, certainly not a negligible result in itself. Now, imagine the temptation when such rhetorical power, by which you can largely control the public's interpretation of a certain threat or potential action, is available to politicians. Such dimension becomes even more critical in a situation in which the activities of the terrorists, as well as those of the counterterrorists, are clouded in secrecy and classified information. In this crucial sense—what matters are the reactions and interpretations terrorism provokes—it is primarily a rhetorical phenomenon. In the 2008 U.S. elections, the last attempt by the McCain campaign to offset Obama's advantage in the polls was to associate him with "the former terrorist" Bill Ayers. Rhetorics and discourse become *constitutive* of the reality itself. The writing of terror becomes inaugural.

States of Exception

A fateful consequence of counterterrorist doctrine is the adoption of the exceptional as norm. Terrorism by its very nature resorts tactically to improvisation and formlessness—the methods, organization, legality, ethics, even the very persona of the terrorist lack stability and coherence. The irresistible temptation for counterterrorism is to fight its enemy by replicating this abrogation of form and law. The informality embraced for tactical advantage by the powerless terrorist, when replicated by the state, becomes a structural state of exception that subverts to its core the ordinary rule of law.

Counterterrorism begins by portraying terrorism as totally unique. It takes for granted that terrorist violence is unlike any other; that the immorality of its actions is an unredeemable atrocity; that it is a form of madness with no possible political legitimacy; that its methods defy rules and order; that the only civilized responses to such aberration are total annihilation (war without quarter) and taboo. In the end, counterterrorist ideology arrives at the conclusion that espousing a perpetual *state of exception* is a necessary condition for fighting the spectral enemy.

The final result of such states of exception has been described by Giorgio Agamben as one in which "it is impossible to distinguish transgression of the law from the execution of the law, such that what violates a rule and what conforms to it coincide without any remainder."[34] Guantánamo, portrayed as the ultimate bastion of civilization against terrorism, became also the symbol of the ultimate denial of any domestic or international law. That which, from the traditional perspectives of civil rights advocates, was the most flagrant violation of legality, was suddenly being tolerated as the law of the land and treated in public opinion and the mainstream media as completely "normal." The anomaly could only be explained in terms of counterterrorism discourse's fundamental premises. According to these, the exceptional became normalized because of the beliefs, fears, and prophecies of a new culture of terrorism that is subversive of what we have known until now as the rule of law. From the perspective of cultural analysis the question that concerns us is the extent to which we can attribute such "exceptionality" to semantic definitions and self-serving political expediency. The critical point, one that can be illustrated with countless examples from Great Britain, Spain, Israel, Chechnya, South America, India, and other places, has to do with the inevitable tendency regarding how the semantics of terrorism work in relation to law: by charging the other with terrorist lawlessness, it allows oneself to dispense with the rule of law.

More generally, information that was previously unimaginable became staple news in the post-9/11 world. It was no longer surprising, say, to hear on NPR a long report on how an Iraqi was tortured to death at the hands of Americans,[35] or to read an editorial in your morning newspaper stating that the White House was "certainly tireless in its effort to legalize torture"[36] or that the president was putting "the full faith and credit of the United States behind the concept of torture."[37] Case after case of outsourcing torture to third-world proxies by the United States, in what is known as "extraordinary rendition," and which has resulted in dozens of deaths, became "normal" reporting in the media. The fate of hundreds of prisoners in Guantánamo was sealed when the Bush administration defined them as "unlawful combatants" and therefore "terrorists." There was no need for a fact-finding process. They could be held indefinitely in legal limbo. Secretary of State Colin Powell argued that the Geneva Conventions should cover the Afghan conflict and asked the president to reconsider. His arguments were rejected by White House lawyers who invoked "the nature of the new war" on terrorism. "The new paradigm rendered obsolete Geneva's strict limitations on questioning of enemy prisoners," and made other Geneva provisions "quaint."[38] All of this led finally to Abu Ghraib and the international outcry over the images of torture and sexual humiliation committed by the U.S. forces in Iraq.

Soon after 9/11 the U.S. Congress enacted the Patriot Act virtually overnight. Defenders of civil liberties criticized the Patriot Act for removing most limitations and judicial controls on governmental abuse, for violating core constitutional principles, for fundamentally altering the power of the Federal Bureau of Investigation and the role of the CIA, and for reserving its harshest measures for immigrants.[39] The Patriot Act has provided the government an extraordinary expansion of surveillance authority that goes beyond the investigation of terrorism and which applies to any federal criminal investigation.[40]

Only counterterrorism discourse could legitimate the practical suspension of habeas corpus in the United States. Anthropologists employ the concepts of ritual pollution and taboo to study the antinomies of norm and anomaly, pattern and chaos, normalcy and pathology. In such primary dynamics of form and formlessness, civilization and barbarism, a key component has to do with lawfulness and lawlessness.[41] Such premises recall ancient notions regarding barbarians as less than human and therefore outside the realm of law. What other phenomenon would belatedly justify the use of torture? In our liberal democracies the tension between civilization and barbarism is now configured by terrorism.

Terrorism goes to the heart of "the paradox of sovereignty" that, in Agamben's formulation, "consists in the fact that the sovereign is, at the same time, outside and inside the juridical order."[42] Guantánamo and Abu Ghraib are instances of the sovereign power's capacity to be simultaneously inside and outside of the law. According to this relation of exception, something is included through exclusion.[43] What happens here to the classical Schmittean definition of politics in terms of the categorical binary friend/enemy? In this view there is no politics without the figure of the enemy and no bigger threat to politics than Friedrich Nietzsche's adage "Enemy, there is no enemy." After the collapse of the Soviet Union, when the world was left with a sole heavily militarized superpower, Schmitt's question would have been: How can you sustain a militarized empire without a real enemy? It is here that the emergence of the figure of the terrorist becomes crucially self-fulfilling to understand the configuration of the new politics. Schmitt differentiated enmity and hostility. The enemy is something "public," and opposition to it has nothing to do with private sentiments of hatred. In the Christian tradition, the maxim "love your enemy" didn't mean love your political enemy. Thus, the distinction between enmity and hostility was the conceptual invention of a medieval Christian Europe intent on liquidating Muslims while fulfilling the Christian duty of loving one's Muslim neighbors. This was not just any war; it was combat with the political at stake. Such struggle over politics is what we are witnessing in the ongoing War on Terror as well. This is not an ordinary "war" between two enemies. It is defined, rather, as a war between civilization and barbarism. The terrorist enemy is dealt with by imposing the cultural premises, laws, and myths of a counterterrorism doctrine for which the state of exception becomes the ordinary rule.

Terrorism and the Betrayal of the Intellectual

How has contemporary violence turned into terrorism narrative and how do its varied versions influence the course of history? "The term history unites the objective and the subjective side, and denotes . . . less what *happened* than the *narration* of what happened," observes Shoshana Felman. "This union of the two meanings we must regard as of a higher order than mere outward accident."[44] Felman concentrated on two of Camus' novels, *The Plague* (1947) and *The Fall* (1956), as exemplary for examining such a relationship.

The Plague describes a town stricken by an epidemic. The protagonist of the novel is a doctor who fights against the plague with dignity and determination. As testimony, the novel is itself primary data documenting unproblematic history. Since the narrator is well informed and is an honest witness, history appears to speak for itself. The narrative is self-evident, the events are literal, and the witness's only task appears to be not to stand in the way of the events themselves by simply stating "this is what happened."[45] The doctor is the one who "has deliberately taken the victim's side and tried to share with his fellow citizens the only certitudes they had in common—love, exile, and suffering."[46] Bearing witness, then, becomes an act of survival. But at the very end of the novel there is a sniper who has gone mad, a proof that not even the honest witness can speak for all, and who raises the question of whether a healing testimony is possible in the contemporary times of the Holocaust and international terrorism. Camus will respond to that very question nine years later with *The Fall*.

In the background of the *The Fall*'s plot there is an emblematic event: the narrator saw by chance the suicide of a woman who suddenly jumps into the Seine. In contrast to *The Plague*, in which the narrator experiences directly the evil that he denounces, in *The Fall* the narrator desires to bear witness to a missed event, yet the absence of the face-to-face encounter reduces the witness to silence. In *The Fall* the death of the Other lacks significance and the protagonist withholds his act of witnessing from the community. It is the failure of the witness that concerns Camus in this novel, the inability to be sure of the value of one's narrative knowledge. "*The Fall*, in opposition to *The Plague*, explores the roots of the disasters of contemporary history not in the evil of the enemies (some external bacillus of Plague) but, less predictably, in the betrayal of the friends," suggests Felman.[47] This is based on the well-known facts regarding the falling out between Jean-Paul Sartre and Camus as the result of the publication of *L'homme revolté* (1951), in which Camus denounced dogmatic Marxism and Stalinism in particular, earning him a negative review in Sartre's journal *Les temps modernes*. Their controversy centered on the role of history and how to be a witness to it; in Sartre's view, the process of dialectical totalization explained Stalin's rule. Camus thought that the totalitarian impulse of historicism was as deluded as its antagonistic ideology—idealist antihistoricism. "There are two sorts of impotence," he concludes, "the impotence of Good and the impotence of Evil."[48] It is preciesely the ideology of salvation and its corresponding witnessing that Camus seeks to question in *The Fall*.

"There are always reasons for murdering a man,"[49] the narrator observes in *The Fall*. The Nazis committed murder in their search for a "final solution." How does that differ from the rationalization of killing in the search for a communist utopia? Thus "Camus now realizes that the very moral core that gave its momentum to *The Plague* . . . was itself in some ways a distortion, a historical delusion."[50] The true witness is beset in the end with issues of knowledge and silence. When Sartre accuses Camus of merely "looking" at history from Hell rather than "making history," Camus replies that Sartre is "making silence" by refusing to look at the horrors of history. Are the political realities of Camus' "view from Hell" over? That which made such realities possible in the past was the wall of silence surrounding them. Isn't the very fact that Guantánamo and a shadowy network of secret prisons can be tolerated by the American public proof of Camus' argument regarding the betrayal of witnessing?

Felman's conclusion is that the premise of the very unmediated access to the evidence of *The Plague*, the very nature of the unqualified testimony given therein is problematic, for it "fails precisely to account for the specificity of a disaster that consisted in a radical failure of witnessing, an event to which the witness had no access, since its very catastrophic and unprecedented nature as event was to *make the witness absent*."[51] *The Fall* seeks to unmask the complacency of the witness who presumes for himself untainted innocence. Because if the witness is truly aware of the criminal history of his times, including the Holocaust, there is no room for pure innocence—"innocence can only mean lack of awareness of one's participation in the crime."[52] Camus' point echoes Fyodor Dostoevsky: "We cannot assert the innocence of anyone, whereas we can state with certainty the guilt of all. Every man testifies to the crimes of all the others—that is my faith and my hope."[53] Since in this perspective there is no longer an innocent platform from which to testify, we are guilty of our own presumption of innocence. Guilt thus becomes not a state opposed to innocence but an element in the process of awakening.

The Fall refers to the turning point marked in history by the events of the Holocaust and the modern crisis of witnessing it underscores. When the narrator witnesses the descent of the suicide off the bridge, whose fall is being narrated? Is it the woman's or the narrator's—who failed to tell anyone what he saw? It is this fall/failure of the witness with which we are confronted. Previously, in 1946, Camus had written in *Neither Victims nor Executioners* that "the years we have gone through have killed something in us. And that something is simply the old confidence man had in himself, which led him to believe that he could always elicit human reactions from another man if he spoke to him in the language of a common humanity."[54] After Auschwitz, the radical crisis of witnessing forces narrative to become writing of such impossibility. Camus wrote faced with the Nazi death camps but also with Hiroshima, Nagasaki, and the systematic destruction of European cities by both sides. The war showed not only a near universal capacity for genocidal murder but also the recourse to massive violence in the name of a just cause. Camus broke with the centuries-old tradition of the just war—a thinking that is untenable during the nuclear era. Camus especially came to abhor the abstract state's role in serving to legitimize murder and the ominous role of lethal technology in the service of national security. It is the bureaucracy that makes the decisions, so individuals are free to deny their responsibility for the potential consequences of such weapons.[55] Mass destruction is thus planned *without witnesses* and everyone is thereby innocent. To this Camus replies, "We are all guilty."[56] The righteous ideologies in the defense of democracy and Western civilization, supported by reason and science, were nothing but masks for murder, since "there are always reasons for murdering a man."

The discourse of "the terrorist" presumably adds a new decisive dimension to the ideological justifications for the just war: it provides the necessary nemesis of a subhuman being who has no moral, legal, or political grounds whatsoever. In President Bush's words, they "hide in caves, [but] we'll get them out" and the "civilized world is rallying to America's side" in an attempt "to hunt down, to find, to smoke [terrorists] out of their holes."[57] Bent on murderous, arbitrary, and random violence, the actions of the terrorist prompt the immediate reaction that the taking of his or her life is not only the only sensible thing to do but a moral duty. Currently the creation of such discourse is in itself the principal ideological construct for condoning an endless War on Terror with many thousands of casualties annually. The terrorist is the new legitimizing signifier (as was "Hitler" during World War II) that elicits, indeed demands, unbridled war by whatever means. Thus the dangers seen by Camus in the ideology that the ends justify the means, that our murders are qualitatively different from theirs, that a conspiracy of silence is warranted because of the nature of the enemy, in short, that our killing is justified, is nowhere more evident than in the War on Terror.

CHAPTER TWO

Who's Afraid of Truman Capote?

Writers versus Counterterrorists

Terrorism is crucially a rhetorical phenomenon—what really matters to the terrorists are the responses to their actions, the interpretations given to the events, the reactions of fear and bafflement they elicit. Rarely does the terrorist action have instrumental military value. Its most important purpose is to become a news event—and thus to have political consequences. The complicity between fact and fiction, reality and discourse, the thing itself and the writing of it thereby become inescapable. The thing itself is the reactions it provokes. Close attention to the writing of terrorism and the narrative plots in which the arguments are couched is thus key to unveiling the genealogy and the very essence of terrorism.

Writing about murder has long been one of the standard literary narratives. Leo Tolstoy denounced Shakespeare for being obsessed with it. We are looking for what is specific to terrorist murder. Perhaps, in order to appreciate how the writing of terror has become constitutive of the thing itself, we should compare and contrast two paradigmatic texts, Truman Capote's *In Cold Blood* and the *9/11 Commission Report*. By examining the writing protocols of a novelist and a commission of counterterrorists, we aim at showing not only that discourse creates in good part reality but that the novelist obtains types of knowledge that are impeded to the counterterrorist. By focusing on such a contrast, our goal is to point out the epistemic impasse of a counterterrorist knowledge incapable of getting into the basic mentality, emotional attitudes, and existential *amor fati* of the subjects it purports to study. The final argument will be that it is the lack of the novelist's subjective knowledge that dooms counterterrorism to dismal failures such as 9/11.

The Shooting Gallery

Here is Capote reporting the confession by Perry Smith who, with his partner Dick Hickock, on one night in November 1959 had murdered the Clutters, a family of farmers in Holcomb, Kansas. The assassins have entered the house and fail to find the safe in Mr. Clutter's office; they decide to wake up the family of four. Perry is relating the scene to the detectives:

"Dick stood guard outside the bathroom door while I reconnoitered. I frisked the girl's room, and I found a little purse—like a doll's purse. Inside it was a silver dollar. I dropped it somehow, and it rolled across the floor. Rolled under a chair. I had to get down on my knees. And just then it was like I was outside myself. Watching myself in some nutty movie. It made me sick. I was just disgusted. Dick, and all his talk about a rich man's safe, and here I am crawling on my belly to steal a child's silver dollar. One dollar. And I'm crawling on my belly to get it."[1]

The soon-to-be-murderer realizes with disgust that his dream of robbing a wealthy farmer is coming down to stealing a child's doll purse; he has been reduced to this—to kneeling for a dollar. Is this a movie? Then Perry remembers the binoculars he saw in Mr. Clutter's office and goes to get them. His narration to the detectives continues:

"It was cold, and the wind in the cold felt good. The moon was so bright you could see for miles. And I thought, Why don't I walk off? Walk to the highway, hitch a ride. I sure Jesus didn't want to go back in that house. And yet—How can I explain it? It was like I wasn't part of it. More as though I was reading a story. And I had to know what was going to happen. The end. So I went back upstairs. And now, let's see—uh-huh, that's when we tied them up."[2]

Perry ties Mr. Clutter to the furnace but not before he puts a box mattress under him for his comfort. While investigating the case, detective Al Dewey argued that there were "indications of ironic, erratic compassion" in the whole gruesome affair and that "at least one of the killers was not altogether uncharitable." The detectives ask Perry about the taping of the victims' mouths: "The taping came later, after I'd tied both the women in their bedrooms. Mrs. Clutter was still crying, at the same time she was asking me about Dick. She didn't trust him, but said she felt I was a decent young man. I'm *sure* you are, she says, and made me promise I wouldn't let Dick hurt anybody. I think what she really had in mind was her daughter. I was worried about that myself. I suspected Dick was plotting something, something I wouldn't stand for."[3]

The woman is telling her future killer that he is a decent young man. A page later, Perry reveals why he was worried about the daughter: "Then he [Dick] says to me, as we're heading along the hall toward Nancy's room, 'I'm gonna bust that little girl.' And I said, 'Uh-huh. But you'll have to kill me first.' He looked like he didn't believe he'd heard right. He says, 'What do you care? Hell, you can bust her, too.' Now, that's something I despise. Anybody that can't control themselves sexually. Christ, I hate that kind of stuff. I told him straight, 'Leave her alone. Else you've got a buzzsaw to fight.' That really burned him."[4]

Mr. Clutter asks about his wife: "I said she was fine, she was ready to go to sleep, and I told him it wasn't long till morning, and how in the morning somebody would find them, and then all of it, me and Dick and all, would seem like something they dreamed. I wasn't kidding him. I didn't want to harm the man. I thought he was a very nice gentleman. Soft-spoken. I thought so right up to the moment I cut his throat."[5]

But Perry has forgotten something. "Wait. I'm not telling it the way it was," he scowls. After they have taped the victims' mouths, Perry takes Dick to a corner to talk it over. "Well, Dick. Any qualms?" No answer. Perry keeps provoking him, looking for a retreat from Dick, who will say nothing. And then:

> He was holding the knife. I asked him for it, and he gave it to me, and I said, 'All right, Dick. Here goes.' But I didn't mean it. I meant to call his bluff, made him argue me out of it, make him admit he was a phony and a coward. See, it was something between me and Dick. I knelt down beside Mr. Clutter, and the pain of kneeling—I thought of the goddam dollar. Silver dollar. The shame. Disgust. And *they'd* told me never to come back to Kansas. But I didn't realize what I'd done till I heard the sound. Like somebody drowning. Screaming under water. I handed the knife to Dick. I said, 'Finish him. You'll feel better.' Dick tried—or pretended to. But the man had the strength of ten men—he was half out of his ropes, his hands were free. Dick panicked. Dick wanted to get the hell out of there. But I wouldn't let him go. The man would have died anyway, I know that,

but I couldn't leave him like he was. I told Dick to hold the flashlight, focus it. Then I aimed the gun. The room just exploded. Went blue. Just blazed up. Jesus, I'll never understand why they didn't hear the noise twenty miles around.[6]

Perry's soft voice rings in detective Dewey's ears to the point of becoming a deafening sound, while he narrates the killings of the son ("Kenyon's head in a circle of light, the murmur of muffled pleadings"), the daughter ("She said, 'Oh, no! Oh, please. No! No! No! No! Don't! Oh, please don't! Please!'"), and Mrs. Clutter ("Perhaps, having heard all she had, Bonnie welcomed their swift approach.") Perry then decides to shoot Dick (he had drummed into Perry over and over *No witnesses*) but something prevents him from doing so.

Capote's writing is focused not only on the murderer's narrative but on the witness of the confession as well, on detective Dewey. "Sorrow and profound fatigue are at the heart of Dewey's silence." Despite the fact that Perry "answered to the questions of how and why," still he

failed to satisfy his sense of meaningful design. The crime was a psychological accident, virtually an impersonal act; the victims might as well have been killed by lightning. Except for one thing: they had experienced prolonged terror, they had suffered. And Dewey could not forget their sufferings. Nonetheless, he found it possible to look at the man beside him without anger—with, rather, a measure of sympathy—for Perry Smith's life had been no bed of roses but pitiful, an ugly and lonely progress toward one mirage and then another. Dewey's sympathy, however, was not deep enough to accommodate either forgiveness or mercy. He hoped to see Perry and his partner hanged—hanged back to back.[7]

After their confessions, the two murderers are taken for trial to Garden City, where a crowd of journalists and townspeople awaits them. Shouts and abuse by the crowd were anticipated, but when it caught sight of the two handcuffed and pale-faced men, "it fell silent, as though amazed to find them humanly shaped."

The simultaneous depths of the murderer' inhumanity *and* humanity is what makes Capote's writing so compelling. Yes, even the killers are humanly shaped. Yes, even they cannot be fundamentally that different from you and me. This might be disturbing for the judge, the policeman, the moralist, but not for the writer Capote, for the detective Dewey, or for Mrs. Meier, the wife of the undersheriff living in an apartment next to the jail who was in charge of cooking and sewing for the prisoners. As the jury sentenced Perry to death and he was led away, he met Dick at the door and said, "No chicken-hearted jurors, they!" They both laughed and the photograph appeared in a Kansas paper with the caption "The Last Laugh?" That afternoon, as he was taken back to the jail, Mrs. Meier shut herself in the kitchen "to keep from having to see him":

> But after everybody had gone, and I'd started to wash some dishes—I heard him crying. I turned on the radio. Not to hear him. But I could. Crying like a child. He'd never broke down before, shown any sign of it. Well, I went to him. The door of his cell. He reached out his hand. He wanted me to hold his hand, and I did, I held his hand, and all he said was, 'I'm embraced by shame.' I wanted to send for Father Goubeaux—I said first thing tomorrow I'd make him Spanish rice—but he just held my hand tighter.[8]

Before the trial, Perry receives an unexpected letter from someone who had served with him in the army in Fort Lewis, Washington (in the fall of 1951). It states, "God made you as well as me and He loves you just as He loves me, and for the little we know of God's will what has happened to you could have happened to me. Your friend, Don Cullivan." Perry, even if he did not care for the religious allusions, was thrilled that a respectable man should call him "friend." Mr. Cullivan testified in favor of Perry at the trial to the bafflement of many. He was a successful engineer who had graduated from Harvard, a husband and a father of three children, and yet, because as a Catholic he believed in life everlasting and had offered his friendship to a murderer, he could not say "no" when Perry's lawyer asked him to testify as a character witness. The Meiers, who were also Catholic and who had been rebuffed by the prisoner when they suggested that he consult with the local priest, Father Goubeaux, invited Cullivan to dine with Perry in his cell. Cullivan offered a blessing before the dinner and told him about his conversion to religion upon his younger brother's death from leukemia. Perry tries to explain the murders to Cullivan, but can't: "I don't know why I did it." He continues: "I was sore at Dick. The tough brass boy. But it wasn't Dick. Or the fear of being identified. I was willing to take that gamble. And it wasn't because of anything the Clutters did. They never hurt me. Like other people. Like people have all my life. Maybe it's just that the Clutters were the ones who had to pay for it."[9]

Cullivan assumed Perry was trying to show contrition, perhaps a desire for forgiveness. Nothing could be further from the truth. Perry's chilling words were an expression of his abyss: "Am I sorry? If that's what you mean—I'm not. I don't feel anything about it. I wish I did. But nothing about it bothers me a bit. Half an hour after it happened, Dick was making jokes and I was laughing at them. Maybe we're not human. I'm human enough to feel sorry for myself. Sorry I can't walk out of here when you walk out. But that's all."[10]

Cullivan could not believe such detachment; it was not possible to be so devoid of conscience. Perry says, "Why? Soldiers don't lose much sleep. They murder, and get medals for doing it. The good people of Kansas want to murder me—and some hangman will be glad to get the work. It's easy to kill—a lot easier than passing a bad check. Just remember: I only knew the Clutters maybe an hour. If I'd really known them, I guess I'd feel different. I don't think I could live with myself. But the way it was, it was like picking off targets in a shooting gallery."[11]

Cullivan's silence is upsetting to Perry: "Hell, Don, don't make me act the hypocrite with *you*. Throw a load of bull—how sorry I am, how all I want to do now is crawl on my knees and pray. That stuff don't ring with me. I can't accept overnight what I've always denied. The truth is, you've done more for me than any what you call God ever has. Or ever will. By writing to me, by signing yourself 'friend.' When I had no friends. Except Joe James."[12]

And Perry can't help but raise the question: "Joe always liked me. Do you, Don?" "Yes, I like you," Cullivan replies and Perry is relieved. Even murderers pathologically unable to feel remorse can make room for a "friend." Capote could allude to all that has been erected by centuries of culture, tradition, Christianity, law, literature in order to humanize someone if he was a murderer. But could you be a friend of a terrorist? Could you write empathetically of a terrorist in Capote's manner?

Perry "wished" he could feel something about the people he had killed, like sorrow or repentance. He couldn't. He could feel sorry for himself, but not for others. He didn't know why he had done it. He had expected that Dick would call his bluff when he took the knife from him, that he would tell him to stop. It was like taking out a target in a shooting gallery. It was some sort of play but with terrible consequences for everyone, himself included. The Clutters were innocent, yet someone had to pay and fate had chosen them. He knew that what he had done was "unforgivable," yet he couldn't feel any responsibility or remorse for it, he was innocent in some dark way that made sense only to him. Just before he was hung, his last barely audible words, blurred in shyness, expressed his dilemma: "It would be meaningless to apologize for what I did. Even inappropriate. But I do. I apologize."

Capote's narrative, word by word, sentence by sentence, chapter by chapter, captures Perry's painstaking portrait with a literary rigor that combines emphatic intimacy and emotional detachment, ethnographic precision and Homeric perspective, relentlessly confronting the reader with "the aura of an exiled animal, a creature walking wounded." With a lover's insight, Capote paints the portrait of Perry, a boy born near Elko, Nevada, half Indian, deeply hurt by witnessing at home sexual promiscuity and violence, taken away from his father by an alcoholic mother, raised in abject poverty—a sensitive boy who spent hours watching the moon and who later joined his wandering father for whom he felt great love. Despite his criminal delinquency and his sense of utter loss, Perry was still able to project the image that he was "a decent young man," as Mrs. Clutter put it before herself being murdered. Mrs. Hickock might have agreed, as she learned in court from detective Dewey that Perry had claimed the two murders committed by her son Dick, because "the Hickocks were good people" and Perry didn't want Mrs. Hickock to suffer for her son's deeds. Mrs. Hickock comes to embody the sorrow and the pity of the entire tragedy. She tries hard to explain to her companion what could have happened to her son Dick:

> Maybe I did do something wrong. Only I don't know what it could have been; I get headaches trying to remember. We're plain people, just country people, getting along the same as everybody else. We had some good times at our house. I taught Dick the foxtrot. Dancing, I was always crazy about it, gosh, he could dance like Christmas—we won a silver cup waltzing together. For a long time we planned to run away and go on the stage. Vaudeville. It was just a dream.... he was sweet, Dick was the best-natured little kid.[13]

All the grief in the world will not make Mrs. Hickock lose her composure and her sense of how to handle such tragic reality: "I can't make any excuses for what he did, his part in it. I'm not forgetting the family; I pray for them every night. But I pray for Dick, too. And this boy Perry. It was wrong of me to hate him; I've got nothing but pity for him now. And you know—I believe Mrs. Clutter would feel pity, too. Being the kind of woman they say she was."[14]

Pity is the feeling of tragedy. Capote captured the tragedy best through the sorrow of the murderer's mother: her pity for the victims and the killers. How else to cleanse the unbearable stain and wounds?

Capote takes the reader to the limit in order to contemplate, from the dark shores of madness, the murderer's subjectivity. He describes Perry on death row dreaming of having unscrewed the bulb of his cell by pressing the broom against it in order to cut his wrists and ankles with the broken glass. "The walls of the cell fell away, the sky came down, I saw the big yellow bird," Perry described the feeling. The yellow bird has soared in his dreams since childhood, an avenging angel and a savior: "She lifted me, I could have been light as a mouse, we went up, up, I could see the Square below, men running, yelling, the sheriff shooting at us, everybody sore as hell because I was free, I was flying, I was better than any of *them*."[15] The summer before he faced the hangman, Perry alternated between half-awake days and sweat-drenched nightmares. "Where is Jesus? Where?" was one of the persistent voices he would hear. "The bird is Jesus! The bird is Jesus!" once he awoke shouting. A recurrent dream had him as "Perry O'Parsons, The One-Man Symphony" in a Las Vegas nightclub, singing "You Are My Sunshine" while wearing a white top hat and white tuxedo:

> [A]t the top, standing on a platform, he took a bow. There was no applause, none, and yet thousands of patrons packed the vast and gaudy room—a strange audience, mostly men and mostly Negroes. Staring at them, the perspiring entertainer at last understood their silence, for suddenly he knew that these were phantoms, the ghosts of the legally annihilated, the hanged, the gassed, the electrocuted—and in the same instant he realized that he was there to join them, that the gold-painted steps had led to a scaffold, that the platform on which he stood was opening beneath him. His top hat tumbled; urinating, defecating, Perry O'Parsons entered eternity.[16]

The Las Vegas theatrical fantasy sums up Capote's America. In the course of its ordinary violence, in any given year close to thirty thousand people die in weapon-related deaths. America incarcerates 2.5 million people, of which 3,350 are on death row. Since Capote wrote his novel, close to a million people have died in the United States of gunshot wounds. None of this produces any special fuss in the American media and it is not a threat to national security. It is simply taken for granted by many people that we murder each other. As the saying goes, "Violence is as American as apple pie."

The reader of Capote's arresting novel comes away with the impression of actually knowing the killers. We learn about their families, listen to their own stories, witness their errors, struggles, attempts at redemption. We enter into the logic of their desires, frustrations, and self-destruction. And even if the unbearable question, *why?*, cannot be answered, the reader comes to understand that it also perplexes the murderer himself. The reader wonders at his madness, at his unforgivable deeds, yet the murderer is also human. Should you doubt that, Capote introduces his childhood through his mother's recollection, the waltzing with her and winning of a silver cup, the dream of running away together and going on the vaudeville stage. Could there be a more American *dream*? A more *normal* boy? A more tragic *American* mother?

Capote's writing makes you see that to be human is to be a potential murderer. Thus Capote provides an Americanized version of the Homeric tragedy—only it is not that of a unique archetypal event turned into legend, but rather of the all too banal killings of thousands upon thousands of people annually. As Patrick Moynihan observed, the upward/downward redefinitions of murder make for its "normalizing/abnormalizing"[17] dynamics; criminal violence, in particular, had been defined downward to the point that what even in the Chicago of the 1930s would have appeared as unthinkable was now trivialized to a "normal" rate for a weekend in any American city. It could be predicted that between 1993 and 2000 there would be something like 350,000 shooting deaths in the United States. Yet there seems nothing anomalous about this number in American public discourse. For anomaly one must look at terrorism. What Capote described was *normal* homegrown American (as opposed to "terrorist") murder. Terrorist exceptionality is altogether of a different order. In the meantime, while the murderer awaits the gallows, his fantasy whisks him away to Las Vegas. It is quintessential Americana.

In short, the collection and selection of "facts" obviously differentiates the novelist and the counterterrorist. For six years Capote gathered documents that could fill an entire room, and wrote four thousand pages on the Kansas murders. Yet for the book to become a seed in the reader's mind, he had to cut drastically the length of his manuscript by paying utmost attention to the choice of elements as well as the organization of the final text. The artist's process is, in the end, reductive—reduce the complexity to its bare bones, its salient traits, its emblematic images. This obliges the reportage to be partial as he cannot bring all the viewpoints into play. But selection according to what criteria? That's where Capote's strength lay: he knew what was relevant to the murderers *from the point of view of their own desires*. This required writing based on the intimate knowledge of the murderers' inner lives, a closeness so perilous that it could scorch and ultimately destroy even someone as infamously frivolous as Capote. The external events were there for everyone to see—the murders, the killers, the biographies, the communities. The artistic challenge was to describe convincingly a world of fears, phantoms, fantasies, memories, and desires that could lead to such horror. In the case of a truthful rendering of the Clutter murders, this relied not upon "making up" the facts, as would a fiction writer, but on the insightful selection and ordering of the multiplicity of actual facts at hand. In a nutshell, the narrative provided the bare essentials of what needed to be known to judge the case.

The *9/11 Commission Report*: The "Facts" and the Confessions

The *9/11 Commission Report* is a genuine effort to find out the facts and see what went wrong. It represents the best of counterterrorist research. It was headed by two outstanding public servants, the former governor Thomas H. Kean and former congressman Lee H. Hamilton. The Report was guided, we are told in the preface, by the following sweeping "mandate": "The law directed us to investigate 'facts and circumstances relating to the terrorist attacks of September 11, 2001.' " It added: "Our aim has not been to assign blame. Our aim has been to provide the fullest possible account of the events surrounding 9/11 and to identify lessons learned."[18] If I am taking this remarkable text as the foil against which to point out critically the limits of counterterrorist discourse, it is to underline the fact that it is the paradigmatic frame that is the problem, rather than the dedication and professionalism of the operatives themselves.

If Capote was primarily interested in the how and why of the murderers themselves—their subjectivities—the Committee's agenda is focused rather on the surveillance and political circumstances under which the attacks transpired. Therefore, Capote's and the Commission's "account of the events," and even what should be considered as event, are quite distinct: for the novelist a most revelatory "event" is, say, the murderer dreaming of a big yellow bird, or his regard for his fellow killer's mother. Such details would not count as meaningful events for the counterterrorist. In short, the novelist is intent on inscribing the *dreams* and *desires* of the murderer as actual events in order to make sense of his senseless behavior; the counterterrorist is policing criminal behavior and looking for actual events that can be documented and taken as proof in a court case.

Unlike Capote's novel, a narrative of thousands of pages reduced to a tight description of the events, the Report begins by stating categorically that "we have endeavored to provide the most complete account we can of the events of September 11, what happened and why."[19] If the novelist works reductively in search of the crucial events that reveal the dynamics of murder, a phenomenon that is as old as the history of mankind, and one that has obsessed canonical writers for centuries, the counterterrorist experts aim at describing everything possible about terrorism, a new and barely understood phenomenon. Commission members profess to be "conscious of our limits," but what they and the writer take to be "limit" is not the same. For the novelist, limit has to do with his or her own powers of insightful description of events that are there for everyone to see and interpret; for the experts of the Commission, the limits derive from the investigative process. They could not interview every possible witness, so additional information will likely eventually come to light. Should they not be aware of some other limits, particularly those imposed from the outset by the discursive frame of the counterterrorist mind-set? The novel format obviously has its own limits, physical as well as discursive: it deals with experience through "fiction." By contrast, the journalist and the social scientist have to portray "facts." Capote's pioneering answer was the creation of "the nonfiction novel" combining reportage and literature.

So the 9/11 Commission's report is a paradigm of the counterterrorist search for the facts of the case. Does the Report succeed in its quest? Consider the following paragraphs as illustrative of the nature of the Report's factualness (italics added):

There is also *evidence* that around this time Bin Ladin sent out a number of feelers to the Iraqi regime, offering some cooperation. *None are reported* to have received a significant response. According to one *report*, Saddam Hussein's efforts at this time to rebuild relations with the Saudis and other Middle Eastern regimes led him to stay clear of Bin Ladin.

In the mid-1998, the situation reversed; it was Iraq that *reportedly* took the initiative. In March of 1998, after Bin Ladin's public fatwa against the United States, two al Qaeda members *reportedly* went to Iraq to meet with Iraqi intelligence. In July, an Iraqi delegation traveled to Afghanistan to meet first with the Taliban and then with Bin Ladin. *Sources reported* that one, or *perhaps* both, of these meetings was *apparently* arranged through Bin Ladin's Egyptian deputy, Ayman al-Zawahiri, who had ties of his own with the Iraqis. In 1998,

Iraq was under intensifying U.S. pressure, which culminated in a series of large air attacks in December.

Similar meetings between Iraqi officials and Bin Ladin or his aides *may have occurred* in 1999 during a period of *reported* strains with the Taliban. According to the *reporting*, Iraqi officials offered Bin Ladin a safe haven in Iraq. Bin Ladin declined, *apparently* judging that his circumstances in Afghanistan remained more favorable than the Iraqi alternative. The *reports* describe friendly contacts and indicate some common themes in both sides' hatred of the United States. But to date we have seen *no evidence* that these or the earlier contacts ever developed into a collaborative operational relationship. *Nor have we seen evidence* indicating that Iraq cooperated with al Qaeda in developing or carrying out any attack against the United States.[20]

Does the reader know "the facts" after reading such a narrative or are we confronted with what the authors of the Report consider to be likely misinformation, yet intelligence that they feel bound to *report* as it was gathered in *reportorial* fashion, but whose veracity cannot be established since there is *no evidence*? In other words, the language of the Report raises the question of whether the "facts" are historical or are being generated rhetorically. If the latter, that is a very significant "fact" in its own right. For a reader sensitive to rhetorical ploys, these paragraphs might serve as prime example of what Hayden White labeled "the fictions of factual representations."[21] As an example, bin Laden has said time and time again that the one thing that pushed him into anti-American jihad was the stationing of military forces in Saudi Arabia. For him it was tantamount to desecration of the holy land. Does the Report recognize this? The information is buried in the larger context of Muslim history and grievances, without ever underscoring its singular relevance as the tipping point in bin Laden's decision.

An obvious question is how the 9/11 Commission collected its information. This goes to the heart of the matter regarding the differences between Capote's narrative and that of the Report. Capote spent countless hours with the jailed murderers and exchanged hundreds of letters with each. Besides the scholarly work of the field of counterterrorism, the Report relies on two main sources. One is classified information: "Depending on the source and nature of the information," we are told, "these reports may be highly classified—and therefore tightly held— or less sensitive and widely disseminated. . . . Because the amount of reporting is so voluminous, only a select fraction can be chosen for briefing the president and senior officials."[22] Secrecy and nontransparency in the selection process are at the heart of such information gathering and its classification. The premises that govern such a process are not aired; there is no external control of possible misinformation. The reasons for this start with something as elementary as knowledge of the language.[23] It is evident that when you don't know the language and culture of someone you have to read meaning into their gestures, facial expressions, and other nonverbal codes. Since you can't speak his or her language, you are reduced to a lot of guesswork. How can you ascertain the "facts" in such a flawed process of communication?

Classified information is supplemented in the *9/11 Commission Report* by another source of information gathering: torture. The torturer may not know the subject's language, but he will surely have many "gestures" of the tortured body that he can "interpret." The Report is candid in admitting that its basic information on the "terrorists" came from "information obtained from captured al Qaeda members."[24] It candidly admitted that "assessing the truth of statements by these witnesses . . . is challenging," and that the authors "had no control" over the interrogations, "[n]or were we allowed to talk to the interrogators so that we could better judge the credibility of the detainees and clarify ambiguities in the reporting."[25] There is no attempt to hide the fact that entire chapters of the Report are exclusively based on information gathered from torture chamber guards.

What would Capote say about gathering information from Perry and Dick through torture? Information extracted through torture is by its very nature untrustworthy—the subject is willing to say anything to the torturers in order to end the ordeal. But beyond the essential unreliability of "facts" reported under torture, there is a larger message in assuming the legitimacy and validity of such information. Capote turned his murderers into tragic figures—by meticulously describing their thoughts and desires in life situations gone wrong. If it was basic human respect, even empathy, that Capote felt for the murderers, the counterterrorist's relation to his subject is obviously not the same. The counterterrorist may go as far as condoning torture if that is the only way to extract a confession. By such utilitarian calculations and consequentialist thinking (wouldn't you torture someone to avoid mass killings?), counterterrorism repeats the arguments of all of the predecessors who practiced torture. It has been said frequently that torture only reflects the inhuman barbarism of its practitioners.

The question that ultimately concern us here is: Who *knows* his subject best, Capote or the counterterrorist? And this implies: Who knows best the decisive facts that help explain the events of the case? In other words, what type of knowledge does the novelist hold that the counterterrorist does not value but might be decisive to predict terrorist behavior? In Capote's narrative we are convinced by the writer that we are given all the relevant facts—in a detailed way, with precision, in a shifting interplay of various contexts taken from life histories, detective reports, community networks, and psychological impulses. Capote approaches the subjects in a manner that is intimate yet distanced, personal yet objective—to "understand" murders that are beyond comprehension even for the perpetrators themselves. In the *9/11 Commission Report* there is a nebulous narrative that ends up including everything (politics, society, ideology, religion, psychology), yet nothing emerges that would explain the terrorists' subjectivity and their decision to undertake violent action.

The Report casts a wide net, in the typical fashion of counterterrorism discourse, in describing the threat as a worldwide phenomenon that is spreading like wildfire.[26] One of the nations to which al Qaeda has also expanded, and which we can perhaps use to test the value of such links, is the United States: "This pattern of [bin Laden's] expansion through building alliances extended to the United States." The Report states: "A Muslim organization called al Khifa had numerous branch offices, the largest of which was the Farouq mosque in Brooklyn. In the mid-1980s, it was one of the first outposts of Azzam and Bin Ladin's MAK [Mektab al Khidmat]. Other cities with branches of al Khifa included Atlanta, Boston, Chicago, Pittsburgh, and Tucson."[27] The Report recognizes that al Khifa was esablished to recruit American Muslims to fight in Afghanistan, but neglects something widely reported and that is not insignificant: the CIA was behind the entire setup, including regular visits from a Green Beret from the U.S. Special forces at Fort Bragg to train its members in the use of weapons.[28] The reasons for such omission are not hard to pin down: the narrative of the terrorist "enemy" against which an all-out "war" has to be waged demands a clear "us versus them" antagonism. Whether it is with the blind Sheikh Omar Abdel Rahman, bin Laden, or Saddam Hussein, the longstanding complicities between "us" and "them" are all too obvious for anyone to ignore.[29] But suddenly any hint of former cooperation with Evil is the first thing that needs to be eradicated and forgotten.[30]

All of this leads us to signal a boundary of counterterrorist thinking that is a condition of its possibility: the exclusion of terrorist subjectivity—a subjectivity that includes the cultural and historial backgrounds, the political motivations, and the unconscious drives of the actors. It is here that the difference with Capote is most striking: he confronted head-on such tragic subjectivity. But delving into emotions is outside its scope of the Report. If anything, the reactions to 9/11 were of shock, awe, fear, anticipation— intense emotions raised by the images of the collapsing towers. Yet all emotion is absent from the Report.[31] The intellectual consequences of the absence of terrorist's political and unconscious subjectivity are decisive in determining counterterrorist discourse and policy.[32] The Report itself provides an implicit admission of this when it lists the lessons that were *not* learned from the first World Trade Center bombing, and which can be traced directly to ignoring the terrorists' intentionality and humiliation. First, this was a new terrorist challenge, with Ramzi Yousef, the leader of the plot, hoping to kill 250,000 people—that is, a radical departure from the constraints of the symbolic economy of traditional European terrorism (kill one to scare a million). Second, the prosecutorial success against the plotters "created an impression that the law enforcement system was well-equipped to cope with terrorism."[33] Third, "the successful use of the legal system to address the first World Trade Center bombing had the side effect of obscuring the need to examine the character and extent of the new threat facing the United States." Fourth, there was the "widespread underestimation of the threat"—"the public image that persisted was not of clever Yousef but of stupid Salameh going back again and again to reclaim his $400 truck rental deposit."[34] Such unknowns clearly constitute ignorance and underestimation of terrorist desire and determination.

The Novelist versus the Counterterrorist

But let us return to the initial question: Would Capote be allowed to write of an Islamist terrorist murderer, say Mohamed Atta or Osama bin Laden, the way he wrote of Perry Smith or Dick Hickock? A comparison between *In Cold Blood*, a novel, and *the 9/11 Commission Report*, representative of counterterrorist writing, is revealing for our main concern here: What do we lose intellectually if we are not allowed to write on subjects from the perspective of a novelist and take into account the political subjectivity of the murderer? Put differently: What sort of "evidence" are we allowed to consider in order to *know* the murderer, the one provided exclusively by the policeman and judge, or also the one provided by a detective and the novelist and the ethnographer?

"How did it happen, and how can we avoid such tragedy again?"—this is the preliminary question for the 9/11 Commission. Its mandate was to investigate the "facts and circumstances relating to the terrorist attacks of September 11, 2001." Capote would agree with such an agenda—it was what he himself set out to do days after he read in the *New York Times* word of the gruesome killings of the Clutters in the town of Holcomb, Kansas. Yet from the beginning the Commission's preface provides an adversarial perspective that is decisive for the counterterrorist's mind-set, yet alien to the novelist: "We learned about an enemy who is sophisticated, patient, disciplined and lethal. The enemy rallies broad support in the Arab and Muslim world by demanding redress of political grievances, but its hostility toward us and our values is limitless."[35] The novelist is dealing with "literature" (fiction, art, and the like), whereas terrorism is stark reality, one might object. But the reality is that Capote was also writing of true events. And what concerns us here is that, regarding reliable knowledge, both texts are in the end *writing*, an activity ruled by all sorts of rhetorical conventions and discursive premises.

Capote's topic is American cold-blooded murder, yet his attitude is not one of confrontation with the loathsome "enemy" nor is he engaged in any "war on murder." He told Eric Norden that the killers were "perhaps the closest friends I've ever had in my life."[36] He added to Lawrence Grobel that "short of actually living in a death cell myself, I couldn't have come closer to their experience," and "I identify with them [Perry and Dick] completely."[37] Perry left all his belongings to Capote—"a heart-breaking assemblage that arrived about a month after the execution. I simply couldn't bear to look at it for a long time."[38] In short, Capote relates to his murderer as an ordinary human being. Can a counterterrorist become a "friend" of a terrorist? In Capote's case friendship does not make him an accomplice in any sense. In the case of the terrorist "enemy," friendship would be regarded as being very close to conspiracy and betrayal.

Capote paid heavily for such "friendship." His initial interest in the case was nothing but literary. But witnessing the tragedy of the murderers transformed him to the core. In the end Capote was utterly shaken by the execution of Perry and Dick and haunted by the experience for the rest of his life. Capote had great difficulty writing the last pages of the book describing the hangings, to the point that he developed paralysis in his writing hand. He was never able to complete another book. In the view of people who knew Capote, there were three deaths that day—the two cold-blooded murderers and the writer. After the book was published, he told George Plimpton, "I'm still very much haunted by the whole thing. I have finished the book, but in a sense I *haven't* finished it: it keeps churning around in my head. It particularizes itself now and then, but not in the sense that it brings about a total conclusion."[39] For Capote, writing that "nonfiction" narrative was like dying. "After I had worked on it for three years, I almost abandoned it," he told Frankel about the writing of *In Cold Blood*. "I'd become so emotionally involved that it was really a question of personal survival, and I'm not kidding."[40] He couldn't bear the morbidity of it.[41] There was only so much he could give to writing before he perished emotionally. This is how the artist works—by giving all to the demands of his craft, by being willing to probe the limits of knowledge, by identifying with his subjects and sharing their emotions.

Capote even theorized that there are types of writing that are possible only after a personal transformation. Trying to unveil the secret of his writing *In Cold Blood*, in his 1966 conversation with Frankel he distinguished between his technical craftsmanship and something else: "All I had to do then was something to myself. As far as technical ability, I could write as well when I was eighteen as I can today. I mean technically. *But I had to do something to myself. You see, I had to recreate myself.*"[42] In another conversation two years later, when Norden asked him what he meant by that, Capote replied: "Most American writers, as Scott Fitzgerald said, never have a second chance. I realized that if I were ever going to have that chance, it was necessary for me to make a radical change; I had to get outside of my own imagination and learn to exist in the imagination and lives of other people."[43] This led Capote to take up journalism, because this medium's criteria forced him to empathize with the characters he was writing about and understand their motives.

Capote did not want to be a mere journalist, however. His aim was a narrative beyond the "I was there" premise—"what I wanted to do," he told Norden, "was bring to journalism the technique of fiction, which moves both horizontally and vertically at the same time: horizontally on the narrative side and vertically by entering *inside* its characters."[44] In other words, like the ethnographer and the detective, Capote had to play with his own subjectivity in order to understand the desires and the motives of the peoples he was going to write about.

Is the counterterrorist allowed to be *inside* his or her characters, or is such an intellectual operation seen to be an exercise in "justifying" terrorism and therefore politically anathema? For any writer of fiction or ethnography, penetration of the subjectivity of the people about whom one writes is nothing less than the precondition for writing. But should you allow yourself to be a Capote when dealing with terrorists given what Capote put himself through? That the counterterrorist may also write is evidenced by the hundreds of books being published on the topic. But the question is whether you are allowed to write with the full range of artistic strategies that a novelist or ethnographer takes for granted. Are you allowed to write as the lover of a terrorist? Oriana Fallaci did write of an affair she had with a Greek "freedom fighter" and Robin Morgan wrote of her experiences with "terrorist activities" and her becoming a "demon lover."[45] But the very fact that they could fall in love with terrorists was implicit proof that in the end they could not possibly be merely monstrous "terrorists."[46]

Why did Capote write the book? The murderers themselves were the first to ask him the question. His reply was that he was not interested in changing the readers' minds nor had he any moral or political reasons for writing such a book, but "it was just that I had a strictly aesthetic theory about creating a book which could result in a work of art."[47] His purpose might not have been to change anyone's mind regarding multiple murderers, but the book did indeed change the writer himself while affecting readers powerfully. But whether one writes about multiple murderers or terrorists, isn't it "truth" that really matters? Capote's answer was telling; he was trying "to make truth into fiction, or fiction into truth."[48] Writing was for Capote anything but trivial. It was in fact a matter of life or death, which is why he found writing *"extremely* difficult,"[49] to the point that he'd as soon have not been a writer. There was nothing banal about his choosing the topic of multiple murders in Kansas; in fact, Capote felt that writing about those murderers had been his vocation, his dark fate, and that "in a very real sense, they selected *me*,"[50] as he told Norden.

The reward of having become an unguarded witness was that Capote came to know Perry and Dick almost to a point of excess. As a result, he became aware that Perry, the one who was actually capable of killing, "had extraordinary qualities" and that he "could have been an entirely different person."[51] Perry wanted intensely to write and paint and had a real talent as a musician; he played five or six instruments, the guitar in particular. This killer was also "quite a little moralist" and a sort of expert on the philosopher George Santayana. Perry's last one-hundred-page letter, received by Capote after his execution, concluded with a paraphrase from Thoreau, "And suddenly I realize life is the father and death is the mother." Above all, the one thing Capote knew about Perry was that he "wasn't an evil person."[52] Perry—a man with an absent Irish father, a Shoshone alcoholic and prostitute mother who choked to death on her own vomit; a recluse in an orphanage where his bed wetting made him the target of scorn and abuse; first arrrested when he was eight and held in confinement in several detention centers; beaten by the nuns, his penis rubbed with a burning ointment by one attendant, while another held him in a tub of ice water until he developed pneumonia; someone who had suffered several brutal assaults by fellow servicemen while in the Merchant Marine, whose brother had committed suicide and whose sister died after falling from the window of a hotel during a drinking spree; a man arrested for theft after his military service in Korea, held in prison for years and, finally, a multiple murderer—he became for Capote a tragic figure rather than the incarnation of evil. Everything would have been so much easier with a simple explanatory principle: poor Perry is *evil* and that is why he is the monster capable of doing what he did. Proof that he was evil incarnate was his lack of guilt—like an animal, he did not even possess a conscience.

In the end, Capote's interpretation of the killer was closer to what Hannah Arendt termed "the banality of evil" than to one of hypostatic, irredeemable Evil. That is why he had no problems believing Perry's confession, not even when he said that he never meant to kill the Clutters and was amazed that he'd done so. Capote agrees with the conclusion of the psychiatrist Joseph Satten that the person Perry murdered that night was a substitute father figure.[53] Capote's narrative is the antithesis of simple dismissal of the murderers as evil persons; Gloria Steinem was right when she wrote of the author that "his great strength is his gift for understanding many worlds and many realities; for writing about both the murderer and the murdered with a compassion that makes the reader trust him completely."[54]

Yet can one *fictionalize* terrorist murder? Hollywood does it all the time, while sensationalizing it. In counterterrorist thinking only real "facts" should be considered. It is a discourse that only allows for the most literal and documented facts, never fantasies or desires per se, and it is anchored in the search for immediate causality. It is the strength of Capote's novel that he escapes the constraints of an easily identifiable causality in order to situate the tragedy in a larger narrative that includes two biographies and the complex interactions between them, as well as between the biographies and the wider American society and culture. The novel itself as a work of art provides a different type of answer, one that is sustained by two individual life histories and revealed through the skillful combination of journalism and fiction. Camus understood the need to fictionalize "the plague" of World War II rather than merely chronicle it, because the unbelievable *unreality* of European barbarism in the twentieth century was such that it required the imaginative powers of literature in order to provoke the transformation necessary for the reader's survival.

A Sense of Evil and the Faltering Writer

Capote's initial commitment was his determination to truly comprehend the murderers. In the end, "What mattered is that I *knew* them, as well as I knew myself."[55] He knew them so intimately that "it wasn't a question of my *liking* Dick and Perry. That's like saying, 'Do you like yourself?' "[56] Such knowledge was not only factual (the result of many hours of visits with them, the hundreds of exchanged letters, the painstaking research), but also and crucially emotional (through intimate identification with the murderers' life situations, catastrophes, desires). Capote led a "monastic life" to be able to write the book, sometimes writing in trance-like states for four or five hours.[57]

But it wasn't merely that Capote was being a good writer, rendering real events with "fictional" techniques and contemplating the simple horror of stark murder with the mantle of psychological insight. Capote had to effect a far more difficult aesthetic operation, which he described thus to Grobel, "I just have a double sense of perception. I sort of see what's good and bad simultaneously."[58] Such a Blakean perspective of talking to angels and demons simultaneously is what comes out of Capote's narrative. Critics such as Newton Arvin suggested that Capote, like Nathaniel Hawthorne and Herman Melville, had "a sense of evil." But it was because he knew evil so intimately, and because of his simultaneous dual vision, that Capote could not reduce the murderers to evil. Also, because of his wider view of their human condition, he could not pass an easy judgment on the murderers' lives; this was the reason why he could relate so well to them and why they would bare their souls to him. It was as if he could see in the murderer his conscious and unconscious lives, his personal and his social selves simultaneously.

In the final analysis, Capote's approach approximates Greek tragedy. Norman Mailer saw in Perry one of the great characters of American literature. Beyond the narrative of gruesome murders, Capote's book makes the killers and their families credible ordinary good people destroyed by social and psychological forces beyond their control. Hence Steinem's apt attribution of "compassion" to Capote's narrative, this being the sentiment of tragedy—we watch the protagonists falling into the abyss of error and death but it is an error that we ourselves could well have committed and therefore we end up pitying them. Such perspective makes Capote's narrative a work of art so compelling that it questions and transforms the reader's consciousness. It is no longer "ordinary" murder, a banal event adding to the annual statistics of crime, but a profoundly unique murder reverberating with the echoes of Greek tragedy.

It was through surrendering his own life to the demands of excessive witnessing that Capote was able to write such a book. But, in the end, Capote had to pay a heavy price for such recklessness. He could not put *In Cold Blood* out of his mind; as his friend Phyllis Cerf put it, "Eventually it began to own him. Emotionally, it became something bigger than he could handle. Those boys began to own him."[59] Despite all his empathy and artistic surrender, there was something Capote could scarcely forget: his deep ambivalence toward saving the lives of Perry and Dick. He was against capital punishment, which he saw as a form of "institutional sadism"; yet he was also opposed to the attitude that criminals were simply the victims of society. His views regarding the culpability of murderers were rather conservative; his final explanations tended to be psychiatric— killers such as Perry were "psychopaths." Obsessed with nothing but the fate of Perry and Dick on death row, Capote, too, was going through the whole excruciating experience, his life turned into a nightmarish state of suspended animation—while hoping that it would all soon end so that he could finish his book and reap the much anticipated rewards of his masterpiece. In other words, he wanted his dear friends, to whom he owed most in his life, hung. This moral dilemma must have consumed him. When, in January 1965, the Supreme Court refused to hear their latest appeal, it was a dark moment for Perry and Dick, but not so for Capote. Finally, he could sigh in relief that the agony of anticipation was ending. "I hardly give a fuck anymore *what* happens. My sanity is at stake,"[60] he wrote a friend.[61]

Among the general praise Capote received there was a personal attack from an old friend, Kenneth Tynan, that touched a raw nerve. He argued that Perry and Dick could probably have been saved had Capote wanted to spend his time and money to prove their insanity: "It seems to me that the blood in which this book is written is as cold as any in recent literature."[62]

Tynan was wrong regarding Kansas law, which did not accept a psychiatric defense, but he was right in his assertion that Capote did not want to save Perry and Dick.

Despite the recklessness of his ordeal, Capote the artist had to put himself through that hell.[63] What he had gone through was simply excessive witnessing, the kind that made him *know* his subjects intimately and feel responsible for their fate, a personal transformation through absorption into a different perspective on life. If the men with whom he so passionately identified were killers, he must also be some sort of potential killer; if, in the final analysis, they were saints, then he was too—or perhaps there was no true distinction between being a "killer" and a "saint." It was the enigma of his "dualism." He was simultaneously the charmer and the avatar of death.

What is the counterterorist to learn from Capote? That it is only by combining "a sense of evil" with "the dual vision" of heaven and hell that a writer or a researcher can grasp the world of the terrorist. This might require something as radical as Capote having to transform *himself* in order to be able to write his book. It was to such radicalness that he was referring when he insisted in interviews that "[n]o one will ever know what *In Cold Blood* took out of me. It scraped me right down to the marrow of my bones. It nearly killed me. I think, in a way, it *did* kill me."[64] Capote's testimony changed our very understanding of the murderer. The terrorism writer, too, has to be willing to endure the rigors of unprejudiced writing if he is to convey to the reader the tragedy he is examining. Such a writer must understand that one's culture and even oneself might first have to be transformed.

What such "dual vision" implies in the end is that the writer must be aware that the subject he is dealing with is deeply engaged in "the politics of the unconscious." The terrorist grounds his personality on the psychoanalytic notion of "the death drive" to the point of openly embracing suicide. Capote's art is consistent with an ethics that derives from contemporary psychoanalysis as well as from the Judeo-Christian tradition, namely, in Eric Santner's words,

> an ethics pertaining to my *answerability to my neighbor-with-an-unconscious*. What makes the Other *other* is not his or her spatial exteriority with respect to my being but the fact that he or she is *strange*, is a *stranger*, and not only to me but also to him- or herself, is the bearer of an internal alterity, an enigmatic density of desire calling for response beyond any rule-governed reciprocity;

against this background, the very opposition between 'neighbor' and 'stranger' begins to lose its force. I furthermore want to propose that it is precisely this sort of answerability that is at the heart of our very aliveness to the world.[65]

Capote delved into the "strangeness" of the action for the murderers themselves who could not understand their own madness. What makes the terrorist really *other* is his or her disturbing alterity that breaks down all the rules of law and ethics. Realizing that an intrinsic aspect of the terrorist persona is the excess of his or her unconscious drive does not imply condoning terrorism. It is by accepting the possibility that such others are strangers that the possibilities of a new community are opened up. Rather than an evil person, in Perry Capote saw the image of what he could have become. It was the kind of "evil" Capote experienced in his own childhood experiences—abandonment, despair, and rage. His identification with Perry meant that he, too, could be a potential killer and still be himself. This is what counterterrorism will not allow itself: to see in terrorism its own potential double. What Capote saw between him and Perry, and what is so difficult for the counterterrorist regarding the terrorist, is that they both, rather than being opposed in their essential humanity, could easily "belong to the same field."[66]

In order to understand their unconscious drives, what Capote did with the murderers was, in the end, *to take their subjectivity literally*. He digged into what constituted the fundamental phantasy of his actors' inner lives. He was not afraid to look into their suicidal madness as a reflection of his own potential one.

Terrorist Subjectivities

CHAPTER THREE

The Terrorist as Lover

Read My Terrorist Desire

"At the risk of seeming ridiculous, let me say that a true revolutionary is guided by great feelings of love. It is impossible to think of a true revolutionary lacking in this quality"—these are the often quoted words from Che Guevara. They need to be taken literally if we are to know what "the terrorist" is all about.

I have argued in part I that terrorism discourse shapes and frequently ends up creating its own reality. But is there nothing to "terrorism" but the discourse itself? In part II I will consider terrorist desire, madness, suicide—the various stages of subjective formation and transformation of the militant. These are indeed *real* things that go beyond the gridlock of discursive categories.

In the present chapter I will look into the terrorist as lover. My goal is to gain awareness of the relevance of knowing the militant's subjective world. Not only is the current taboo on the terrorist person intellectually self-defeating, not to mention politically disastrous, but we are unable to read the terrrorist's viewpoints because the very premises of enquiry prevent us from considering the evidence that really matters. By ignoring the terrorist's perspectives and desires we make all possible mistakes in dealing with his or her activities—a certain path to a circular course of action. In what follows we look into three texts in which "terrorists" are described as lovers and the writers themselves are "prisoners of love" regarding terrorists.

The Demon Lover: Robin Morgan

Robin Morgan wrote a book on terrorism based on her own life history: "My expertise is experiential. Because once I participated in what some call terrorist activities, and extricated myself barely in time to avoid the fate of a number of colleagues—fugitivity, prison, or death—I especially want to understand the phenomenon."[1] The title of her book, *The Demon Lover* (1989), signals from the beginning the relationship between terrorism and eroticism. Morgan had been with the Weatherman organization that got involved in acts of terrorism in the United States in the early 1970s. Her group expressed admiration for the murder of pregnant actress Sharon Tate by Charles Manson's group in these terms: "First they killed the pigs, then they ate dinner in the same room with them, they even shoved a fork in the victim's stomach. *Wild*."[2] Morgan ended up leaving the organization and being accused of "betraying the revolution"; consequently, two assassination attempts were made on her life. Writing becomes for Morgan a means of confession and exorcisim of her past.

From the outset, Morgan grasps directly the linkage between violence, death, pity, and sexual politics. Her view that terrorism marks the intersection of violence, eroticism, and masculinity is backed up by the history of most organizations. She observes that over 80 percent of terrorists are male; their typical age is between twenty-two and twenty-five years. The 9/11 terrorists were all male as well. The terrorist belongs largely to the realm of the imagination, Morgan reminds us: "Yes, the murder exists. The fear exists. The grief exists. But yes, the terrorist *is* a figment of our imagination."[3] A figment of the imagination, 9/11 included? Her point is not to deny the existence of terrorist actions but to insist on the imaginary and erotic involvement with the figure of the Terrorist. Because, in the final analysis, he is "the ultimate sexual idol of a male-centered cultural tradition."[4] No wonder that renowned terrorists such as "Carlos the Jackal" have a "harem" of female lovers. Morgan's mythical name for her terrorist is "the Demon Lover."

My own ethnography of ETA in the early 1980s[5] found that the role of women conforms to Morgan's description of their being "token terrorists." Many women have been affiliated with ETA, but their involvement was articulated through their male partners. When an important action was planned, women were excluded. At most they ran errands and carried messages. Rarely did a woman participate in the "executive committee" of the organization. "We were never equals with the boys; we were there to be mothers or prostitutes," one told me.

Still, there have been rare cases of ETA women who did achieve legendary status. One of them is Maria Soledad Iparragirre, known by her alias "Anboto"; it is believed that she swore eternal hatred of the Spanish police after one shot her boyfriend dead. Another, arrested some years ago in France and currently in a Spanish prison, was Idoia Lopez, known as "the Tigress" because of her irresisitible beauty: "Spanish police folklore has transformed the attractive green-eyed blonde bomber into a sexually voracious killer whose favorite pastime while serving in the Madrid commando is said to have been picking up police officers in bars, normally ETA targets, and having one-night stands with them."[6] This is the female archetype, the "demon lover" of the sexual politics of terrorism. A third high-ranking woman in ETA was Maria Dolores González Catarain, known as Yoyes; chapter 5 examines her extraordinary career in and out of ETA.

Morgan describes the image of the terrorist in pre-9/11 times: "The terrorist has been the subliminal idol of an androcentric cultural heritage from prebiblical times to the present. His mystique is the latest version of the Demon Lover. He evokes pity because he lives in death. He emanates sexual power because he represents obliteration. He excites with the thrill of fear. He is the essential challenge to tenderness. He is at once a hero at risk and an antihero of mortality."[7] The archetypal image of the Terrorist is for Morgan a "he," despite the fact that she herself participated in a terrorist group as a woman. The feminist Morgan situates him in the long patriarchal history of political violence: "The terrorist is the logical incarnation of patriarchal politics in a technological world."[8]

The value of Morgan's book rests on the contribution of her own "experiential perspective" as a feminist ("the personal *is* the political"). Regarding such a tabooed phenomenon, her unflinching affirmation of gender as a necessary approach to understanding terrorism marks a rare voice among American writers. Morgan's perspective is the struggle between the principles of life and death. Her final words in the new introduction she added after 9/11 are: "Who stands a better chance of survival, after all: those enamored with death? Or those in love with life?" In short, Morgan's honest portrayal of American terrorism, including herself as a participant, provides a crucial perspective that undermines the irreconcilable "they" versus "us," "good" versus "evil" dichotomies underpinning standard counterterrorism discourse.

A Man, a Woman: Oriana Fallaci and the
Terrorist Lover

The terrorist as lover has an exceptional narrative in Oriana Fallaci's
A Man, the novel/memoir in which the Italian journalist narrates her
affair with a Greek revolutionary. Alexandros (Alekos) Panagoulis was
a Greek antifascist fighter who became famous for his failed attempt to
assassinate dictator Georgios Papadopoulos in August 1968 by planting
a series of bombs along the route frequented by the leader. Panagoulis
was arrested and tortured for months. He was condemned to death but
the junta refrained from executing him because of international political
pressure. He refused to succumb to years of psychological torture and
made repeated attempts to escape. In 1973 he benefited from a general
amnesty. Two days after his release he was interviewed by Fallaci; they
became involved and had a tempestuous affair for three years. After he
died in a suspicious car accident (Fallaci always thought he had been
assassinated), she wrote *A Man*, dedicated to him, in which she attempts
to immortalize the martyred poet and resistance figure.

What is most remarkable stylistically is that each line of the book is
addressed to an Olympian "you," a second person singular addressed to
her man Alekos, a pronoun that punctuates every sentence and provides
the rhythm of the entire narrative, while standing for the presence of the
absent hero. She speaks only to him, not to the reader who is the spectator
of the drama unfolding between two lovers. The "you" is a larger-than-
life dead hero, presented to the reader on the first page as a cult figure
mourned and worshipped upon his death by a million and a half Greeks
gathered together in Athens from all over the country. They roar in grief
and rage, "He lives, he lives, he lives!" Panagoulis is the superhuman god
worshipped by a nation rendered subhuman in a "roar that had nothing
human about it. In fact, it did not rise from human beings, creatures with
two ears and two legs and a mind of their own; it rose from a monstrous,
mindless beast, the crowd, the octopus."[9] This projected "you" is
portrayed as nothing but pure heroism, capable of enduring months of
torture without ever flinching, a figure of Greek tragedy—except that,
unlike Greek classical heroes, Panagoulis is unaffected by any weakness
or hubris whatsoever.

And who is the "I" in this narrative about the "you" of a worshipped
fallen hero? There is no mundane "I" of the man who embodied such
a "you" now converted into the nation's heroic Other. It is squarely the

"I" of the narrator, but not the day-to-day conflicted "I" of the former lover uncertain of her man's love, only the "I" of the adoring lover of the departed fighter, bent on deifying the martyred hero. In fact, as Fallaci repeatedly observes, the encounter was strictly the work of Fate. The destiny of the hero and the narrator, the "you" and the "I," are so intertwined that, when they first meet two days after his release from prison and she is still resisting his erotic attraction, "I met those eyes and a terror restrained me: because there was death in those eyes. . . . I tell you there was death in those eyes, the announcement of everything that was to happen in the years to come and couldn't have happened without me, if I were not the instrument or the vehicle of your fate, already written."[10] And after his death and apotheosis—he lives, he lives, he lives—she has to fight her cynicism and tell herself "that maybe it was true. But if it was not true, something had to be done to make it seem true or become true."[11] That is, she had to write the novel of their fateful encounter and make it true. Alekos was truly her "only possible interlocutor,"[12] the only one who fully knew how much he relied on her to make him a god. Thus, she had to write their story, make the world know the gospel of their love, resurrect him in every believer. But she was also his Mary Magdalene. The first time Fallaci and Panagoulis made love, a child was being born in the next house, to whom they give the name Cristos. The atheist Fallaci wrote as if the Christian mythology of her Italian youth had finally become flesh in her lifetime, as if her love affair with the superhuman hero was the revolutionary substitute for the birth and resurrection of Christ.

This I/you relationship recalls the I/you of religious transcendence. But, again, the godliness of the "you" requires the belief and the worship of the "I." She admits that "sometimes I use the word 'you' to describe my own feelings."[13] By comparison, Capote's "I" is scrupulously absent from his Kansas murders' narrative, yet his presence could not be more palpable, his relationship to the actual murderers more intimate; there is nothing like Fallaci's "you" in Capote's narrative, only the real "you" of the two pathetic imprisoned murderers awaiting the gallows. Fallaci's "I" is ubiquitous as the lover and accomplice of the man, yet her presence is projected toward an utterly distant and otherworldly superhuman being. Capote watches the humanity of the inhuman, the banality of the evil, the perpetrator's incomprehensibility of his own actions. Fallaci writes a paean to godly heroism, sings of the utter victory of courage and freedom. Capote "is owned" by the presence of an intense mutual friendship with his subjects and is ravaged beyond repair, destroyed by having witnessed their hangings; Fallaci "owns" her hero after his death, writes a novel about him from the subject position of an eternal "great faithful love," and, by turning him into the protagonist of her own journalistic novel, "bursts forth from the same pages as the heroine who stands up to a military regime and sustains her lover in his struggle against power."[14]

Far from the real time of actual revolution and terror, Fallaci's narrative can only be framed in the past—a sacralized past in which everything did happen to the extent that the writer can remember, assert and reenact it, a perfect past with no danger any longer of future hubris. The role of the narrative is to show the reader the interaction between the I and the you, and the extent to which the Olympian you is the creation of the narrator/lover.

Fallaci's hero is in a sense the antithesis of Roland Barthes, who wrote, "To know that one does not write for the other, to know that these things that I am going to write will never cause me to be loved by the one I love (the other), to know that writing compensates for nothing, sublimates nothing, that it is precisely *there where you are not*—this is the beginning of writing."[15] In Fallaci's long "novel," the solemn and self-conscious proclamation of heroic love beyond the grave appears to the be the writer's ploy to achieve something else: writing one's own autobiography through the mythification of the love object. And such mythification is in the end an escape from the real dilemmas of political involvement.

By using Christian and Greek classical archetypes, Fallaci turns Alekos into a mythical figure. She uses history, journalism, and literature to create a "you" who "represents more than a historical hero and [who] emerges as a poetic figure or as a protagonist in an ancient fable."[16] "Death," what else, is a central protagonist of the narrative. Fallaci used to tell her interviewers that Death was ultimately the topic of her books. "You fell in love with the idea of dying,"[17] she tells Panagoulis, who writes in prison poems in praise of death: "Don't weep for me / Know that I die / You can't help me / But look at that flower / the one that is withering I tell you / Water it."[18] When a petition of pardon might free him, Panagoulis refuses to sign it; when he is finally given an amnesty, he seems indifferent to leaving his cell. Aricò says Fallaci makes him into a hero: "In the final analysis, it matters little whether the protagonist of *A Man* lived in the real world, whether he supported a leftist, rightist, or centrist regime, or whether he courageously opposed power in favor of individual freedom. Panagoulis emerges from the book's pages as an exciting combination of such heroes as Odysseus and Roland—a magical warrior armed with his lance in pursuit of twentieth-century tyrants."[19]

Does such an archetypal figure tell us anything about the ambivalence and madness of plotting and attempting actual murder, as Panagoulis did in real life? Was he in fact a real killer? The lines that are most memorable in her portrait of him are these: "I didn't want to kill a man. I'm not capable of killing a man. I wanted to kill a tyrant." [20] But he was, of course, capable of killing a man and it was the attempt to kill Papadopoulos that made him a hero. Fallaci's hagiography required that her hero should not be a murderer, that he be entirely good, only about life and not death. This is her sentimentalist big lie.

Early in the book Fallaci's hero is asked whether he knows how to shoot, how to aim, how to make a bomb. He does not. But, "Are you ready to die?" "Yes."[21] He is ready to die but he is not yet ready to kill. Still, in the same paragraph, "But now you were shuddering, thinking that it wasn't a game, it was the killing of a man. You never believed you could kill a man; you weren't even capable of killing an animal. This ant, for example. An ant was crawling up your arm. You picked if off with delicate fingers and set it on the table."[22] The delicate soul of the hero is unable to kill a man, unable to kill an animal, unable to terminate even the ant crawling up his arm. All he desires to do is to kill the *idea* of the tyrant. Thus he refuses to look at the face of his intended victim, because "if you look an enemy in the face" you might "realize that despite everything he's a man like you" and then "killing him becomes difficult." Thus it is "better to deceive your-self and imagine you are killing an automobile."[23] Fallaci's heroic "you" is not a born killer—"even holding a gun nauseated you." But this is not the Kansas multiple murder about to transpire on August 13, 1968, in Athens; it was happening in archetypal time and space. The reader should know that "in ancient Greece tyrannicide was honored with monuments and a laurel crown. And the phrase you had learned by heart: I am not capable of killing a man, but a tyrant is not a man, he is a tyrant."[24] This is the time of Greek heroes—except that this time Achilles need not kill in order to become the hero.

The only persons who will call Panagoulis a "murderer" are the torturers of the military junta: "Talk, murderer, talk! . . . If you don't answer me I'll kill you."[25] "But you never talked," Fallaci adds.[26] The narrative makes Panagoulis the innocent man paying with months of torture for simply desiring "a bit of freedom." Who are the real murderers here? Fallaci describes in detail an event that takes place in Panagoulis's jail cell that elicits the discourse of the murderer. He spies a cockroach on the floor and establishes an hypnotic relationship with it. He names it Salvador Dali because its antennae remind him of the painter's moustache. When the guard enters the cell and sees Dali, he crushes it under his foot; Panagoulis is furious and attacks the guard while calling him "Murderer!"[27] Crushing a cockroach is murder; but killing a tyrant and his driver is still tyrannicide situated in ancient Greek tragedy. In another episode, Panagoulis is visited by his mother, who bursts into tears, and he shouts at the jailers, "Murderers!" Fallaci reminds the hero that it is because "[y]ou would never have believed your mother capable of crying."[28] No wonder Panagoulis's mother was furious at Fallaci's book for having misrepresented and trivialized her son's life.

Recalling her encounter with Panagoulis, Fallaci contended it was the work of Fate. From the moment they met—he greeted her: "I was waiting for you. Come in"; and he takes her by the hand to "a bedroom . . . transformed into an altar"[29]—their encounter became "a duel, the meeting between a man and a woman that led to a love for each other, the most dangerous love that exists: the love that mixes ideals and oral commitments with attraction and with emotions." The agonic struggle is described in terms of warfare: "From that interview was born a great love and an immense tragedy."[30] Still, writes Judy Harris, this was "true only to a point, for it was neither a particularly great love, nor was the tragedy hers, except in the telling."[31] Even if couched in the mythical "you" of Greek drama, in the end Panagoulis was still a human being. Fallaci recounts how at one point they got into a fight and she, pregnant, lost their child after Panagoulis kicked her in the stomach. She also narrates the battles to dissuade him from suicide guerrilla attacks. She describes herself as the Sancho Panza to the fighter Don Quixote, although some have come to the conclusion that "she comes across more as a nanny to a juvenile delinquent."[32] In fact, at the time of his death Panagoulis had a Greek fiancée he was expecting to marry.

Fate, an avowed substitute for God in Fallaci's view, determines the encounter and the unfolding of the events; the frivolity of contemporary times is best expressed, for Fallaci, in skepticism toward Fate: "But if the gods were to announce it to us, or put us on our guard, if they were to tell us that this is your fate, already written, we wouldn't believe it and I would answer, mocking, that fate doesn't exist."[33] Fate is presaged by a series of dreams that recur throughout the story, tragic admonitions that are reminiscent of the Delphic oracle in ancient Greece. Since destiny has in the end determined this story, it is a rather moot point whether the two heroes bear any responsibility for what is transpiring in the narrative. Fallaci was infuriated with Robert Scheer when, in their interview, he insisted that there was not a single moment in her book in which Panagoulis felt any responsibility for another human being, not even her. He had even considered bombing the Acropolis and taking American tourists as hostages because of U.S. support for the military junta—forms of terrorism that Fallaci seemed to endorse. Fallaci replied that, with such questions, Scheer would make a good dictator. Asking that the Olympian "you" who had sacrificed everything for freedom should also be responsible for actual human affairs was a failure to understand anything about the mythical Other she had created.

What can we learn from Fallaci about the freedom fighter? She had, as Vivian Gornick put it, "a mythic sense of political evil" that was a residue from her youthful experiences with clandestine activism—carrying explosives, delivering messages—against fascism. The same determination shows in her legendary interviews in which she challenged the masks of the powerful as did no one else. But she had been blinded by the mythic struggle against absolute Evil. The violence of one side was pure good, the violence of the other consummate evil. Her hero Alekos could never be a killer and consequently had to be elevated into an Olympian god. The superhero "you" of her narrative, created by her love and writing, is presented as a worshipful figure—not as a real human being who can teach us about the dilemmas of violence.

Unfortunately, the same moral absolutism made Fallaci predisposed to fall, after 9/11, for George W. Bush's "axis of evil." The Quran became now the new *Mein Kampf* for her, and Europe a colony of Islam—Muslim migration was as dangerous as Nazism. She became paranoid about homosexuals and Jews. Suddenly her soulmate was not a revolutionary figure like Panagoulis but Cardinal Ratzinger who, as Pope Benedict XVI, offended Jews and Muslims worldwide with his insensitive remarks at Auschwitz and against the prophet Muhammed. The partisan who fought valiantly against fascism ended up becaming a rabid racist, an exhibitionist posing as the Joan of Arc of the West, as the newspaper *La Repubblica* described her.

In the final analysis we are confronted with the question of whether any narrative of contemporary violence framed from a position of absolute self-righteousness can be morally and intellectually valid. Isn't such pontification an instance of Camus' "the impotence of Good" and a denial of the modern history of crime? What kind of testimony did

Fallaci's book provide for the freedom-fighter hero? The one thing she never questions is the meaning of the killing of the dictator and the subject who plotted it. She seems to be saying: "I was his lover for three years. I know that he was a hero and that he was right in everything he did." But did she really know him? His mother and brother were outraged by her book. It is a long confession, but confessions can be notoriously false.[34]

Given the constant rhetoric of revolutionary freedom and sacrifice in Fallaci's book it is unclear whether she is narrating the events of Greece in 1976 (the year Panagoulis died) or reenacting the antifascist drama of her Italian youth. The same moral absolutism that covers the distant tragedy of the Holocaust seems to apply again and again, including the situation after 9/11. The Nazis in the 1940s, the Greek junta in the 1960s and 1970s, and the 9/11 jihad in 2001 all appear to be the same. Is she really being a witness of her times or is she projecting, employing facts that are deemed to be journalistically true although couched in novelistic fiction, an archetypal allegory of Good versus Evil? Fallaci certainly is not the witness transformed by the very act of bearing witness to the horrors of her times. For such transformation, we need to look at the figure of Yoyes/Antigone in chapter 5.

Prisoner of Love: Jean Genet

Jean Genet, the "Black Prince of French Literature" as Jean Cocteau called him, the infamous transgressor, the one and the same time saint and canaille, during the last twenty-five years of his life wrote nothing but an hallucinatory report of his sojourn in Jordan and Lebanon among destitute and armed Palestinian fedayeen. He titled his book *Prisoner of Love*.[35] This *captif amoureux* acting "like a little black box projecting slides without captions"—a literati who "settled for witnessing" and produced a work that, in Clifford Geertz's assessment, "is, disconcertingly, a surprising success" [36]—can serve as a guide on how to write about terrorist subjectivity. The philosopher Gilles Deleuze could compare Genet's book to the Bible—with his stories about a chosen homeless people, it is a book of memory that alternates serenity and hate, mixes history and poetry.[37] Affection and empathy, more than ideology, bound Genet to the Palestinians' fate, yet his rejection at one point of the existence of God scandalized his "terrorist" friends. The public debate between their leader,

Abu Gamal, and Genet was settled with the bond of a final promise from Gamal: "If a Jordanian soldier . . . threatened you, I'd kill him"; to which Genet replies: "I'd try to do the same if he threatened you."[38] By their willingness to shed blood for each other, the fighter and the writer were bound by the same tragic fate.

As in the case of Abraham, ready to kill his son Isaac following a higher call, it is the closeness between sanctity and murder that throws into relief the difficulties of theorizing and moralizing when writing about contemporary terrorism. There is no ethical posturing in Genet, no unctuous rhetoric of witnessing, no unquestioned memory or unreviewed truth. The last thing Genet wants to establish is his own innocence. Whatever they are—revolutionaries, madmen, terrorists—he wants to be one of them. The self-questioning is radical. He asked himself why they needed him there. For what purpose was "this grey, pink, round head for ever in their midst? Use it as a witness? My body didn't count. It served only to carry my round grey head."[39] It is when we look through Genet's bare lenses that we become suspicious of moral grandstanding.

Genet acted as a provocateur by simply witnessing the armed fedayeen, becoming incautiously "responsible" for their fate beyond any personal reserve, while still remaining quite conscious of the uselessness of his presence. He didn't need to dress up his writing as moral imperative. As he put it in a 1974 interview, "It was completely natural for me to be attracted to the people who are not only the most unfortunate but also crystallize to the highest degree the hatred of the West."[40] He was acting like "a prisoner of love." Yet he forced himself into watching the bulls, not from the safety of the stands, but from inside the arena, while he kept recording the fascination that made them leap to their deaths. By witnessing the horrors of their sacrifice, he was quietly defining the genesis of a people. He was also inscribing his own view of the mission of the contemporary intellectual regarding the violence of those abandoned by the West. It is "the need to call the whole of society into question"[41] that drives Genet to write about the Palestinians in Jordan and Lebanon as well as the Black Panthers in the United States.

Genet does not favor patriotism, "generally an inflated assertion of imaginary superiority or supremacy,"[42] and he admits that when the Palestinians become a nation-state he will lose his interest in them. But he is for those who, like the Panthers and the Palestinians, possess no country and no home, even if he refuses to have one himself. This mystical atheist who earnestly pursued sainthood had been struck by Raskolnikov's revelation in *Crime and Punishment*: everyone is worth the same. He was at home among the wretched of the earth, in the renunciation of material things and Western values.

These were for Genet "days of great love"[43] and he knew that passionate love may not endure for long. His feelings changed after the 1973 war: "I was still charmed, but I wasn't convinced; I was attracted but not blinded. I behaved like a prisoner of love."[44] It is only through love's captivation that Genet can still go on having the courage to witness the horrors and the ecstasies of the destitute, still discern universality in the fleeting particularities of marginal societies and persons. He cannot resist the invitation by the Panthers and the Palestinians who call to him; it is his weakness for love that betrays him: "The call to love came not from voices and things, perhaps not even from myself, but from the configuration of nature in the darkness. A daylight landscape, too, sometimes issues the order to love."[45] When he asks the fedayeen about "love," whether they would go "so far as to call the friendship you speak of, love," he elicits this reply: "We may be revolutionaries but we're only human. I love all the fedayeen, and you too. . . . Yes. It is love. Do you think at a time like this I'm afraid of words? Friendship, love? One thing is true—if he [the friend who is going on a dangerous mission] dies tonight there'll always be a gulf at my side, a gulf into which I must never fall."[46] It is a feeling of "faint intoxication . . . the shining eyes; the complete openness of the relations. . . . There under the trees everything and everyone was quivering, laughing, filled with wonder at a life so new to them, and to me too. . . . Everyone belonged to everyone else, yet each was alone in himself."[47]

Genet claims he does not believe in God but the fedayeen know better, because "if you didn't believe in Him you wouldn't have come"[48]—thus echoing the view that there can't be true love without willingness to surrender one's life, and that true religion is nothing but readiness for self-transcendence. Genet observes pointedly that what matters in a revolution is liberation, "not the interpretation and application of some transcendental ideology. While Marxism-Leninism is officially atheist, revolutionary movements like those of the Panthers and the Palestinians seem not to be, though their more or less secret goal may be to wear God down."[49] What Genet discovers among the fighters is not the righteousness of ideology or lofty values, but the centrality of decision and surrender.

For someone who in his youth as a thief and prostitute found prisons "rather motherly" and a place whose "corridors were at once the most erotic and the most restful places I've ever known,"[50] his fascination with the soon-to-die fedayeen is colored with eroticism. He sees the young soldiers "in love with their guns," turned into signs of "virility triumphant,"[51] and sexual images crop up everywhere "because they are unavoidable."[52] Genet describes the departure of a fedayeen selected for a dangerous mission: "He seemed to go there quite peacefully, aware of his beauty and the glory surrounding it, and aware of the glory that would surround his death. Did his beauty help him to die?"[53] Genet "is full of love, but a love as chaste as Muslim puritanism might demand."[54] And then the trees:

> I talk about the trees because they were the setting of happiness—happiness in arms. . . . War was all around us . . . every fedayee was just doing what he was fated to do. All desire was abolished by such liberty. Rifles, machine-guns, Katyushkas—every weapon had its target. Yet under the golden trees—peace. . . . The yellow leaves were attached to the branches by a fine yet real stalk . . . more like a sketch of a forest, a makeshift forest with any old leaves, but sheltering soldiers so beautiful to look at they filled it with peace. Nearly all of them were killed, or taken prisoner and tortured.[55]

When Genet hears about a virgin of sixteen blowing herself up among Israeli soldiers, "it's the lugubrious yet joyful preparations that intrigue me. . . . [H]ow was the bodice arranged to make the girl's body look womanly and enticing?"[56] It is the strength of Palestinian women who impress Genet the most.

In the early 1970s he meets a mother and her soldier son Hamza right before he is going that night on a mission. As he hears rumors of Hamza's death, they became for Genet the image of the Pietà, one that becomes larger over the years. Genet is bothered by "the strength of the Hamza-Mother image, linked to that of the Pietà and Christ,"[57] and wonders whether both are "obeying a general law among the Palestinians whereby a widowed mother and a beloved son became one."[58] In 1984, at the end of his life and of the book, Genet undertakes a journey to find Hamza and his mother: "The fixed mark, the pole star that guided me was still Hamza, his mother, his disappearance, torture and almost certain death. . . . My fixed mark might be called love, but what sort of love was it that had germinated, grown and spread in me for fourteen years for a boy and an old woman I'd only ever seen for twenty-four hours? It was still emanating radiations—had its power been building up over thousands of years?"[59] In the end the *captif amoreux* finds the sacred couple alive and realizes that his final quest for the Pietà image took place because, abandoned as an infant by his mother, "in fact I was haunted by an inner dream dating from when I was five years old."[60]

Genet details a card game that becomes his conceptual anchor: yet it was a game played by Palestinians *without cards*, by gesturing. Games are connected to chance and to a question about divinity: "Can such solitary God (He is called the One, the Alone) coexist with chance? Or is what is called chance willed by God? Is the outcome of a game of cards something divine?"[61] No matter how clever the players, "it's Zeus who decides."[62] It is by chance that Palestinians received their fate and Genet his to join them: "What am I doing here? If chance exists then there's no God, and I owe my happiness on the banks of the Jordan to chance. But though I may be here through the famous throw of the dice, isn't every Palestinian here by chance too? I was brought here by a series of extraordinary events, and it is equally strange that I should choose to exult in it."[63] Leaving aside the weight of religious belief, the idea of chance brought "lightness and laughter" to Genet, Paul Claudel's "jubilations of chance."[64] But the wretched of the earth had been handed a deck with no high cards to play, no real chances to win. Genet could add: "The Palestinian revolution was no ordinary battle to recover stolen land; it was a metaphysical struggle."[65]

But is Genet's narrative for real? Or is it a dream? He is haunted by the possibility that everything is a fantasy produced by his own delirium. Did he fail to understand the Palestinian insurgency? he asks himself on the first page of the report, and leaves no doubt, "Yes, completely." Was there any "reality" to it all? "The reality lay in involvement, fertile in hate and love."[66] His questions are never ending: "By agreeing to go first with the Panthers and then with the Palestinians, playing my role as a dreamer inside a dream, wasn't I just one more factor of unreality inside both movements? Wasn't I, a European, saying to a dream, 'You are a dream—don't wake the sleeper!' "[67] Because certainly, "[t]rying to think the revolution is like waking up and trying to see the logic of a dream."[68] It was "the dream" of the fedayeen against the league of Arab nations and against America, pushing to a sacrifice that "results not in altruism but in a kind of fascination that makes them jump off a cliff not to help but merely to follow those who have already leapt to their deaths."[69] At one point he realizes that "the Palestinians' struggle meant protecting a fantasy."[70] It is a fantasy lodged in Genet's memory: "The Palestinian revolt was among my oldest memories." It is not ordinary memory he is talking about, but he "might as well admit that by staying with them I was staying—I don't know how,

how else, to put it—in my own memory"[71]—as in the memory of the Pietà
and the Christ from his childhood made flesh in Hamza and his mother. It
was a way of saying that he was acting, not out of ideology and belief, but
as a prisoner of love and as a prisoner of his own past: "My heart was in it;
my body was in it; my spirit was in it. Everything was in it at one time or
another; but never my total belief, never the whole of myself."[72] It is such
awareness of the link between desire and dream, writing and fantasy, that
grants hallucinatory power to Genet's narrative.

Is Genet in the end an impostor? Long fascinated with treachery, he
will of course confess that "I was an impostor, too" and that "these lines,
this whole book, are only a diversion, producing quick emotions quickly
over."[73] In his sensitivity to the dream and the emotion, Genet is the true
witness of the violent desire of the damned. He understands intimately
Camus' *The Fall*—not only because of the failures of Communist regimes
and European democracies and memories of abandoned Republican
Spain and Greece, but also because "I discovered there'd long been a sort
of debacle inside me, and it's from that moment I date my certainty of a
shipwreck to come."[74] He is the writer of a delirium of love and death that
has overpowered the wretched revolutionaries.

And what does writing mean here? How is writing about "terrorists"
concerned with "truth"? Genet's radicalness in demolishing his own text
parallels the self-destruction of his subjects: "But what if it were true that
writing is a lie? What if it merely enabled us to conceal what was, and any
account is, only eyewash? . . . [W]riting presents only its visible, acceptable and, so to speak, silent face, because it is incapable of really showing
the other one."[75] Yes, he will write about Hamza's mother and the scenes
"ooze love and friendship and pity, but how can one simultaneously ex-
press all the contradictory emanations issuing from the witnesses? The
same is true for every page in this book where there is only one voice.
And like all the other voices my own is faked."[76] Genet wonders what we
really know of people and whether all we write "may only have been invented to hide the abysses of which life is made up."[77] Yasir Arafat asked
him to write the book, but "I didn't believe in the idea of that or any other
book";[78] the events and words remain set in his memory and gradually
he warms up to reliving them. He began writing the book in 1983, long
after his sojourn with the Palestinians was over. He is acutely aware that
by writing that "by transforming a fact into words and characters you
create other facts that can never recreate the original one," he must stress
that "it's my eyes that saw what I thought I was describing, and my ears

that heard it." But, like the detective, he cannot take at face value the evidence in front of him; what he does have to take literally are the workings of desire. Is Genet certain whether he is telling the truth? If the truth is "only a question of ordinary morality, I don't care whether someone's lying or telling the truth"; and certainly "this account was never designed to tell the reader what the Palestinian revolution was really like."[79] And yet, nearing the end of his own life, his writing is concerned with giving the most truthful account of witnessing of which he is capable. He knows that the book will have few readers in France and the rest of Europe, and that it will not be translated into Arabic. "Who is it for?" he asks.[80] This was simply his throw of the dice.

It is by mistrusting his own evidence, by relentlessly questioning his writing and his role as a witness, by admitting his lies, that he can aim at giving us a glimpse into the terrorist subjectivity's *real*, made up simultaneously of trauma and dream, hate and love, death and life. He will not "deliberately . . . *betray* the facts" and he will manage to "seem to be a privileged witness";[81] he will even tell of being there when Beirut was "reduced to dust" by the bombs from the Israeli planes from June 12 to September 8, 1982, and of having "gone down the main street in Chatila having almost to leapfrog over the corpses blocking the streets."[82] Regarding truth, for Genet a book of reminiscences is no different from a novel. But there is one thing he is truly sure of, one event he will return to once again in the final paragraph of the book, after having reminded the reader that the witness is supposed to say "I swear to tell the whole truth . . ." That truth is the image of the mother and son that forced his last journey before death: "what will remain with me is the little house in Irbid where I slept for one night, and fourteen years during which I tried to find out if that night ever happened."[83] That archetypal Pietà, reverberating with his own childhood, the son dead and the mother crying out to the heavens, seemed to be in the end the one universally "transparent" truth.[84]

What he saw, Genet confesses, "caused a kind of collapse in my vocabulary." He used to avoid "words like heroes, martyrs, struggle, revolution, liberation, resistance, courage and the like. I probably *have* avoided the words homeland and fraternity, which still repel me."[85] How can you answer a dead man if not by silence? Silence "may apply to all words, but it's certainly true of words like sacrifice, self-sacrificing, abnegation, altruism. To write them down as a tribute to someone who dared to live them, and live them to the point of dying for them, is indecent."[86] It is Genet's delirious awareness that "words are terrible" and that what the political enemy is doing is "carry[ing] the war right into the heart of vocabulary"[87] that makes his report compelling. Murder is, after all, as Thomas de Quincey wrote, one of the fine arts. A crucial aspect of art, Genet reminds the reader, is for powers to make everyone abide by differences such as murders that are "assassinations" and murders that are "terrorism,"[88] or the difference between terrorists who risk their own lives and those who "terrorize by proxy."[89] But how can you account for something as ordinary as the activist's self-sacrifice, the distant, sublimated relation to it of the reporter, and the even further distanced reader, dawdling over her morning coffee and newspaper?

Genet is in a hotel room listening to a Walkman, "and then the *Requiem* descended on me with full choir and orchestra. The music conjured up not death but a life, the life of the corpse, present or absent, the one for whom the mass is sung."[90] It is the play of death and life as experienced by the insurgents, filtered through Mozart, through Dostoevsky, "[t]he journey through the underworld, the terror of the grave, all that was there, but above all the gaiety, the laughter overlaying the fear," the intensity of "Dies Irae" and "Lacrimosa," "music that permitted hilarity and even liberty, that dared all," because "[t]he *Requiem* says as much: joy and fear. And the Palestinians, the Shiites and the Fools of God . . . came together in a thousand roars of onward-rushing laughter, mingled with the fierce retreat of the trombones. Thanks to joy in death or in the new, despite bereavement, and in contrast to ordinary life, all moralities had broken down."[91] In the end, the Palestinian revolt on the banks of the Jordan River was "a party that lasted nine months."[92] This is also the laughter and lightheartedness I recorded among armed Basque underground rebels during the mid-1970s.[93] Genet must be a witness to the madness and joy of the kamikaze, "the cheerfulness of those who have ceased to hope,"[94] and for whom "death was just as much a part of life as the shower of steel and lead nearby."[95] While the feeling among the comrades was of the "almost joyful passage in the 'Kyrie' of Mozart's *Requiem*,"[96] they all knew intimately what Sigmund Freud meant by the "death drive" and its erotic sources.

The Terrorist as Lover

The previous stories of terrorists and their writers as "prisoners of love" provide a glimpse into the radically militant subjectivity of underground activists. Our concern is once again epistemological: What can we *know* of this type of political subjectivity? In order to gain knowledge of it, we ask what does the terrorist's discourse share with that of the lover. They do share a subject's extreme solitude and abandonment. In their despair, they are both expressions of the "unreality" of subjective engulfment. "Engulfment is a moment of hypnosis," comments Roland Barthes while analyzing the lover's language.[97] How will the lover and the terrorist give an account of what has made them fall hypnotically and fatefully into such an emotional state? The lover understands John Keats's hyperbole of being "in love with easeful death." The world will never fully understand a lover's madness, his or her willingness to embrace even death. It is such *excess* of subjective desire that afflicts the terrorist as well. Che Guevara's words that revolutionary violence is a work of love are simply a truism for the violent militant.

The temporality of anticipation characterizes terrorism. What actually happens is nothing compared with the sense of impending catastrophe. There are usually long periods without anything happening, yet it is the very waiting itself that creates a state of terror. Anticipation is also what marks falling in love. "Am I in love?—Yes, since I'm waiting."[98] Waiting is, of course, a state of suspended animation, the absurdity of being agitated by something that is not happening, a sort of fever over the imminence of an upcoming event. The terrorist is deeply embedded in the experience of such fear and trembling. It is an emotional state that can't be easy to hide. The terrorist, as is the lover, is also one who is waiting. Capote's murderers on death row are also waiting for the gallows; such state of anticipation is the ultimate torture. The agony of the "dead man walking" suffuses everything the terrorist does.

The underground activist is sworn to secrecy. He has to assume that nobody knows what he is up to. But how is he going to hide his delirium? How can a lover not show in his face, body, and manner of speaking the inner turbulence of overpowering passions? The novelist, like the therapist, like the detective, will naturally assume that this cannot be concealed. The terror of the impending death, the *jouissance* of a desire taken to the limit, is too much to be able to disguise completely. Besides, if you are sacramentally committed to the cause, if your love object is so adorable, why shouldn't the world know about it? Hence the lover's paradox:

> To impose upon my passion the mask of discretion (of impassivity): this a strictly heroic value. . . . Yet to hide a passion totally (or even to hide, more simply, its

excess) is inconceivable: not because the human subject is too weak, but because passion is in essence made to be seen: the hiding must be seen: *I want you to know that I am hiding something from you*, that is the active paradox I must resolve: *at one and the same time* it must be known and not known: I want you to to know that I don't want to show my feelings: that is the message I address to the other. *Larvatus prodeo*: I advance pointing to my mask: I set a mask upon my passion, but with a discreet (and wily) finger I designate this mask. Every passion, ultimately, has its spectator . . . no amorous oblation without a final theater: the sign is always victorious.[99]

As I will show in chapter 8, the terrorists of 9/11 had also been pointing to their masks. But the counterterrorist system didn't know how to read the obvious signs. The intellectual consequences of such ignorance will prove fatal in the end. No matter how much information is made available—no matter how many times the terrorist points at his mask, saying, "I want you to know that I am hiding something from you"—nothing will happen because the system does not know how to record and read such obvious messages. One could argue that, in the events leading to 9/11, future suicides were repeatedly caught pointing to their masks and shouting, "Read my terrorist intentions!" But this was a foreign language to the counterterrorism system. Terms such as "will," "subjectivity," "emotion" are likely to elicit the counterterrorist's scorn. The writers of the *9/11 Commission Report* were, of course, looking for "facts" that could be presented in court as evidence. What does "terrorist subjectivity" mean? For counterterrorism, in principle the terrorist has no conscience, no common sense, no reliable humanity. He is the embodiment of the in-human. Isn't listening to the terrorist the last thing that we should do? The terrorist persona is simply *taboo*. In fact, it could be said that the terrorist has no fixed persona. Rather, he is the subhuman or at best an "uncivilized" wildman.

Language itself becomes one more mask of the person tormented by love, anxiety, foreboding. Terrorists, too, need language to hide their intentions. They will need to create slang and secret codes to silence their true messages. The enormity of their desires requires a language of deception. This should be the first premise regarding the lover's or the terrorist's discourse: words are masks to conceal the excess of the subject's feelings. Taking such pronouncements literally is a sure recipe for disaster. Americans graduating in Arabic studies in a given year can be counted on the fingers of two hands. To our primordial linguistic ignorance must

be added our incapacity to read the coded messages of the terrorists—
"coded" both in the sense of encrypted terms as well as the words selected
to mask the militant's true intentions. How is one to know what lies behind
the masks? One needs to use the skills of the detective who is not easily
fooled by the criminal's tricks. Or one needs to be the Capote who told
George Plimpton, in reference to the multiple murderers, "I could always
tell when Dick or Perry wasn't telling the truth."[100] Perry and Capote had
established the closest of friendships, including the language of "love."
Representing a terrorist in the capacity of an attorney is dangerous
enough; falling in love with one would not only automatically disqualify
the writer but certainly makes him politically and ethically a pariah.

Words can be easily deceptive, not so the body. One can speak falsely
or lie by omission, but it is not so easy for the face, the eyes, the voice to
conceal the truth. The body can't help but betray by showing the truthful
fears and desires of the subject. As in the case of the lover, the terrorist is
so burdened with anxiety that the true meaning of the words can only be
grasped by understanding his spontaneous body language.

The one thing that the waiting terrorist does know is that he or she is,
literally, *moriturus*. Whether committed to suicidal action or simply willing
to carry out proscribed "illegal" missions despite the vastly superior force
of the state, the terrorist is someone prepared to die. At the very least the
terrorist must anticipate likely capture, incarceration, and probable torture.
There is no return. "There are thousands of young men who look forward
to death," al Qaeda has bragged periodically. "The *goal* is martyrdom,"
in the words of Taliban leader Mullah Omar.[101] In short, as bin Laden
put it in his "Letter to America," the Islamic nation "desires death more
than you desire life."[102] The *9/11 Commission Report* puts this statement
as the last words of the section devoted to "bin Laden's Worldview."
The quote is intended to summarize the viciousness and absurdity of his
Islamist project. Yet such willingness to die is the indispensable subjective
condition to act that can only be sustained by a frightening intensification
of a sense of despair.

But tomorrow's martyrdom is today's anticipated *excess*. There perhaps
will be harems of brides awaiting the martyr in paradise. Previously, in
order to remain unpolluted, avoidance of the other sex may be a strict
requirement. This was the case of Mohamed Atta, as we will see in the
next chapter.[103] But such ritual purity admitted for an exception two days
before his self-sacrifice when he and two of his companions visited a strip
club in Daytona Beach to drink vodka, play video games, and indulge in

lap dances. Hours before their martyrdom, they anticipated the pleasures to come in the paradise of the big Other. Martyrdom would soon cleanse all personal sin. All the ravages of humiliation and anxiety from years of waiting were soon to be erased forever. In their religious vassalage to the god that had to be avenged, they could not escape their catastrophic fate. But final liberation was at hand and their desires were going to be fulfilled to the brim—they could raise their cup of vodka and drain it. In the initiation ordeal of ritual drunkenness, they were swearing for the last time their oath to destroy America.

"Why did they do it?"—the question keeps returning. From the perspective of the terrorist engulfed, as is the lover, in his or her passionate madness, any explanation given is tantamount to mockery. Why do I believe like this? Why am I in love? "I think nothing at all of love," observes Barthes. "I'd be glad to know *what it is*, but being inside, I see it in existence, not in essence."[104] This was Perry's situation in Capote's narrative: as Capote told the interviewer, "He [Perry] was always trying to find out in his own mind why he did it. He was amazed he'd done it."[105] The genius of Capote's narrative is that he convinces the reader of Perry's sincerity, that he truly did not know "why?" Because the writing is aimed at depicting the intentions of the murderer well beyond the facile explanation that he did it for money (all they stole was about forty dollars), the reader is confronted with the abyss of the killer's madness. The terrorists have recourse to ideological rationales but, in the final analysis, their destructive fury is "explained" or "understood" through the act of acting out.

The terrorists' explanation of "why" they did it would make as little sense as the lover's story—"this declamation of a *fait accompli* (frozen, embalmed, removed from any *praxis*) is the lover's discourse."[106] The amorous seduction transpired *before* and *beyond* the conscious drama of the now hopeless situation. The terrorist's decision to commit personal and possibly fatal surrender is also something prior to the violent action. The terrorist cannot write that story himself, just as Perry cannot say why he killed the Clutters. Whatever the terrorist says will be simultaneously too much and too little.

"Talk is cheap" was the slogan I heard most from ETA activists. "In the beginning was the *act*." Action for action's sake becomes *ritualized*—ritual being a device to eliminate the ambiguities and deceptions of language.[107]

For a terrorist mentality in which activism is quintessential, action and talk belong to two altogether separate domains. If anyone, it is the terrorists who know that they cannot write themselves. The militant philosophy of the underground activist has always been "don't explain anything; let the action speak for itself." In such a view nobody is more suspect than the talker. There is an abyss between "talking" and "doing." The doer knows best that language is at best irrelevant, at worst a mask for impotence. Don't offend the terrorist by asking "why?" something is being done. If you don't already perceive the outrage, no words will convince you. The man of action agrees with Barthes's lover that writing is basically "*there where you are not.*"[108] The murderer and the lover are confronted with such reality every day.

The terrorist is *not* primarily in one's proclamations. The terrorist is in the *passage à l'acte* forced by the situation. To know the terrorist requires delving into the realm of his or her subjectivity. This confronts the writer with the opacity of the other's desire—and we can only surmise it by having recourse to the analogy of our own. This is where Capote was pathbreaking in his understanding of the murderer. Only by taking desire and love literally can the writer grasp the terrorist subject.

The Ground Zero of Terrorist Desire: The Detective versus the Policeman

Terrorism studies are still awaiting an epistemic shift, as made obvious by the group of scholars banded together under the journal *Critical Terrorism Studies*. As noted earlier, one way to illustrate such break might be by the analogy of the difference between the way a policeman and a detective handle murder. In the end, terrorism writers are also confronted with what Joan Copjec labels "the locked-room paradox,"[109] a defining element of classical detective fiction. She illustrates the paradox with a scene Hitchcock planned for one of his movies: we witness a car being put together by an assembly line part by part, and when it is completed and ready to drive off the line, after the protagonist's comment, "Isn't it wonderful!" they open the door and a corpse falls out. How was it put there? The detective has to show his special skills by solving the unsolvable. Terrorism studies seek to elucidate all the nuts and bolts of the terrorists' personalities, ideologies, backgrounds, and networks. The only problem is how to explain the incongruity that, seemingly against all logic and reason, in their self-destructive rage of suicidal madness the terrorists refuse to go along with civilized designs and inexplicably strike again—what is the origin of the dead body center stage?

Experts and journalists of terrorism have a hard time interpreting it to the anxious public. Just when we thought that we had it all under control, and globalization was lifting everyone, the West was dumbstruck by 9/11. In the tragedy's aftermath it seemed that the world was with us. Our invasion of Afghanistan was accepted by most people as part of the War on Terror. Yet with the Iraq conflict we are again confronted with the locked-room paradox. Far from escaping the presence of the corpse, we seem to be more and more entangled with it. Where did it go wrong?

Given the dismal failure of counterterrorism in preventing 9/11, the question is: What are the *blind spots* in such knowledge? What type of "locked-room paradox" is blinding the counterterrorist episteme? Why couldn't it find out that Saddam Hussein was bluffing? In solving detective puzzles one can begin as does the proverbially dumb policeman, by sifting through the literal evidence, or one can adopt the approach of the more sophisticated detective who seeks to understand the murderer's *desire* as a prerequisite to resolving the crime/paradox. Detective fiction teaches us that the literalist cop is always outsmarted by the apparently clueless detective who ends up resolving the conundrum. The detective is confronted with a paradox that, in formal terms (as shown by Copjec), is like the paradox studied by Frege regarding set theory (the categories of counting create the very objects in the sets). But Jacques Lacan gives a different reading and argues "that there are real objects that are not reducible to any category" and that derive from logical insight. For counting to be possible, "the set of numbers must register one category under which *no* objects fall. The category is that of the 'not-identical-to-itself'; the number of objects subsumed by it is zero."[110] Copjec's point is that both statistics as well as the detective paradox of the locked room are linked by this Fregean principle. In a situation of terrorism, too, as in solving a crime, the actual evidence might be minimal or missing altogether—zero—yet we can still infer its reality from the traces left by the actors' subjectivities. Once we project intentionality and desire into it, no terrorist threat, no matter how preposterous, can be deemed vacuous. It is our sheer ignorance of terrorist desire that makes us so vulnerable to the threats. The terrorist threat becomes so unbearable, its capacity for bluff so potent, because the public situates it in *the ground zero of terrorist desire*—a seeming black hole capable of devouring the world.

The locked-room paradox is articulated by logicians in relation to set theory as the inability of an infinite series of numbers to *close* itself. The endless waiting for terror, its ever-present threat, is also premised on this inability to close the field. The entire theory of set numbers hinges on the internal limit of the series, but one that is impossible to determine from the logical functioning of numbers whose sets are closed or "sutured" by such limit. The logical suture is empty of content, but at the same time it determines the autonomy of the series of numbers: "Suture, in brief, supplies the logic of a paradoxical function whereby a supplementary element is ADDED to the series of signifiers in order to mark the LACK of a signifier that could close the set."[111] Applied sociologically, it is this nonempirical "addition" that closes the field in order to confer a differential (superior) quality on "our" side. We identify with our group because it is formally different from any other group. It is the internal limit, the "addition," that guarantees the endless combinations, expectations, fears, and fulfillments of desire that give our group its identity.

If modern nations are the product of counting diverse peoples as citizens, as members of an identical set after having discounted all their particularities, in the post 9/11 world what really matters is whether you and your group belong to the set labeled "terrorists": "You are either with us, or with the terrorists." Hence the inaugural relevance of the performance itself of naming and counting. The concept of "terrorism" per se is like the "addition," the suturing point that differentiates them from us, and it is in itself devoid of content; it is the "zero" of set theory that allows for the internal limit. In the United States there were about one hundred thousand "ordinary" murders between 1980 and 1985, but only seventeen "terrorist" murders. There is a vast difference between types of murder due to the autonomy of each statistical field constituted by counting. The central social bond between those who belong to the opposing fields of terrorism/counterterrorism emanates more from that formal difference than from feelings of hatred or solidarity. The autonomous statistical fields are, however, situated in larger juridical and political arenas in which they become related and contrasted to each other; the extraordinary abnormality of the seventeen terrorist murders can, by default, "normalize" the other one hundred thousand deaths. The operation of tabooing one event or person is far from innocent, as it affects dialectically the entire social or political field in which the suturing and the tabooing transpires.

The semantics of "threat" are quintessential to terrorism: the very "reality" constituted by a threat is entwined with the perception of it. The same threat can be dismissed as irrelevant, fantastical, or be deadly serious. The credibility of a threat depends on the context and our *interpretation* of it. The Unabomber managed to bring the traffic in California airports to a halt by simply sending a letter to the *San Francisco Chronicle* that said that within a week he would blow up an airliner (at the same time he sent another letter to the *New York Times* stating that the threat was a "prank"). The actual reality of such a catastrophic threat might be sheer play but can still be deadly serious. What leant credibility in the case of the Unabomber was that he had previously shown his capacity to outmaneuver the police and engage in lethal action. The August 2006 terror scare in London—the alleged plot to blow up ten airliners with liquid explosives—might also be a case in which those arrested were to some degree "playing terrorist,"[112] yet the precedent of the previous year's coordinated subway attacks in London by Islamist suicide bombers, killing fifty-six people and wounding more than seven hundred, gave catastrophic urgency to the surveillance of the airline plotters' activities, whatever they were. The perception of why the London plotters were suddenly such a threat derives from recent history, as well as from the fact that we can guess their intentions; that is, we assume that the "really real" of their lives must be their burning antagonism against the British state and the Occident in general. Once again, we are forced to take into account the motives of the plotters as much as their capabilities and actual deeds.

In short, terrorism is for contemporary politics what the paradox of the locked room is for detective fiction. The excess element in terrorism is not so much the state of terror and its corpses, but its capacity to appear out of what should be a sealed space in the hierarchy of international relations. Therefore, one has to read terrorism as might a detective, and not as the policeman who is blinded by the literalness of the corpse and is unable to see that the point of the entire exercise is to take into account the internal limit of the paradox, that is, the *zero* that makes the series possible. The point is that a performance in the space of such deep play leaves so many traces and alternatives unaccounted for that it can never be fully described. Furthermore, the very meaning and perpetuation of the catastrophe—the appearance of the obscene corpse in the middle of the field—depends to a large extent on the interpretation given to it.

The detective pays attention to the law of limits, of ignorance, and the degree to which all premises fail and therefore have to be abandoned. There is more to the evidence than meets the eye—the way it is given, that which is hidden, the gap between evidence and that which it confirms. In Lacanian vocabulary, the *real* is always lurking around ready to intrude upon the symbolic. The detective, like the psychoanalyst, has to try to read what remains hidden, the *real* of desire—desire that is ruled by the law of the negative, the lack, the zero that closes the series. While the policeman is looking for the clue, the index that will clarify the ambiguous situation, the detective is looking for the clue that cannot be sorted out merely by the symbolic (language, law, the Other), because it belongs to the *real* (trauma, anxiety, the impossible). "There is a gap, a distance, between the evidence and that which the evidence establishes, which means that there is something that is *not* visible in the evidence: the principle by which the trail attaches itself to the criminal."[113] Both the police and the detective are looking for evidence, but the detective knows that the evidence per se cannot account for the way it reveals itself.

The terrorist is a subject whose desire speaks and writes in ordinary language, but whose truest statements are marked by the failure of language—the recognition of language's insufficiency to speak the whole truth. Suicidal actions underscore that inability of language to produce the message that matters. No terrorism discourse will be able to decipher and absorb them. In the absence of words by the suicide terrorist, what we must take literally is the terrorist's and her public's desire, a desire that does not register in speech.[114] This requires that we take the subject himself/herself as a primary and autonomous locus of investigation and not merely as the reflection of a system of power relations or a sediment of social and historical forces. Traumatized by 9/11, the last thing counterterrorism appears interested in is whether the suicide bombers have specific grievances, goals, and motivations. Some expert might know that what enraged bin Laden most was the U.S. military presence in his native Saudi Arabia, which for him amounts to occupation of sacred lands by the invader. But these are small details largely left out of a public debate. The mere act of paying attention to what they have to say appears as a step toward perhaps making an effort to understand their motives, which in turn might lead to somehow "justifying" what is unjustifiable.

Counterterrorism experts and commentators are for the most part like the literalist policemen pointing at the evidence of the corpse at the center of everything, yet unable to follow the paradoxical logic of the desire that fuels the act and the role of interpretation in establishing (for "them" and for "us") what the evidence means (success or failure, martyrdom or catastrophe). Interpretation being in part the work of desire, as well as fear, it implies acceptance that one does not know everything, that the evidence does not tell us how it should be interpreted. Desire is not a bias that contaminates thinking and makes objectivity impossible; it is the principle by which the detective or the novelist will end up finding the truth as a result of applying the very logic of desire to the criminal. As a result, in terrorism, as in detective fiction, it is not the *evidence* that has to be taken literally, as does the dumb policeman, but rather "*desire must be taken literally.*"[115] Intrinsic to desire is the inner gap that results from the absence of a final signifier. In short, to understand the horror and the *jouissance* of terrorist martyrdom, one has to take into account the logic of desire by which lack turns into excess.

CHAPTER FOUR

Eros, Terror, and Suicide

Life against Death

The fanatical embrace of what Freud called the "death instinct" is what typifies terrorist psychology. This is the politics of the unconscious and its study takes us to psychoanalysis. In *Civilization and Its Discontents* Freud spoke of the "battle of the giants" between Eros and Thanatos as the most decisive struggle of civilization. It is no accident that he developed his seminal ideas regarding the death drive during the tragic period between the two world wars. The critical point for Freud was that *both* Eros and Death are necessary to preserve life and that both spring from the same libidinal source. Sexual and aggressive instincts go together, he realized, and love and hate can be interchanged easily. Furthermore, eroticism and moral masochism can act jointly—love and death, pleasure and pain, the sublime and the perverse. Such a perspective of sublimated destructiveness finds a paramount expression in terrorism.

The current intellectual climate, with an increasing threat of renewed nuclearism and the alarming prospect of nuclear terrorism, is reminiscent of the 1950s when, for the first time in history, the reality of a nuclear arms race made the world aware that our species could be obliterated. Confronted with such an unprecedented crisis, during that decade the Freudian paradigm was further developed and applied to the analysis of contemporary culture in the work of Herbert Marcuse (*Eros and Civilization*) and Norman O. Brown (*Life Against Death*). The point emphasized by both authors is that erotic and death drives overlap and share a fundamental unity.

Marcuse proposes eschewing such dualistic treatment of the two drives, which for him are subject to historical change, by reducing human needs through greater tolerance and the use of more technology. Brown was skeptical of such historical "progress"; he believed that the general awareness that the nuclear arms race had brought the world to the brink of an apocalypse demanded utopian thinking. In the end, the role of culture is to resist death. But it is not the consciousness of death that concerns psychoanalysis; rather, it is the unconscious *death drive* that becomes aggression and deserves study. "What would he say about today's universal adversary, the terrorist?" asked James Clifford at Brown's memorial service.[1]

The Death Drive

If there is a contemporary figure that radically embodies the Freudian "death instinct," it is the suicidal terrorist. Freud turned such "instinct" into the cornerstone of his psychoanalytic theory, thereby effecting his semantics of desire and his entire notion of culture. Previously, he had developed a more "scientific" theory of the instincts around the regulative notions of "the reality principle" and "the pleasure principle." In his 1920 essay *Beyond the Pleasure Principle*, Freud takes a more mythical approach in which he broaches of the interplay of love and death by adopting the archetypal terms Eros and Thanatos. For Freud this was the most definitive struggle of contemporary life and it was the task of culture to engage in this battle.[2] War is the great cultural invention of the death drive. Current terrorism is but its latest incarnation.

How does Freud characterize the "death instinct"? Initially, he did not introduce it to account for aggressive destructiveness and in opposition to Eros, but rather as a hypothesis to explain the patient's compulsion to replicate repressed pesonal trauma. In his own words, "It seems, then, that an instinct is an urge inherent in organic life to restore an earlier state of things."[3] The life instinct is equivalent to such inertia and its aim is nothing but death. If everything in life is a path to death, the libido/Eros is the exception that resists it. Hence the apparent dualism of the instincts. If the inner movement of life leads toward death, the counterforce must come from the outside, from the desire of Eros for the other. This translates not only into sexuality but also into the view that the dualism is in fact an overlapping of coexisting instincts: "In a sense, everything is death . . . In another sense, everything is life."[4]

It is only later that Freud used the notion of a death drive to examine clinical phenomena. Finally, shifting from biology to culture, particularly in *Civilization and Its Discontents*, he casts it against Eros in an apocalyptic battle. Thus Freud formulated the theories of masochism and sadism (pleasure in pain). Reading the superego from the perspective of the death drive underscores the enigmatic trait of its harsh cruelty, derived from the Oedipus complex, to the point that, in its sadistic rage, "what is now holding sway in the superego is, as it were, a pure culture of the death instinct."[5] Melancholia to the point of suicide illustrates the point. Terrorists are regularly described as "giving their lives" for the cause of their country or their jihad. It is not some criminal instinct that compels them to martyrdom and destructive rage; following Freud's insight, it is their religious or ideological superego that drives them to suicide and death.

Freud also examines the implicit links between eroticism and moral masochism. In Ricoeur's words, "With the resexualization of morality the possibility of a monstrous fusion of love and death arises; such a fusion on the 'sublime' plane has its counterpart on the 'perverse' plane in the phenomena of pleasure in pain."[6] The death instinct is part of the superego's sadism, "the result being what might be called a deathly sublimation."[7] A sublimated destructiveness is what counterterrorism writers have frequently attributed to terrorists. In Freudian thought, the instinctual basis of this sublimated death drive is fear of castration. For example, we are told that Mohamed Atta, the leader of 9/11, grew up in terror of his strict disciplinarian father; that his father complained to his mother that she was raising him as a girl; that his only means of rebellion was to become extremely religious; that he was shy with women; that he wrote in his will, as a future jihadist, that he wanted a strict Muslim burial in which the person who would wash his genitals must wear gloves.[8] Thus, the Freudian connections between fear of castration, superegoic sadism, and the death instinct are brought home.

Symbolic castration consists in the subject acting in *the name of* a big Other. The subject pays with his own symbolic castration for the fact that he is acting not in his own name but as a representative of some other authority. "You need to have balls" was the expression that, in my youth, summed up what was most necessary in order to join an armed group such as ETA. Everyone agreed that the antifascist struggle was legitimate, but only those who had the balls joined the underground. Those of us who did not have them were useless; but even those who joined needed to have them essentially in order to then undergo symbolic castration by surrendering their lives to the big Other of the nationalist cause.

Potentially suicidal activists are, by the very nature of their circumstances, like the *morituri* of the initiation rituals—subjects profoundly transformed by their experience of symbolic death and resurrection. As part of their initiation they must give up normal sex. Similarly, soldiers, to the extent that they share such an initiatory culture of being ready for death, are also asexual beings who are left with only two outlets: sublimation or prostitution.[9] Nothing is more dissonant with the image of a symbolically castrated terrorist, ready to die at any moment, than the rare photo of him in the company of a wife and children. The same can be said of soldiers ready to die while attempting to conceal their terror with machistic bravado, but who are essentially sexless adolescents whose lives have been surrendered to the mandates of the big Other. The English colonel in Kurt Vonnegut's *Slaughterhouse-Five* says it best: "We had forgotten that wars were fought by babies. When I saw those freshly shaved faces, it was a shock. My God, my God—I said to myself, 'It's the Children's Crusade.'"[10] The U.S. Department of Defense has an annual budget of $3 billion to recruit kids from middle and high schools through the Middle School Cadet Corps and Junior Reserve Officers' Training Corps programs.

The Study of Death: From Capote to Mishima

In addition to psychoanalysis, literature also has been engaged with the study of Eros and its destructive power. Earlier I paid attention to the ways in which Capote's art revealed the inner self of the multiple murderer—the talent in the madness, the humanity in the inhumanity. It was the Japanese writer Yukio Mishima, world renowned for his novels and for committing ritual hara-kiri at the Self-Defense Force headquarters in Tokyo in 1970, who confidently predicted that Capote would commit suicide. Capote was perturbed by the prediction, which in the end proved to be true.[11] In their writings, Capote and Mishima are both keenly cognizant of the power of the "death drive" in their own culture and life. As different as were the ways in which they embraced death—an overdose in a Los Angeles mansion versus public hara-kiri at Tokyo's military headquarters—they knew that death and killing are keys for diagnosing contemporary times.

President Bush's War on Terror was regularly portrayed around the world as a Western movie in which the Texan shouted "Bring' em on!"

while twirling his pistol, or leaped onto the deck of an aircraft carrier in a pilot suit in front of the "Mission Accomplished" banner, in the service of a simple romanticized morality tale of Good versus Evil. If the cowboy of the "Old West," with his gun and horse and sense of justice, is the prototype of the American western, the warrior figure of the mythified samurai is its counterpart in Japanese film. Samurai ethics in traditional Japan, a classical locus to explore the military culture of kamikaze suicide, has been immortalized by films such as Akira Kurosawa's classical *Seven Samurai*, which itself came to influence Hollywood westerns. One's viewing the War on Terror from the perspective of a western, while the enemy sees it from the perspective of a kamikaze film, suggests the fundamental misunderstanding between the enemies regarding the very nature of the war in which they are engaged.

Yukio Mishima dwelled on this culture of death in his best-selling *The Way of the Samurai*,[12] written in August 1967, three years before he committed his own ritual suicide. The book is a personal interpretation of the classic samurai text *Hagakure*, whose foundational motto is "I have discovered that the Way of the Samurai is death." Mishima, considered by many to be the most important Japanese novelist of the twentieth century, applied the samurai warrior code of ethics to a modern society unable to feel intense emotional or spiritual passion.

Hagakure became, after the war, "a loathsome, ugly, evil book, a tainted book to be wiped from memory," yet for Mishima this "book destined to paradox" was "like a luminiscent object in broad daylight," the one book that could support his creative loneliness and anachronistic ethics. While it was seen as "a book of odious fanaticism," it was at the same time "a book that preached freedom, that taught passion."[13] Its central irony is "the discrepancy between knowledge of proper conduct and decision to act."[14] This is, of course, the fundamental paradox of militant decision: you cannot know in advance all the consequences of the *passage à l'acte*, while at the same time you cannot remain passive.

The samuari is the subject who is not running away from death. It is the medicine of death against death that the samurai displays. Mishima knew from his own experience that in such tradition there was "an astonishing understanding of human nature."[15] In modern life, on the contrary, we don't want to focus on death; we attempt to banish it from our consciousness. The military is the only modern institution that, following the orders of the commander in chief, has to answer the call to die for the community.

Despite their different costumes, protagonists of the western and the samurai film do share the core value that death is their "way."

Suicide terrorists are the latest group to openly embody the shocking medicine of death as the only means of escape from the maddening paradoxes of their societies. But are their "suicides" freely chosen or imposed on them by their communities? If we consider the kamikaze suicide pilots of World War II, we find that many volunteered, but others went to their deaths against their wills. Mishima undermines the distinction by raising the key question: "Can righteous death, death chosen by us for the sake of a self-chosen righteous goal, can such a death in fact exist?"[16] Mishima's thinking, like all military thinking, is that, even when faced with an unjust war, and because people live their lives within the framework of a nation, we cannot limit ourselves to what we believe to be the righteous cause—righteousness being a relative concept that is subject to revision or change.

For Mishima, who was excused from military service and then was plagued by the shame of having survived the war in which so many others had died, no death is in vain. "What is important is purity of action," according to the *Hagakure*, Mishima writes, and therefore "on the point of death one is by no means able to evaluate the justice of a cause."[17] It is because the individual lives within the framework of a larger community, thought Mishima, that one is not allowed to discriminate between right and wrong causes. This is the logical extension of the military's hierarchical reasoning. It is vehemently opposed to the Oxford oath of Norman O. Brown and others during World War II: "I will not die for God and country." But even Brown, who was no pacifist but rejected mindless patriotism, later devoted the best of his intellectual energies to "the study of Death."

Self-Immolation as Weapon

What appears most shocking about post-9/11 jihadist terrorism is its primary reliance on the activist's willful acceptance of self-immolation. Willingness to risk one's own life for the cause has been a feature of insurgent groups everywhere, but historically it was acceptance of unavoidable possibility, as unwanted failure of planned escape from a course of events. Self-immolation was not embraced per se and was to be avoided by all means. The "fallen comrade" was an unwanted by-product of the struggle. Achievement of the political goal was paramount. If this meant submission to torture and even self-immolation, so be it. But one's own death was never the desired outcome. In yesterday's terrorism, the "political" message of militant activism was framed by writing and by largely symbolic actions designed primarily to attract attention in order to articulate for the general public a set of historical grievances and demands. Terrorism was largely an attempt to construct an alternative discourse, backed up by the willingness to use violence, which might include as a by-product risking the lives of the activists.

Ambushing the victim and then running away can be seen as an assassin's capricious and cowardly murder. But the meaning of the killing changes radically for the actor when it entails deliberately and willingly paying with one's own life for the decision to kill someone else. Compared with ordinary murder, the decision, the purpose, the future, and the meaning of the suicide action has shifted radically. The "revolutionary" discourse of militant groups has always relied ultimately on the self-proclaimed willingness to risk one's life for the cause—"fatherland or death," "revolution or death."

In the case of ETA, for example, it is noteworthy how the true model of the heroic-tragic subject predisposed to self-sacrifice for the homeland was created. In July 1968, nine years after ETA's creation, a young economics student named Txabi Etxebarrieta, ETA's ideological leader at the time, killed a Spanish policeman when he was stopped for a traffic violation. A few hours later, he was himself killed by the police, or, according to his closest friends, "he practically let himself be killed."[18] Knowing that all the roads were under police surveillance after the initial killing, instead of remaining hidden in the apartment where he took refuge, Etxebarrieta took the fatal decision to venture forth in his car to his death. Such suicidal component has in principle always been alien to ETA's modus operandi, as observed by Robert Pape and Mia Bloom.[19] The very suggestion that this might explain Etxebarrieta's death still elicits strong reactions of disbelief and even resentment from his sympathizers. But from the perspective of terrorist suicide that we are implying here, such possibility is far from scandalous. This was ETA's first killing and it was still an unknown how the Basque public would react to it. Was it really necessary to kill a policeman who had merely stopped Etxebarrieta because of a traffic violation? (His companion that day in the car, in an interview given decades later, blamed Etxebarrieta for the killing of the policeman). By then, ETA's propaganda was taking for granted the need for revolutionary violence to counter the violence of the state. Yet what made such violence "revolutionary" in the eyes of the Basque public was the willingness of the activists to face torture and even death for the cause.[20]

Etxebarrieta was the ETA leader who, almost a decade after its formation, had pushed the armed organization toward taking seriously the road of armed violence. It was by the force of his personality that the new ETA was going to start killing. Even if he was a member of an organization, basically he was not following anyone else's order. Rather, he was imposing his own Nietzschean will and the suicidal component is intrinsic to this type of will. Nothing could have been more tragically ironic for Etxebarrieta than that history should record his killing of the policeman as a criminal murder. His disposition to put his own life on the line was the one thing that proved that he was not a common killer. But one can hear the inner voice of the activist asking himself whether he really meant it when it came to willingness to surrender his own life. And in that very foundational moment of a tragic-heroic subject, readiness to die would mark from then on the criterion for ETA's patriotic model. Whether his obviously reckless behavior can be construed or not as implicit "suicide," the political and ethical justification of the inaugural killing by ETA demanded that it be governed by the logic of revolutionary sacrifice. Thus, even for armed groups such as ETA, for whom suicide has never been a prominent tactical option and whose public would not appreciate it, the suicidal component is never far away. If the axiomatic alternative is "Freedom or Death," only Death can guarantee that you were truly for Freedom.

What is specific to the latest wave of terrorists is that the suicidal component becomes a primary and decisive element of the entire strategy. The new type of terrorism heralded by 9/11 seems to find the classical modus operandi of militant armed struggle too cumbersome, its politicized message too diluted. It rather starts by making crystal clear that suicide is the primary decision as a way of stating that no metalanguage is possible, no communication between the two fronts viable. Self-immolation is the only way of stating that there is no negotiating position—the only language is that there is no language, no dialogue postsuicide. This is the message of converting planes filled with passengers into missiles.

So how can we read such a message of self-immolation when language itself has been abolished and the issuer of the message is no longer here to reply? When the purpose of an action is to seek one's own death and that of others, all of our deeply buried mechanisms for adjusting to life are contradicted. We feel defenseless when confronted with such an "unnatural" intentionality. Nothing can terrorize us more than the proximity of such a willingness to self-immolation, which contradicts all of our ordinary expectations regarding human behavior. The fear derives from the future action of the subject who, by having decided to die, has, so to speak, eliminated the ordinary course of time and replaced it with apocalyptic waiting.

The conventional wisdom, as summed up by Robert Pape,[21] explains the phenomenon of suicide terrorism in terms of religious fanaticism, psychological imbalances, social isolation, deep poverty, or as the product of domestic competition. The work of Yoram Schwitzer,[22] Christopher Reuter,[23] Mia Bloom,[24] and Pape himself, among others, dismisses each one of these explanations as unfounded: most of the suicide terrorists have emerged from secular backgrounds; their profiles do not fit that of the suicidal individual; 95 percent of all of the suicide terrorist attacks take place as the result of organized campaigns in a given time frame; a comparison between the economic indicators of the countries producing suicide terrorism and those without it shows that poverty is not a factor; domestic competition among suicide bombers may explain some behavior in the Palestinian situation but overall it is inadequate as explanation. For example, the Quran explicitly prohibits suicide; when bin Laden's lieutenant, Ayman al-Zawahiri, had to justify the suicide bombing of the Egyptian embassy in Islamabad, Pakistan, in November 1995, which resulted in the deaths of sixteen people and the wounding of sixty, and which became the prototype for future al Qaeda bombings, he had to first reverse the doctrine of the Prophet by explaining that martyrdom is a weapon denied to tyrants and accessible only to those who believe in the greater good of Islam.[25] The question is why it has been so easy for bin Laden/Zawahiri to reverse the official Quranic doctrine and turn "suicide" into "martyrdom"; why, eschewing the traditional religious outlook, believers and nonbelievers opt for espousing Lacan's view that "suicide is the only successful act"[26]—that is, the only way to erase the utter humiliation of current living conditions and the only hope for creating a new status quo. Indeed, "[w]hat is frightening is not the abnormality of those who carry out the suicide attacks, but their sheer normality."[27] This is not to deny that the individuals who choose suicide are likely to have experienced some deep personal trauma.[28]

Suicide serves as a "way out" for the madness that has engulfed the militant who has embraced the terrorist act. The terrorists find themselves in the situation of the desperate "prisoner of love" who wants to find a solution to the crisis, but there is no way out. In the words of Barthes, "Idea of suicide; idea of separation; idea of withdrawal; idea of travel; idea of sacrifice, etc.; I can imagine several solutions to the amorous crisis. . . . [T]he lover's discourse is in a sense a series of No Exits."[29] All the various alternatives have been eliminated in a sort of reductio ad absurdum and finally there is no solution within the system but suicide. The lover is trapped inside his or her own system and does not have any other framework—has fallen into a type of madness.

Thoughts of suicide come easily to the subject who has succumbed to the unconscious—"For the slightest injury, I want to commit suicide."[30] The idea of suicide can be spoken of, used as blackmail, turned into fantasy. It is a way to have the last word. As in Johann Wolfgang von Goethe's *Werther*, the announcement of suicide makes the unrequited lover the stronger of the two. The lover knows that without the truth of his love, life is not worth living. For him there is no question that what the world takes as error and madness is in fact the only real truth; and what it is regarded as real by everyone else is but illusion. There might not be anything original about the object of love, but what matters, the truth, is the indestructible relation to such an object. If that truth were to be taken away, it would be better to die. What the suicidal terrorist action confronts us with in the end is the nonmastery of the political unconscious.

The Terrorist *Homo Sacer*

The figure that underpins the post-9/11 political horizon is a newly redefined "terrorist." But a terrorist that is no longer portrayed as the historically ambiguous figure of the underground activist who could be defined simultaneously as killer and hero, assassin and priest ("one man's terrorist is another man's freedom fighter"). The new figure of the terrorist has been reduced to the "bare life" of Agamben's *homo sacer*: "The sacred man is the one whom the people have judged on account of a crime. It is not permitted to sacrifice this man, yet he who kills him will not be condemned for homicide."[31] If the concept of taboo in anthropology carried an ambivalence between sacred and damned, killer and priest, horror and fascination, that was applicable to the classical figure of the terrorist/free-dom fighter.[32] The figure of *homo sacer*, reduced to bare life, corresponds better to the post-/11 figure of the terrorist.[33]

But it is the second trait, exclusion from sacrifice, that goes to the heart of the archaic figure in Roman law called *homo sacer*. Military, religious, and legal institutions have required sacrificial victims in every society. Yet the bare life of the man who could be killed but not sacrificed is something different. This type of man is exempted from every form of ritual killing or death penalty. To the exception that he could be killed with impunity we have to add that he could not be ritually sacrificed. Thus he is excluded both from *ius humanum* (killing him is not homicide) and *ius divinum* (he is unsacrificable). Agamben concludes that "[w]hat defines the status of *homo sacer* is therefore not the original ambivalence of the sacredness that is assumed to belong to him, but rather both the particular character of the double exclusion into which he is taken and the violence to which he finds himself exposed."[34] Does the terrorist partake in any sense of the economy of *ius divinum?* Could we say of him, as we say of a soldier killed carrying out his duty, that his death partakes of the sacrificial sense of a victim who gave his life for the good of the community? Holding such a view would amount to an apology for terrorism. In the past, various European governments have executed alleged terrorists in the streets under "shoot-to-kill" policies with a degree of impunity.[35] It was always a gray area that triggered internal investigations to calm public outrage, but there no longer seems to be any squeamishness or ambivalence when it comes to treatment of the Terrorist under the law. Basically, killing the terrorist is not homicide. And neither is the terrorist's death a sacrifice. This is what we find in the archaic Roman law's figure of *homo sacer* and which in the end sums up the true nature of sovereignty, that is, "the sphere in which it is permitted to kill without committing homicide and without celebrating a sacrifice." In the post-9/11 politics of counterterrorism, a major task of sovereign power is to decide who has fallen into this space.

The terrorist's suicidal martyrdom acquires a new dimension when seen from this perspective. The terrorist's message is the following: Yes, I can commit self-immolation, I can be sacrificed for my people, I can be a martyr for my community. Self-sacrifice is a way to assert the humanity otherwise denied by Western counterterrorism jurisdiction.

The age of terrorism brings to the fore the politicization of bare life itself. If the original fact of sovereignty is the production of the biopolitical body, in the current imperial order what is at issue is the bare humanity of peoples and entire countries deemed "terrorist" or "rogue." What matters is the relationship of inclusion/exclusion, of bare life transformed into the sphere of the biopolitical, of power defined by the capacity to establish a state of exception. To this imperial sovereign whose first avowed task is to prevail in the war on terror, all other peoples are potentially *homines sacri* unprotected by any rule of law.

The figure of the terrorist closely resembles Agamben's description of bare life having to do with biopolitics, not religion or politics per se. His suicidal fury, we are frequently told in what is intended to be a display of Western liberalism, has nothing to do with religion, for Islam is not such a mad religion. Nor does it have a political rationale, we tell ourselves. With any truly religious or political motivation denied to him, the suicide bomber becomes a puzzling aberration of bare life beyond the pale of any country, religion, community, or political agenda. Agamben wonders, "If today there is no longer any one clear figure of the sacred man, it is perhaps because we are all virtually *homines sacri*."[36] But for this to be the case one condition is necessary: the doctrine of counterterrorism must be imposed politically and turned into law. We are all virtually *homines sacri* if we all can easily become terrorists' accomplices in the War on Terror's proclaimed polarity of "with us or against us." Such biopolitics of terrorism has to do with a power intent, ultimately, not on passing judgment on political views, religious perspectives, or cultural values, but simply on deciding on the very value—or lack thereof—of the lives of alleged enemies.

Dancing with Chance, Innocence, and Suicidal Purpose

The terrorist's suicidal madness has to do with the logic of sudden chance, "purposeless" action, and ritual sacrifice. In order to understand the cruel "arbitrariness" of terrorist action and the "innocence" of its victims, there is a key conceptual issue that requires investigation, namely that it takes place within a logical space dominated by *random election*. This does not deny that the target might have emblematic value. Such logic of chance, which ensures that the innocent victims are chosen arbitrarily, removes the action to an entirely different realm of possibility and meaning. Only an enquiry into its purposefulness, a strategy that is different from the usual analysis of its "causes," can reveal the true conceptual nature of terrorist self-immolation. This type of enquiry overcomes false dichotomies such as whether suicide terrorism should be understood primarily in psychological terms or as an "organizational phenomenon,"[37] or whether the entire field has "a strong intentionalist bias."[38]

In cultural anthropology this conceptual interdependence between chance election and the innocence of the victim has been central to the widely recorded institution of ritual sacrifice. To ensure the innocence of the sacrificial victim, societies instituted the practice of drawing lots.[39] Guilt by association has been common in military institutions: upon the desertion of a soldier or the escape of a prisoner ten other soldiers or prisoners might be picked out randomly and punished (even executed) in retribution for their comrade's action. Thus the chosen victims are not sacrificed as the result of some known personal fault but merely because circumstances demanded that "someone" be sacrificed. Random election guarantees that an innocent victim be sacrificed ritually in retribution for a collective crime.

Terrorist action also assumes this ritual logic of random election among members of a population targeted by the militants as "guilty" for whatever reason. Hence the logical economy of terrorism whereby attacking one member stands for attacking the entire collectivity, the clear message to each member of the target group being "you too could have been picked out; you might be elected next time." Whether the terrorist is or is not a suicide, typically his victim is chosen randomly and is therefore innocent. But do these components of randomness and innocence touch in any sense the terrorist perpetrator himself? At first blush, we would reply in the negative: the victimizer and the victim must belong to different categories; the victim is a passive recipient of someone else's random selection, while the victimizer chooses at will; the victim has no option but to sacrifice his or her life, while the victimizer does not have to be the sacrifier; if the victim is "innocent," then the victimizer must be guilty.

And yet the terrorist embodiment of such Evil would disagree—the terrorist would argue, against all logic, that the horror of such defferred retaliation is a higher form of justice. The terrorist would begin by proclaiming his or her "innocence." But how can the terrorist send such a message? It is at this point that suicide becomes key, as if in their delirium the terrorists aim at making the statement that "we are also innocent victims, chosen randomly, by historical forces we can't control." The terrorist suicide attempts to break down the innocent/guilty, good/evil dichotomy of terrorism discourse. The message is "yes, my victims are innocent, but so am I." Or else: "Yes, I am guilty of murder, but so are you, my victims."

If for historic armed militaries the "gift of death" (Derrida)[40] was in the ideological and operational background, for the suicide terrorists it is the foreground. Derrida has seen at the heart of the Western religious and philosophical tradition such a fundamental premise whereby there is no greater gift of faith (Abraham), love (Christ), or truth (Socrates) than the readiness to die. Yet even in this tradition, suicide, for the most part, has been treated as a crime or as a sin. You had to be willing to give up your life but never to kill yourself. Abraham being ready to kill his son was the supreme act of faith, whereas Isaac killing himself would have been the most sinful act. It is killing or letting yourself be killed in the name of the big Other that is permitted, not self-immolation. The military man's actions are likewise embedded in a hierarchical order; the decisions are organizational, not personal. To the extent that suicide is in the end a personal choice, it goes against the military ethos whereby the soldier surrenders his life to the army's goals and decisions. Even when the suicide is sought and orchestrated by the collective organization, the individual has to concur and make it personal.

Conventional military behavior also has to take unpredictable chance into account and exploit it to strategic advantage. But it is guided by its best-laid plans and clearly stated goals that attempt to rule out chance as much as possible. If, in a conventional military organization, the surprise element of chance is a mere tactical component at the service of the overall strategy, in a terrorist organization the formlessness of chance per se becomes the key strategic condition for success against a far better organized power. If the strength of a conventional army is its organizational formality and hierarchical complexity, the strength of an insurgent armed group is its organizational informality and its aleatory strategy.[41] Not surprisingly, students of al Qaeda have "concluded with the crucial role played by weak acquaintances that provided the critical bridges to the jihad,"[42] rather than explicitly strong organizational linkages.

If chance behavior is key to terrorism, this leads us to the investigation of *purpose* as a crucial field for studying the entire phenomenon.[43] Terrorism typically engages in a course of behavior that deliberatedly and strategically rules out feedback. Once the airplane has been hijacked, it can be taken for granted that there is no way back. If feedback is required for teleological behavior, "by non-feed-back behavior is meant that in which there are no signals from the goal which modify the activity of the object *in the course of the behavior*."[44] Such "purposelessness," once the course of action has been put in motion and logically implicated with the innocence and impotence of the victims, is what makes terrorism so frightening. This does not mean, of course, that terrorist behavior is devoid of purposes. Yet what is typical of terrorism is the use of a nonfeedback strategy, a situation without exit, in order to call attention to and achieve their goals. It is this combination of purposeless behavior in the service of a purposeful platform that makes terrorism such an aporetic and unpredicatable phenomenon.

Intimately associated with this logic of nonfeedback chance are the ethics of personal martyrdom. If "transcendence" derives initially from the logical terms of higher external purpose, its subjective implication is that the actors relinquish any control over the purpose of their own lives. Election by chance will make the lives of the terrorist perpetrators and their victims subject to such systemically "purposeless" courses of action. To be effective, many types of military and nonmilitary violence incorporate a dimension of nonfeedback or deliberate purposelessness. Yet "terrorism," ideal-typically, is a strategy that plays Russian roulette with the general public in order to convey the message of chance terror to thereby provoke uncontrollable fear. Personal suicide is the one action that unmistakably conveys to oneself and the others such a message of no return. It is a way of saying: this action is so out of control that I will not even bother to spare my own life. The premise of nonteleology covers not only the fate of the victims but also that of the perpetrator. Suicide by the perpetrator of violence attempts to bring to the fore the message that (although on the basis of different criteria for decision making) both the victim and the perpetrator have been chosen randomly for ritual sacrifice.

This terrifying logic of deliberately random action is no invention of terrorists. Warfare has always accessed this type of action as its ultimate resort; the bombing of cities with tens of thousands of civilian casualties, deemed "collateral damage," can easily be justified by the laws of warfare. Nagasaki was chosen by chance for attack after a city that had been targeted originally for the bombing awoke that morning to cloudy weather and was ruled out. With nuclear arms the very distinction between military and civilian targets can even be considered an anachronism. Speaking of the deliberate military use of nonteleology, nuclear arms are perhaps the best example. Nations allowed their proliferation premised on the belief that they would never be used, as resort to them would result in mutually assured destruction. The missile targets the enemy but its purpose is to avoid its own use, thus to become ultimately "purposeless." Targeting the enemy is tantamount to targeting oneself. As will be discussed in chapter

7 in a larger political context, to a great extent contemporary terrorism is a parasite of the existence of nuclear arms. Western nuclearism and its readiness for destruction on a global scale provides the primary context of such willingness for suicidal self-immolation.

Life against Death

In his study of narcissism Freud had come close to abandoning his preference for the instinctual dualism of Eros and Thanatos when he admitted the preeminence of the libido as the single source of energy. If both Eros and Death are conservative of life, what differentiates them? Brown and Marcuse will depart from "instinctual dualism" into an "instinctual dialectic." For them, the overlapping of the erotic and death drives, their intimacy so to speak, is the crucial point that needs to be grasped: "The difference between a dualism of the instincts and a dialectical unity of the instincts is small and elusive; but slight shades of difference at this fundamental level can have large consequences."[45] Freud had undermined his own dualism of love and hate with empirical data suggesting that sexual and aggressive instincts acted jointly, and by showing how easily love can transform into hate, as in the phenomenon of sadism—the desire to die turns into the desire to kill, "a transformation achieved by Eros so as to reduce the innate self-destructive tendency in the organism and turn it into a useful ally in the erotic task of maintaining and enriching life."[46] Such primary drives "are subject to *historical* modification"[47] and reflect the subject's intersubjective situation in a dialectical process. The Hegelian dialectics of domination over the objects and of mutual recognition assumes that the subject risks negation, that the universal recognition of equality may require risking one's life. Thus, the essence of what a subject is consists of the contradictions of his or her actual existence. In the end, Freud's insights led to the conclusion that "the dualism between life and death is only a misreading of a fundamental unity which denies the difference between life and death."[48] As summed up by Paul Ricoeur, "the death instinct . . . is not beyond the pleasure principle, but is somehow identical with it."[49] Such a precedence of Death in the history of civilization, and its alliance with pleasure, is the psychoanalytic perspective that sheds light on contemporary suicidal terrorism.

"History is shaped, beyond our conscious wills, not by the cunning of Reason but by the cunning of Desire,"[50] argued Brown. From the perspective of the precedence of desire and the realization that "repressed Eros is the energy of history,"[51] the challenge is then how to turn the death drive, the ultimate horror of Freudian pessimism, into an ally of life, into "the only way out of the really pessimistic hypothesis of an innate aggressive instinct."[52] Repression of unconscious desires implies that the subject must protect himself from death and from sexuality. History is for G. W. F. Hegel what man does with death; he also links individuality with death, a view stressed later by Martin Heidegger; and society is ultimately a community built around the dead and in flight from death—hence the group's need for historical or religious immortality by denying death. In their madness, suicidal terrorists have understood this; as bin Laden stated in his 1996 declaration of war on America, "These youths love death as you love life."[53]

"Terrorists," and their communities, are people who recognize the normalcy and necessity of such willingness to die under situations of intolerable repression—a condition that might even require suicidal action. This is action that might fall into the category of "madness" yet is also the disposition of a "liberated body" willing to satisfy to the end the death drive in the hope of affirming the life of one's community. It is as if "the terrorist" and his community are forced to admit the unbearable truth: we have fallen into a state of nonrecognition and undignified slavery, we have become a people afraid to confront our masters, our community is nothing but a social shield in our flight from death—ergo, confronting suicidal death head on is the only way to regain digntiy and overcome the fear of death that has made our life unbearable. Only a body reconciled with death becomes a body worth living with. Suicide becomes liberation. This is the message of suicidal terrorism that the West is unwilling to read: in its delirium, the mad *act* of terrorism, like the act of Antigone resisting Creon's order, attempts a reconfiguration of what is possible in the political field. Such a reconfiguration can make sense to a given community because of its conditions of political subordination or subjective dejection. Only a radical subjective transformation may explain that a community sees as legitimate suicidal behavior that also takes innocent victims. Reading nothing but mindless "terrorism" into the acts of suicidal martyrdom is in the end self-defeating. It refuses to acknowledge the potent connection of such desperate behavior by powerless people with the repressed desires of their political unconsciouss.

The potential of acting out such a self-destructive delirium gets magnified in the contemporary world of nuclear and biological technologies.

Terrorism has been called "the weapon of the weak," that is, the suicide bomber is the underdog's reply to the overwhelming technological superiority of the "smart bomb." In a world in which the old arms race ended in nuclear deadlock, and in which the West keeps building smarter bombs, the terrorist's response is not less smart—a body turned into a bomb and directed by a reasoning and desiring human brain rather than a computer. If technology bombs anonymously from forty thousand feet, the self-immolator shares death in the proximity of the victims—the very essence of the successful action. If the Western nuclear arsenal is death instinct in its pure madness, the lone terrorist embodies its suicidal potential through personal self-destruction, hoping perhaps to visualize in his body the obscenity of nuclearist culture and thus further its demise. In this sense, the terrorist could see himself allied with "eternal Eros," the force Freud called for at the conclusion of his *Civilization and Its Discontents* in its struggle with Death, "his equally immortal adversary." As Ricoeur noted, "culture places death at the service of love and reverses the initial relationship between life and death . . . culture comes upon the scene as the great enterprise of making life prevail against death: its supreme weapon is to employ internalized violence against externalized violence; its supreme ruse is to make death work against death."[54] The terrorist is the epitome of the "death drive" of current times. The insights from psychoanalysis, literature, philosophy, and other disciplines beckon us to transcend the simplistic dualisms of life/death instincts—or its moral version of the irreducible good/evil dichotomy—when dealing with contemporary terrorism.

CHAPTER FIVE

Antigone, the Terrorist

The Passage à l'Acte *That Traverses the Subject's Fantasy*

Counterterrorist thinking is grounded in the figure of an unchanging Terrorist who is immune to any transformations brought about by political process or personal change. This is typically a figure unaffected by experience or circumstance. But terrorist action is conducted in historical time by subjects who have been shaped and transformed by powerful political sequences. The Terrorist might be the latest embodiment of diabolical Evil, but it is self-deceiving to assume that he or she is unsusceptible to persuasion or other forms of change. Hence, what concerns me here in the study of the terrorist subject is the *crisis* that leads to the decision to act, the consequences of accepting death and killing, and the subsequent fidelity to and transformation of that subject.

I will address the subjective transformations of the terrorist by considering the militant who, during her time, held the highest leadership role of any woman in the history of ETA and who subsequently abandoned the organization only to be murdered by her former comrades—María Dolores González Catarain, known as Yoyes. What is of particular interest to me is the capacity of such radical subjectivity to keep faithful to its original commitment to Freedom or Death not through a blind subservience to ideas such as Fate, Fatherland, or any other big Other (such as ETA itself), but by the reevaluation and almost impossible transformation of self, including the willingness to sacrifice that big Other for which one was previously willing to die.

The revolutionary insurgent willingly embraces death as the ultimate option, but it is the desire for freedom and life that mark the *passage à l'acte* and the acceptance of a radical subject. "What is a rebel?" asked Camus. "A man who says no: but whose refusal does not imply a renunciation. He is also a man who says yes as soon as he begins to think for himself."[1] The goal that ultimately matters for the rebel is to radically transform the basic power structure of an intolerable situation. The revolutionary subject has internalized the belief that "only such an 'impossible' gesture of pure expenditure can change the very coordinates of what is strategically possible within a historical constellation."[2] If this demands the possibility of death, so be it.

Armed resistance groups, in their rebellion against the state, have been seen at times through the lens of Sophocles' heroine, Antigone. The 1978 film *Germany in Autumn* did so with the Red Army Faction after the collective suicide in prison of several Baader-Meinhof members. Antigone buried her brother Polyneices in defiance of the prohibition on doing so by the king, her uncle Creon, even though she knew that it might cost her own life. Antigone thereby represents a negation of established power in the name of a different ethics. Antigone's paradigmatic tale, discussed by a long array of authors, provides crucial insights into the meaning of a radical activism that challenges the rules of the existing order. Antigone falls into the symbolic death of being excluded from the social-political order. The terrorist who has accepted self-immolation for a political cause is also excluded from society and exists beyond life and death—the *decision* places her in a situation in which the symbolic order has been suspended.

Yoyes is a contemporary Antigone. In her youth she followed the steps of hundreds of Basque youths who joined ETA to fight Franco's dictatorship. Yoyes traded her dreams of being a school teacher, even a religious missionary and a pacifist in Taizé (France), for the martyrdom of armed struggle. It was in her post-ETA political life, with democracy restored in Spain, that ETA had become a law unto itself and Yoyes could no longer agree with its agenda. It was then that she became Antigone in defiance of ETA's power. Through such evolution no other Basque figure is more emblematic of the dilemmas and transformative potential of political rebellion. Yoyes's case runs contrary to the stereotype of "the terrorist" as an unyielding, potentially suicidal, subject bent on nothing but death. By persevering in her struggle, like Antigone, she was confronted with her own desire's self-realization and with the need to overturn her past completely. The ultimate test of her revolutionary calling was not her willingness to surrender her own life for the cause of her country's independence—something she did for seven years in ETA—but her willingness to *surrender even her cause*, that "primary fantasy" that constituted her political self.

Hero, Traitor, Mother: The Collapse of Gender Models

After being a member of ETA from 1972 to 1979, Yoyes decided to abandon the armed organzation and to start a new life in Mexico. She had been in disagreement with the organization's increasingly militaristic stance. In Mexico she studied sociology and in 1982 had a son. She returned to Paris in 1985 and, unable to get a grant that would allow her to keep studying sociology there, she settled in the Basque Country, in San Sebastian, with her partner and son. She took advantage of a de facto amnesty offer by the Spanish state and was at liberty. But ETA did not welcome her return. As one of its former leaders, ETA saw her return to family life as a victory for Spanish counterinsurgency. During her town's annual festivities, in September 1986, ETA killed her. The killing shocked the Basque Country—the "freedom fighters" were also cold-blooded and vengeful killers who murdered a young mother in front of her three-year-old son. Her only crime was her determination to quit ETA and live a "normal" family life. Yoyes had attained mythical status in the Spanish media. She was the avenger of the Spanish state during the difficult years of transition from Francoism to democracy. In the end, she owned her life but not her myth.

The killing of Yoyes posed a conundrum. Other male ETA members had returned to the Basque Country after a period of prison or exile and had resumed a normal civilian life. Their cases had not posed an irreconcilable dilemma with their former status as underground freedom fighters. So why was Yoyes's return different? Begoña Aretxaga wrote an incisive reply to this question; she read the death of Yoyes through various cultural frames and her insights are disturbing: "Hero, traitor, martyr— Yoyes was everything that, from the cultural premises embedded in nationalist practice, a woman could not be. Moreover, Yoyes was a mother. In the nationalist context, the models of hero, traitor or martyr and the model of the mother are mutually exclusive. It is precisely, I believe, the synthesis of these models in the person of Yoyes which made her 'treason' much more unbearable than that of other ex-militants."[3] In traditional Basque nationalist discourse, the militant is typically a son who is ready to die for the "motherland." In the funeral homages that are ritually performed for dead ETA members, their mothers have had a central role, frequently holding up the ashes of the dead son. The mother represents the continuity of both generational and historical lineages. In the absence of a church burial, the mother validates the figure of the redeemer-hero.

These traditional roles pose problems for female activists who can identify with them only by denying themselves as female and on an exceptional basis: "Yoyes was an anomaly in the radical nationalist world, as much in terms of the political role she assumed as in terms of the images that were projected onto her. Yoyes was treated as a hero and as a traitor, but she was also a mother at the same time. A mother by definition cannot be a hero or a traitor in the cultural context of radical nationalism; she is beyond these categories. Yoyes collapsed gender differentiations at a moment when ETA(m) needed them more rigidly than ever."[4] Ironically, Yoyes could have joined the ranks of "repented" ex-militants, and this would probably have saved her life. But, as she made clear in her own diary, she refused to be a repenter; she did not want to fall into one of ETA's polarized categories, hero or traitor. She was neither. Plus she was a mother. Her unclassifiable ambiguity generated by the reversal of all the traditional roles was too much to bear for her former male associates.[5]

The Diaries: Writing under the Volcano

But Yoyes was not only the guerrilla who had risked everything on the battlefield; since adolescence she had been a compulsive writer. She wrote for years a diary that became her refuge and her testament of the fight for personal and political freedom. In moments of crisis, she tells herself, "I have to write, it is something indispensable if I want to continue evolving."[6] She writes, "To thus know my deepest desires and not confuse my way. . . . And always without betraying myself, without betraying the cause of freedom . . . a cause that is inseparable from my collectivity and my individuality."[7] One such moment was when Argala (nom de guerre for José Miguel Beñaran Ordeñana), her close friend and the undisputed leader of ETA, was killed by the Spanish police in December

1978. Yoyes became entrusted with Argala's documents and occupied his position on the council of the armed organization. She was at the time the only woman in the upper echelons of ETA. She soon became disillusioned with the new direction of the organization and ceded her position to another member. This was the period after formal democracy had just returned to Spain, but nevertheless ETA had decided to carry on with the armed struggle. Her mentor Argala's advocacy of continuation had prevailed, but he had also been in favor of a gradual negotiation with the Spanish state rather than the uncompromising stance favored by some others. Yoyes was arrested and exiled to Valensole, eight hundred kilometers from the Basque Country in southern France. Two months later, and after refusing to obey the orders of the authorities, she returned and rejoined ETA. The attacks against ETA members by Spanish paramilitary groups were evident and Yoyes feared for her life. But as disturbing were the ideological differences with her comrades—two of them threatened that she would end up "in the hole." For Yoyes it was a period of intense anxiety that evolved into a personal crisis. Finally, after months of reflection, she decided to leave the organization. This implied radical change, since she had to transform her self-image from that of a leading ETA militant to a suspect veteran exiled in Mexico. Writing became her refuge.

On April 26, 1977, she writes, "I need to start writing again on paper my thoughts, my concerns, my fears, my problems and my moments of happiness."[8] During her moment of crisis and separation from ETA she writes a poem. She hears "women's voices that are vibrant to make me vibrant."[9] These women were her friends, her sisters, her feminist networks. She was also sustained by the voices of her favorite writers—Emily Dickinson, Virginia Woolf, and Simone de Beauvoir in particular.[10] When de Beauvoir died, Yoyes writes in her diary that "I feel as if my mother had died, for there is no doubt that she has been my 'intellectual mother,' my mother and my father."[11] Previously she had taken note of the death of Sartre, another fundamental author for her. If Yoyes had done something in her life, if she had become the best-known activist in ETA, if she had decided to transcend ETA, she owed it all fundamentally to these authors. Her "terrorist" self was primarily the result of reading and writing.

Writing was her pathway to self-discovery. In the difficult days after she had broken with ETA, she wrote that "these are days of reflection, and I no longer dream with a happy future; I am beginning to scrutinize and delve into my past; it is the only thing that provides me with reliable data because I know they have happened and they are real. I am trying to discover them again so that I know my deepest desires and I don't take the wrong path."[12] Writing was her way to uncover her "deepest desires." Her former ethics of martyrdom had turned by then into an ambivalent love: "I cannot love you more / Country of mine / I cannot love you more / There are loves that kill, they say / Love may turn into hatred / and this one can truly kill."[13] Yoyes was aware that she was writing not only for herself but possibly also for others,[14] that what was happening to her was something beyond her individual consciousness, that some paradigmatic shift was perhaps taking place within ETA's history.

When years later, in October 1985, she returns from Mexico to the Basque Country with her son only to be received as a "traitoress," she describes the commotion in her diary: "the volcano has erupted."[15] As she fears the fate that is awaiting her, Yoyes records her body's reactions to the anxiety, the difficulties of menstruating, her profound sense of loneliness. In what turns out to be the last entry of her diary she concludes, "I think that only writing could save me."[16] But this writing is different from the sociological papers she wrote for her professors at the National Autonomous University of Mexico (UNAM): "I don't believe in the objectivity [of sociology], again this cannot be separated from one's own subjectivity."[17] She had been undecided for a while as to whether to study sociology or literature; now she outlined the plot of a novel.

Yoyes was the first feminist in ETA. She began by questioning the male models of activism and ended by problematizing the entire revolutionary sense of ETA's modus operandi. As soon as she became an exile in the French border town of Hendaia, Yoyes realizes, in the words of a friend, that among her comrades, "the macho mentality had no limits: women were sexual objects or couriers for certain errands. Yoyes used to say that she [as an ETA operative] did not want to be the patient woman waiting for her husband to return from his activities."[18] Her feminist concerns are explicit from the beginning of the diary as a "most urgent task." Not only does she reject the machismo of her colleagues, she is afraid that it might infect her as well: "I don't want to become the woman who is accepted because men consider her in some way macho."[19] She felt that the organization had to change its ways to absorb more women: "What should I do for these men to understand and fully assume that women's liberation is a revolutionary priority?"[20] A revolution that would keep women subjugated as "second class citizens" had no worth for her.

Life against Death

"How many times can you start a new life!"[21] This was the sentence Yoyes had appropriated from Tina Modotti. As a leader of an armed organization deemed "terrorist" by the Spanish state, Yoyes's life had been for years a tightrope act. She could say with no hyperbole that "I have always lived with the presence of death" and that "I am not afraid of dying."[22] Furthermore, she would never renounce the years she spent in ETA. "I left my home because of my commitment to the struggle and if I were to be reborn I would do exactly the same," she writes in the last year of her life.[23] But in September 1979, in the midst of the personal crisis that is forcing her to leave ETA, threatened on both sides, she confides in her diary: "I cannot let myself be killed, let myself die, I believe I should not allow it, and in the event that one day I should [allow myself to die], this is not the moment, I want to live, I still have many things to live through, that I have not lived yet, and in this struggle against death I miss them more than ever."[24]

In the same paragraph she used Antigone's precise word to describe her situation—"entombment." She decided "to speak up to get out of this tomb, of this entombment in life that was beginning to suffocate me and in which I felt I was dying physically." She repeats the sentence, "And it is a true struggle against death."[25] At one point she spends two days with her lover; after he leaves she goes for a walk and the world of desire takes over her writing in a list of things "I have desired so much!"—including "I have desired children, to make life sprout . . . to use my capacity to give *life* physically."[26] Yoyes's first love was an ETA member who shared her militancy. But personal relations had to be subordinated to the demands of one's first love, the Revolution. She writes to him, "No, I am not tied to you, I don't know what I feel, I don't know whether I am able to fall in love with a man . . . you have to forget me."[27] Days later, in December 1972, he dies while planting a bomb and she is devastated. Annually her diary will record the anniversaries of his death. Later, in the fall of 1975, Yoyes meets another man, a philosophy professor, who will be her lifelong companion and the father of her child.

"I have felt death so close on quite a few occasions and now I feel life by my side and I have all the right to it. . . . it is my life, my son, my right, my pleasure."[28] She feels that maternity is regenerating her body: "my skin is now softer, my nails grow quicker, as well as my hair. . . . Marvelous life!"[29] She feels in "total communion" with the child inside her, "someone with whom

I have dreamt to the *summum*, someone whom I have adored so much during these months."[30] Akaitz is born and paradoxically something changes: in her dreams "the theme that predominates now is death . . . Life is outside, it is in Akaitz."[31] As she begins to think of her return from Mexico, death becomes a presence again: "Everything is getting complicated as I face an uncertain future and I am beginning to think of death again, although there is a substantial change, the fact that Akaitz exists changes my feeling towards death, the idea of leaving him without a mother horrifies me."[32]

What had happened? Already while pregnant there was news that members of ETA, including her, were recruiting money for the organization in Mexico, an accusation that put her life in peril and that she "felt like a dagger."[33] While she was nursing her son in Mexico, the Spanish media sizzled with news of women terrorists, including reporting falsely on her terrorist activities in France and Spain. On June 21, 1984, *El País* reported: "Even if she has resided in Mexico since the year 1982, after resigning her position in ETA, the Spanish police situates Yoyes currently in France, where she resumes her tasks at the direction and organization [of ETA] since 1983."[34] Yoyes's partner felt compelled to reply to *El País* that the news was false, that she had quit the organization five years earlier. Publicity about Yoyes leaving the organization was the last thing ETA wanted, of course, and she is reminded so in a letter received from an ETA operative. Yoyes is at a crossroads. The situation will worsen after she returns to the Basque Country. In October 1985, the Spanish weekly journal, *Cambio 16*, will publish a digitized photo of her on its front cover. She has the feeling that "they have all agreed to murder me." But she will not run away. The last thing she wants is a confrontation with the press or ETA. But nothing will stop her either.

Yoyes/Antigone

Yoyes had a poignant analogy to judge ETA's unwillingness to let her return from exile: "[ETA] cannot accept it, as if it were a husband abandoned by a wife who hopes that some day she will return, even if the entire world knows [that she will not]."[35] She had quit ETA in the summer of 1979 "due to important tactical and political differences" between her and the organization.[36] ETA kept the schism secret, something she wrongly assumed would be transitory. In a letter she wrote for the media but did not make public, she wrote that by the time she finished sociology courses in Mexico, "nothing or almost nothing tied me to ETA's and [its political wing] Herri Batasuna's projects as expressed in their activities."[37] Herri Batasuna had distorted the meaning of ETA's platform "by confusing means and goals"[38] and by giving to it a militaristic rather than a political interpretation. Still, when she met with ETA's leadership in the summer of 1985, she was still wanted back in the organization. Yoyes refused the invitation categorically. But the spurned husband would not take no for an answer. Yoyes knew that her situation was becoming increasingly precarious. In the summer of 1985 she is despairing that ETA will deny her the right to return to her native country with her son and has chilling premonitory dreams. In one of them, "a kind of religious sacrifice" takes place.

The premonitory dream in Paris had forewarned Yoyes that her death might be a foretold reality. She had been told by the Ministry of the Interior that there were no longer charges against her after the 1977 amnesty and that she could return. She had made it a condition that she would not seek protection under any of the "reinsertion" laws, construed as "repentance" by the Basque supporters of ETA. The ministry agreed that Yoyes's return was a serious coup against ETA's public image. But she was not going to be able to escape her past, nor even abandon her name. Both ETA and the press would deny her a new identity. She was used to facing up to death, but she was not used to confronting ETA. But if she had to do so, there was no other alternative. When she arrived in San Sebastian in the company of her partner and son the first thing she did was to walk by the sea. It was again her sea, her city, her life. It was all there, including the "volcano" that was waiting for her as soon as she arrived.

The press heralded her return. The graffiti on the walls of several towns read "Yoyes traitoress." That Yoyes was perfectly aware of the risks she was taking is reflected in the letter she wrote, days before her return to San Sebastian in October 1985, "To Public Opinion: I, Maria Dolores González Catarain, declare that I have been threatened by ETA after letting it know of my intention to return from exile to live in South Euskadi with my family. . . . I affirm that the responsibility of my death corresponds to ETA." And she adds: "I am aware of the consequences of this statement, but even if I don't agree with the politics of the Spanish government regarding the Basque problem, it is unacceptable that an organization that considers itself revolutionary should use fascist or Stalinist tactics, as one prefers, with members who in the past (long ago in my case) belonged to it. Silence is complicity."[39] She described the organization to which she had surrendered seven years of her life as being involved in "a fight that has degenerated into something terrible, dictatorial and mythical, contrary to my values and deepest feelings and to the permanent features of my trajectory."[40] Yoyes had fully embraced the fate of Antigone.

At this point Yoyes introduces in her diary the figure of "madness": "madness is or starts perhaps just as an idea or, in this case, a small melody with lyrics that you cannot get rid of, and that is constantly present . . . and you tell your thought: leave me alone! . . . and it all returns, the melody and the obsession of, what can I do? How could you believe in friends who today threaten your life? They are now your enemies . . . they think they are the pure ones, but what demonic purity!"[41] An enduring image of hers, the one which gives the title to her diaries, is "Yoyes at the window"—back from exile, the news of her return having exploded, she looks down from the window at one of those rare snowfalls in San Sebastian on a late November day in 1985, "everything is white, including my window. . . . I sit in a chair, by the window, and I watch the snow fall, engrossed."[42] The window allows her an escape from the madness of her new entombment. She can still enjoy it all in quiet defiance.

"I don't like the business of heroism," she observes in April 1984. "I never felt a hero, nor do I believe in heroes, because it leads to an absurd mythification that is an impediment to individual and collective development."[43] And later in San Sebastian she adds that "I never considered myself a hero, I cannot consider myself an anti-hero, nor was I a terrorist, rather a political militant."[44] Initially, it was her antifascist struggle in ETA that required the violent metamorphosis of having to take the identity of a "terrorist," always bordering on arrest, torture, or death. But when, in the fall of 1979, she is immersed in the crisis that will lead her to abandon ETA, she has to reconsider the ideology of martyrdom that has nourished her throughout all those years; " 'to be ready to give your life' cannot mean 'to be ready to surrender your life to the enemy,' they are two totally different things, I would say they are opposed."[45] Her understanding of "the enemy" had evolved, as her own comrades had threatened her with "the hole." She now realizes that the sacrifice of her life might no longer mean martyrdom but simply a settling of old scores by revengeful comrades.

Yoyes's case goes against the stereotype of "the terrorist" as an unyielding suicidal subject bent on nothing but death. She *perseveres* in her struggle until she is murdered, but her true struggle is with her own desire's self-realization. There was initially the fight against Franco's dictatorship. But it was far more than that, as shown dramatically by her subsequent evolution. It was having a son, studying sociology, being a feminist, writing a diary, having a life of her own—in short, her true struggle was to be faithful to the unyielding responsibility to be herself by thinking on her own and fulfilling the demands of her own personal freedom—such being her truest "political" act.

Yoyes had risked everything for the patriotic community. But after her ETA years she had to confront death without the protection of such a big Other. Now she had to be true to that initial project of freedom while radically changing its subjective forms. What Joan Copjec wrote about Antigone applies to Yoyes as well: "[Her] perseverance does not consist in the repetition of a 'pattern of behavior,' but of the performance, in the face of enormous obstacles, of a creative act, and it results not in the preservation of the very core of her being—however wayward or perverse—but of its complete overturning. Antigone's perseverance is not indicated by her remaining rigidly the same, but by her *metamorphosis* at the moment of her encounter with the event of her brother's death and Creon's refusal to allow his burial."[46] It is ETA's refusal to allow her to have a family life that turns Yoyes into an unyielding rebel once again, but this time cast totally differently and in defiance of the power of her former comrades. She perseveres by keeping the faith, not to any nationalist calling or ethnic allegiance, but to her inner ethical core, which requires that, pursuing her desire to the end, she transforms herself. It was no longer enough that she is willing to surrender her own life—something she was willing to do for seven years in ETA—but also, if freedom so demanded, to something altogether different—*to surrender the cause itself.* This is what Lacanians call the "primary fantasy" that constitutes the subject. She had to be ready to abandon the big Other of ETA and still keep faith in the cause of liberty. She surrenders the old ground of foundational culture and political violence for the sake of simultaneously "giving ground" to a new world. [47]

But one may ask: Why did she have to choose death? She did not directly choose it but it was the result of the slogan "Revolution or Death" that her former self had embraced and that was still in force in ETA. In Yoyes's case such an either/or had the structure of lose/lose alienating alternatives, as Copjec explains: "If you choose freedom and thereby lose the threat of death . . . you have no way of demonstrating that your choice is free. So, in this case the only real choice is death, since it alone proves that your choice has been freely made. But once this decision is taken, you lose all freedom but the freedom to die."[48] By tacitly assenting to her own death, Yoyes was in fact telling ETA, "I am ready to die for my new type freedom as much as you are for yours." Since the only way to proclaim "truth" in ETA's frame was through the "Freedom or Death" alternative, one that she knew intimately after her years of underground militancy, she defied them by not running away. Thus, her former comrades were forced to face the fact that she had not only rejected their shared revolutionary commitment but had radically embraced it in a new form that was beyond their scope.

Hegel provided the classical interpretation of Antigone versus Creon as the opposition between the two spheres of kinship versus the state, blood versus norms, particularity versus universality. As Judith Butler observes, Hegel and most other commentators see in Sophocles's heroine someone "who articulates a pre-political opposition to politics."[49] Since it has to do essentially with "blood," kinship is at the limits of ethical rule, which is properly the state. Yoyes radically questions the validity of these Hegelian polarities, for she makes inseparable her struggle against the Spanish state (of her ETA period) and her struggle against ETA itself. She was obviously as *political* when she left ETA, forcing upon her as acute a personal crisis as when she was militating inside ETA. Her decision to have a son and return to her native country despite ETA's threats and the media's assault on her privacy was political through and through. Rather than "pre-political," Yoyes's behavior was *metapolitical*—in Alain Badiou's sense that "[a]n event is political if its material is collective" and "'[c]ollective' means immediately universalizing"; that thought and truth procedures must be "considered subjectively"; that an event presents itself as "the infinite character of situations" summoned politically "as subjective universality"; and that "it puts the State at a distance."[50] A year before she was murdered, Yoyes wrote in her diary that "in Euskadi, in the minds of many, the 'universal' aspect is being lost for the sake of excessive praise of the 'particular,' the 'typical, what is in their words the 'national identity,' and which can devastate all the militant work done until these last years in terms of searching for a more just, progressive, open, creative society, in which all the members could have better possibilities of personal evolution."[51] Yoyes's subjective transformation into her "new life," which carried with it ETA's threat to her life, was avowedly metapolitical.

Thus, Yoyes as Antigone contradicts Hegel's assumption of the separability of kinship and the state, prompting Butler to question whether there can be one without the mediation of the other, and leading her to the conclusion that "Antigone emerges in her criminality to speak in the name of politics and the law: she absorbs the very language of the state against which she rebels, and hers becomes a politics not of oppositional purity but of the scandalously impure."[52] Yoyes complained about the "demonic purity" of her former ETA companions. By contrast, she was "scandalously impure" because, like Antigone, she was privileging kinship (by living a normal family life in the open) to the point of defying the orders of ETA as big Other. And Yoyes was doing it by implicitly assuming at an existential level the very terms of ETA's definitional alternative, "Freedom or Death." ETA could kill her, of course, but it could not rob her of her freedom. Yoyes's death was ETA's ultimate admission of impotence.

Antigone's "crime" was that she did not respect the sovereign's edict denying burial to her brother. But what kind of law was this? Antigone considered that her relationship to her brother was something unique, hence this was "a law with no generality and no transposability, one mired in the very circumstances to which it is applied . . . and, therefore, no law at all in any ordinary instance of its application."[53] Thus, rather than being law versus crime, the actions by both Creon and Antigone mirror each other in their exceptionality. Antigone not only defies the law, but "she assumes the voice of the law in committing the act against the law."[54] ETA's sovereignty emerged from its direct armed antagonism against state sovereignty—both warring forces do not permit a no-man's-land between them. Therefore, her abandonment of ETA was for her comrades, in principle, like passing over to the enemy. But Yoyes had fulfilled her promise not to issue public statements. She had not subscribed to the state's "repentance" rules. When the governor of the province offered her protection, she refused. What she really desired was to be left alone outside the war between ETA and the state. But returning meant to be in the cross fire of the two warring parties. It was a direct defiance against both powers. Yoyes was risking a double death.

"Oh Tomb, My Nuptial Bed"

While waiting alone in Paris for the papers she needed to return to the Basque Country, in the summer of 1985 Yoyes dreamed that, to please her mother, she had decided to have a white wedding. But things went awry. She arrived at the restaurant late and with her hair undone. Her white dress was already used and had stains—"I feel ridiculous doing something I did not want to do, with pretty disastrous consequences, because in the end I am doing it all by myself, with no help, and completely humiliated by everyone."[55] White weddings were not for her. Just the day before she had had another dream in which she was with the leadership of ETA and "they, of course, assumed that they had the right to decide my life"; she tells them that they don't and "I try to explain to them that there is a confusion, that I am not here to place myself under their orders, that I wanted to suggest something else" but they won't let her explain herself "and insist on talking as though they had that power." In her dream some people leave and she tells those remaining that she is going to continue living her own life and return to San Sebastian "because I have no other option." Someone tells her she cannot take that risk because she has a son, to whom she replies, "Are you going to kill me or what?" In her dream the ETA leader Txomin jumps from his chair to reply to his comrades, saying, "You will do so only under your personal responsibility, not that of the organization."[56] A few days later she will awake in anguish from a nightmare in which a girl is sacrificed in her own natal home and in whom she recognizes herself. Yoyes had described her quitting ETA as getting "out of this tomb, of this entombment in life that was beginning to suffocate me and in which I felt I was dying physically."[57] "Oh tomb, my nuptial bed!" had been Antigone's exclamation after Creon's punishment. Now Yoyes was facing her second entombment; a blood wedding had been prophesized by her dreams.

Yoyes's decision to leave ETA and return to her country, although quite legitimate at a personal level, was not free of political ambiguity. She had been a leader in ETA and she had quit it years ago. She did not agree with the latest course of action by ETA and its political wing Herri Batasuna, but neither did she renounce her past. Nor did she have to escape because that could be interpreted as admission of guilt. She had nothing to deny or to declare; she just wanted to live and be left alone by the state and by ETA. She needed no protection from either of them. But such independence would make her vulnerable to both.

It is legitimate to ask: What else could ETA do but to combat the state and therefore frame the situation in terms of war and treason? Which leads us to the question: To what extent was Yoyes the author of her own death? Her situation was analogous to that of Antigone. Butler's questions regarding the latter apply in essence to Yoyes:

Her act leads to her death, but the relationship between the act and her fatal conclusion is not precisely causal. She acts, she defies the law, knowing that death is the punishment, but what propels her action? And what propels her action towards death? It would be easier if we could say that Creon killed her, but Creon banishes her only to a living death, and it is within that tomb that she takes her life. It might be possible to say that she authors her own death, but what legacy of acts is being worked out through the instrument of her agency? Is her fatality a necessity? And if not, under what non-necessary conditions does her fatality come to appear as necessity?[58]

Even if an implicit suicidal component can be seen in Yoyes's defiance, consciously choosing death was the last thing Yoyes wanted. Her son Akaitz had been her vote for life. Still, in her unconscious, in her dreams, Yoyes accepted her destiny as part of her freedom. Had she wanted to fully protect herself from the risk of a fatal outcome, all she had to do was to leave the Basque Country and go live in Paris. Antigone's duty to bury her brother was also self-imposed. What does this partial authorship reveal of the true nature of Yoyes's historic action? The radical inter-pellation presented by Yoyes's transformation was ignored at the time. Currently even the leaders who decided to kill her espouse her positions; some of them have been expelled from ETA because, like Yoyes, they have questioned the value of the armed struggle in the current situation. Yoyes's truth does not derive from her innocence but from her willing-ness to engage herself fully in a process of constant personal and political transformation. Her life and her death changed the coordinates of ETA. Her politically radical act—not simply her willingness to surrender her life but even to sacrifice the cause itself—is, for her generation, the model for a new post-ETA subject.

Delirium and Prophecy

"Antigone entered her tomb . . . delirious," writes María Zambrano. "And only then she glimpses . . . the law beyond gods and men, older than them . . . then she breaks down at once in tears and delirium. The girl cries—as Joan cried on her way to the bonfire, as have cried without being heard those women buried alive in tombs of stone or in the solitude of time. And delirium springs from those lives, of those living beings in the last phase of their achievement, in the last time in which their voice can be heard. And their presence becomes one, an inviolable presence; an intangible consciousness, a voice that emerges once and again. While the history that devoured the girl Antigone continues, that history that demands sacrifice,

Antigone will continue delirious."[59] Zambrano dedicated her book to her sister Araceli, whom she called Antigone—her first husband had committed suicide after being interned in the Soviet Gulag in Siberia; her second husband, a Republican, was executed by Franco. Zambrano would have seen in Yoyes as well a woman "who first of all could not kill herself, not even die in an ordinary way, as it happens to personages who embody truth to the point of becoming prophecy."[60]

In which political context has one to situate the conversion, the delirium, the final destiny of Yoyes? The context of such conversion had to do with desire and the inherent internal gap of desire. If feminine desire was perhaps an unessential distraction while she was in ETA, in her post-ETA period Yoyes realized that desire and its antinomies were now her true field of knowledge: "the goal is to know myself, to know myself more each day, to reach the unconscious and remove it with the conscious, to know myself for the sake of knowing."[61] Sacrifice was no longer enough; she also had to love herself, because "it's only myself that remains now and I constantly search for myself to protect myself, to love myself more without conditions."[62] It was desire that had taken her initially into intense religious experience and then into ETA, into reading and identifying with de Beauvoir, then into sociology, and now into motherhood and literature. During her ETA period, taking refuge in "a personal solution" was the coded expression of selfish escapism and betrayal. Now this self-love was going to rescue her from herself.

Lacan's analysis helps us understand the internal conflict of desire on which Antigone is based. From this perspective, espoused earlier by Goethe, Antigone and Creon are not opposed as two principles of law. Creon, too, is driven by desire and its deviations. Yoyes's challenge was to present an alternative subject position that eclipsed ETA's from inside without relinquishing to her ex-comrades an exclusive right to interpret the revolutionary law "Euskadi or Death." Antigone stood against Creon reinforced by her personal conscience alone. Butler says this was how "Lacan resituates the problematic of *Antigone* as an internal difficulty of 'the desire to do good,' the desire to live in conformity with an ethical norm."[63] In this light, Yoyes's drama is not the result of the conflict between the Basque Country and living an ordinary live with her son, but rather, as Butler wrote of Antigone, "a conflict internal to and constitutive of the operation of desire and, in particular, ethical desire."[64] Yoyes could and perhaps should have abandoned the Basque Country considering the threat against her. But she was acting ultimately in the inalienable field of desire as her supreme power, desire that had been made flesh in her son, desire that originated in the gap essential to the subject and that since adolescence had propelled her to search for truth by means of self-transformation.

But desire cannot avoid something intrinsic to it: the phantom of death, or, as theorized by psychoanalysis, "the death instinct." Such "instinct" (a mythical term to refer to what remains in the psyche between the known and the unknown) must be situated in the Freudian context of Eros and Thanatos, two forces that are better understood not as antagonistic but as complementary. In such a dialectic view according to which self-consciousness is *desire*, there is no dualism between the life and death instincts but a fundamental unity that manifests itself in the contribution of both to the principles of pleasure and reality. Thus Eros is not only a preserver of life but is also conducive, through nature, to death; and Thanatos is not contrary to the pleasure principle but can identify with it.

It is not only that the revolutionary cause forces the subject to surrender to the death drive, but that the passion of desire may inherently, beyond family ties, propel the subject to self-destruction. Her dreams would remind Yoyes, "you are dead," but there was no question that her desire was alive. By desiring to live while dead, she was using the power of death both to define the radicalness of her position while placing a limit upon death. This recourse to considering death as intrinsic to her life appears more frequently as her diary evolves and defines once again Yoyes's subjective changes, but with a different dynamic than that of Thanatos when she was in ETA. Now it is with an Eros transformed into family, literature, individuality. She could watch the snow falling in San Sebastian and realize that everything had been worthwhile. She could tell herself again what she had once written in Mexico, pregnant, brimming with happiness, "Marvelous life!"

Still, Yoyes, like Antigone, represents a figure "between two deaths" or a figure "beyond life and death." These are the words that Zambrano has Antigone say: "Because now I know my sentence: 'Antigone, buried alive, you will not die, you will remain like this, neither alive nor dead, neither alive nor dead.'"[65] The Lacanian position is that the elementary ethical act is the result of a desire that goes beyond the imperatives of the big Other and thus risks a sort of "death," an act that cannot be reduced to mere language. Antigone represents this figure "beyond two deaths." As Zizek observes, this act is not the same as the subversive displacement within a hegemonic order; it is rather "the much more radical *act* of a thorough reconfiguration of the entire field which redefines the very conditions of socially sustained performativity."[66] This requires "traversing" the fundamental fantasy that grants consistency to the subject.

This "traversing of the fundamental fantasy" of the subject is what Yoyes illustrates both in her initial *passage à l'acte* of joining ETA as well as in her subsequent post-ETA *passage à l'acte* of not submitting to ETA. For her initial act she had to admit, in a moment of "madness," the nonexistence of the big Other of her religious adolescence and of the big Other of the Spanish state; for her second act she had to admit, in another moment of "madness," that likewise, ETA as big Other was no longer operative for her. The second act was as politically radical as the first. This was something that from her former subject position was "impossible," yet she had made it happen. As with any act of political radicalness, this required not only that she put her life on the line but also the "gesture of pure expenditure" that can change the coordinates of what is possible: "This is the key point: an act is neither a strategic intervention *into* the existing order, nor is it its 'crazy,' destructive *negation*; an act is an 'excessive,' trans-strategic intervention which redefines the rules and contours of the existing order."[67] This is exactly what Yoyes's *act* achieved in the history of ETA: she changed its coordinates, she made ETA's sacrificial ethos obsolete, her death overcame ETA's heroic subject.

Yoyes's life had been, as she insisted in her diary, "a fight against death." She had accepted its possibility in an act of defiance against ETA. Her determination had implied subjectively the victory of life. What Zambrano had written about Antigone could be applied to Yoyes, that hers could only be "a mode of death that is revealing and with it gives a new life to it. For death conceals certain 'beings' when it reaches them and reveals others revealing inextinguishable life." And Zambrano does not hesitate to situate certain archetypal figures in a "time of germination in the obscurity that is due, more than to anyone, to those who actualize somehow the promise of resurrection, as individuals, and to the law of reparation that modulates history."[68] Yoyes would have understood intimately Zambrano's "resurrection." Both Saint Paul and his anti-Christian rival Nietzsche are Dionysian affirmers of life, of the savage happiness of "Oh death, where is thy victory?"[69] The militant atheist Badiou, much like Zambrano, sees in such affirmative subtraction of death the foundations of Christian universalism.[70] Beyond religious belief, Yoyes's subject position itself is, in this affirmation of life, irreducible to death.

Face to face with the ETA assassin who aims the pistol at her, in that final moment of delirium Yoyes finally sees and lives everything, like Isaac contemplating Abraham's raised knife. Not only Yoyes, but also her three-year-old son Akaitz, the *life* she had produced, saw it all. "The cowboys came with pistols and killed Mom," he told the family. On that day in September 1986 ETA had been vanquished, not by its political enemy and the three decades of police repression and media manipulation, but by the bare *act* of a silently defiant pale woman in the company of her son—by Yoyes/Antigone. It is the prophecy of the city of brotherhood, the one demanded by Yoyes/Antigone, that is still waiting for fulfillment.

The fate of "the terrorist" Yoyes/Antigone heroine was also in the end a tragic self-fulfilling prophecy. Her story demonstrates the extreme difficulty, once caught in the web of terrorism/counterterrorism, of extricating oneself from its dynamics, no matter how intense the desire to do so. Yoyes felt compelled to become a figure of "delirium" in her defiance, first against military dictatorship, later against revolutionary dictatorship. But by then she had been overtaken by her involvement in an armed organization that would evolve into adopting "terrorist" methods against a democratic regime. And afterward she would not be allowed to escape the dynamics of the mutually reinforcing violent antagonisms. ETA, the Spanish state, and the media all made certain that she would not regain her civilian status. They all used her to score points in their particular war game plan. In this regard, Yoyes is paradigmatic of the current struggle to bring closure to ETA's traumatic history.[71]

What matters to us here, the one component that is essential for the perpetuation of the violent standoff, is the semantics of "terrorism," with the mantra that you cannot negotiate with terrorists. In the Basques' recent attempt at negotiating a solution this resulted in the obscene spectacle of judges and political parties taking to court and criminalizing the very democratically elected officials who tried to broker a negotiation. The legal and political implications of "terrorism" are such that they lend themselves to all sorts of judicial and electoral manipulations disguised as respect for the rule of law and the moral high ground. The last thing "terrorism" and "counterterrorism" seeks in the Basque/Spanish situation is its own dissolution, even if every single political party, social organization, and cultural group in the Basque Country has demanded it for years. Once set in motion, "terrorism" is a powerful tool for self-deception; facing reality without it is far more difficult politically and ethically. The temptation to follow the self-fulfilling prophecies of Evil in order to be always "right" becomes irresistible for both terrorists and counterterrorists when the alternative is having to confront the revolutionary *act* of a Yoyes/Antigone that dissolves the terrorist/counterterrorist edge and demands a radical change of the very coordinates of what is politically possible. Such is her mad delirium and her prophecy.

PART III

Self-Fulfilling Politics

CHAPTER SIX

The Cold War Is Dead, Long Live Terrorism

"Terrorist" is a word coined during the French Revolution. Maximilien Robespierre was its main referent. He saw himself as the apostle of a new religion—the Cult of the Supreme Being. Robespierre preached virtue and terror: "virtue, without which terror is fatal, and terror, without which virtue is powerless."[1] This man of terror, known also as a "virtuous man," opposed war and made impassioned pleas for public morality and civil liberty. Above all, he was "not afraid to die."[2] Other terrorists would later imitate his mixing of religion and revolution, morality and violence.

After World War II a group formed in the United States that had the hallmarks of Robespierre's revolutionary passion for virtue and terror. Its focal point was Georgetown in Washington, D.C.; its mission was to halt the spread of the evil of communism ; it gathered secret information and engaged in covert subversive action; it was composed of enlightened men, converted to a higher cause, possessed of an urgent call to preserve freedom and order at any cost. They remained underground and frequently operated beyond the law; they were willing to risk everything, including their own lives; in short, they had what it took to assert that Western freedoms were so inalienable that any means of defending such beliefs was acceptable, including the *passage à l'acte* if necessary. This organization was the Central Intelligence Agency. These men were the new Robespierres; theirs was a mixture of freedom and intransigence, virtue and terror; their cause was called the cold war.

The journalist Steve Coll argues convincingly in his highly praised, Pulitzer Prize–winning *Ghost Wars* that the attacks of September 11 cannot be assessed without grasping the role of the intelligence agencies and informal secret networks that preceded them in Afghanistan. Bin Laden's group was at once being pursued by the CIA and supported by Pakistan's ISI (Inter-Services Intelligence)—the two intelligence agencies that battled side by side in the closest partnership in Afghanistan for two decades. Coll emphasizes the central role of the CIA, or more generally "counterterrorism," in the entire story. This is indeed a struggle among ghosts—the ghosts that are at the heart of counterterrorist thinking and require exorcism.

A Crusade for Freedom

Take all the defining traits of "terrorism"—action for action's sake, secrecy, higher purpose, madness, suicide—and the CIA, that bastion against communist and revolutionary subversion, displayed all of them. Consider suicide, deemed the salient mark of the "new" terrorism after 9/11. The CIA sent thousands of agents on missions that turned out to be fatal and could in fact be deemed almost suicidal after World War II. The man in charge of covert operations and responsible for recruiting agents for such missions was Frank Wisner, a dashing lawyer, the son of landed gentry, burning with exorbitant zeal and intensity. He recruited his agents among refugees from the Soviet sphere in postwar Germany. In 1949, the CIA was allowed to enlist one hundred foreigners a year and bring them to the United States. One of the first recruits was Mikola Lebed, someone who, according to the agency's own files, had headed "a terrorist organization" in the Ukraine and who had considered the Nazis to be his allies. That same year the CIA "welcomed dozens of prominent war criminals"[3] housed in Nazi headquarters outside Munich, Germany, as well as émigré groups with fascist backgrounds. And soon there were dozens of Hungarian and Ukrainian agents dispatched by land and air behind the Iron Curtain, destined to be quickly captured and eliminated. The abortive missions continued for five years. Other agents were parachuted into Albania on commando missions, each more frantic and desperate. "Hundreds of the CIA's foreign agents were sent to their deaths in Russia, Poland, Romania, Ukraine, and the Baltic States during the 1950s."[4] This was a matter of national survival; their fates were unrecorded, yet (Robespierre would agree) their deaths were more than justified if the cause was the triumph of Western civilization.

But this was only the beginning. During the Korean conflict, "thousands of recruited Korean and Chinese agents were dropped into North Korea during the war, never to return."[5] That wasn't enough, of course, and "[h]undreds more Chinese agents died after they were launched onto the mainland in misconceived land, air, and sea operations."[6] The CIA dropped 212 agents into Manchuria—101 were killed, 111 captured. These paramilitary missions had nothing to do with gathering intelligence. In the words of the station chief in Hong Kong, "[t]hey were suicide missions."[7] "I wouldn't worry if there were a few casualties or a few martyrs behind the iron curtain," observed Allen Dulles, the powerful director of the agency from 1952 on. "The blood of martyrs"[8] was needed to discredit the Soviets around the world. What mattered was to prove to the enemy that you had Robespierre's will to back your values with suicidal terror.

The purpose of all this was to provoke and support armed revolution in Eastern Europe, Russia, and China. Several of the top CIA officers committed suicide themselves; Wisner went mad and started raving about Adolf Hitler, and then at age fifty-six killed himself with a shotgun. James Angleton, the legendary counterintelligence chief from the beginning of the agency until 1974, a literary radical who had introduced Ezra Pound to Yale and who was the inspiration of the poet-spy for many romanticized myths about the CIA, became so paranoid that he accused CIA director William Colby of being a Russian spy. These were men who risked everything, including their own sanity. They were true believers, as must be any genuine revolutionary. In the words of Richard Bissell, who became the chief of clandestine operations in 1959, "we're the real revolutionaries."[9] It is perhaps not surprising that, in cases such as the French-Algerian war, local CIA officers' sympathies were closer to the FLN (National Liberation Front) than to Charles de Gaulle's government despite the official Washington position. They held visions that the world at large might well consider mad—as when George Shultz took over as Reagan's secretary of state and found that CIA director William Casey was planning something as "crazy" as the agency's invasion of Suriname with 175 Korean commandos. "The CIA's intelligence," summed up Shultz, "was in many cases simply Bill Casey's ideology."[10] Casey, like other CIA directors, was a man of abiding faith; he had been educated by Jesuits, he was a Catholic Knight of Malta, he attended mass daily. "He believed ardently that by spreading the Catholic Church's reach and power he could contain communism's advance."[11] The cold warriors "were all Christians, in a non-sectarian, T.S. Eliot kind of way. They believed in a higher authority, a higher truth which sanctioned their anti-Communist, anti-atheist crusade."[12] It was the titanic struggle between good and evil; the God-fearing and the godless. But above all, they were men who, like Robespierre and so many contemporary terrorist groups around the globe, understood the necessity of accepting death as that ultimate paradox of Abraham's sacred terror—if the Higher Being requires the sacrifice of the beloved son in order to fulfill one's duty, so be it.

If anything, the cold war was a battle to turn peoples' minds against the false idol of communism . It involved eminent conservatives and liberals alike in a truly bipartisan cause. A Marshall Plan was not enough; cultural warfare was also necessary. A sense of mission consumed these Ivy League mandarins. As Irving Kristol put it, "The elite was us—the 'happy few' who had been chosen by History to guide our fellow creatures towards a secular redemption."[13] George Kennan, the diplomat-scholar and one of the founders of the CIA, was the man who articulated the new doctrine of containment. He had worked in Moscow's U.S. embassy beginning in 1933 and written his famous "Long Telegram" (1946) portraying a Soviet Union sensitive only to the logic of force. Kennan introduced the concept of "the necessary lie" as a crucial aspect of American postwar diplomacy; he argued that the Communists had won a strong position in Europe through a skillful use of lies. He posited that "they [the Communists] have fought us with unreality, with irrationalism. Can we combat this unreality successfully with rationalism, with truth, with honest, well-meant economic assistance?"[14] The answer was no. Covert warfare and lying were a historical necessity.

Three seminal books appeared in 1949: a collection of essays about the failure of communism, *The God That Failed*; Arthur Schlesinger's *The Vital Center*; and George Orwell's *Nineteen Eighty-Four*. What their authors sought was, in Schlesinger's words, "the restoration of the radical nerve" and the creation of a noncommunist Left that believed that democratic socialism was the most effective weapon against totalitarianism. But practical issues would soon overtake the cold warriors. For example, at the first conference of the Congress for Cultural Freedom, organized by Arthur Koestler in Berlin in June 1950 with secret funds from the CIA, James Burnham distinguished between "good" and "bad" atomic bombs. Others, like Hugh Trevor-Roper, were appalled at the crusading tone set by Koestler. "Equidistance" and "neutralism" between the contending superpowers were anathema for the hardliners. At the conclusion of the conference, "Koestler, a modern-day Robespierre (though his two American bodyguards hovered close by), thrilled to the occasion"[15] of triumphantly reading the Freedom Manifesto, a litmus test for liberty against totalitarianism and, they insisted, those who had violated the principle of habeas corpus. In Washington the conference's sponsors were ecstatic—a Defense Department representative thought it had been "a subtle covert operation carried out on the highest intellectual level."[16]

Burnham wrote a book entitled *The Machiavellians*, which became a manual for CIA agents. In 1953 Burnham played a vital role in the CIA's Operation Ajax to depose Mohammed Mossadeq, the nationalist prime minister of Iran, and enthrone the shah. It was the burden of the elite to combine theory and practice, which he did by bringing together major European thinkers. As Assistant Secretary of State Edward Barrett had declared, "Truth can be peculiarly the American weapon. It cannot be an isolated weapon, because the propaganda of truth is powerful only when linked with concrete actions and policies. . . . [A] highly skilful and substantial campaign of truth is as indispensable as an air force."[17] Truth and freedom would not come cheap and the CIA pumped hundreds of millions into the campaign. The personnel of only one of its organizations, the Free Europe Committee, numbered 413; its fund-raising arm was the Crusade for Freedom and its leading spokesman was a young actor named Ronald Reagan. Even the promotion of abstract expressionism and other American products became part of the cultural cold war—"the CIA were the best art critics in America in the fifties."[18] The CIA was de facto America's ministry of art and culture.

Intelligence and Covert Action against the Great Enemy

But let us return to the beginning. Throughout the cold war the White House needed a clandestine corps to conduct espionage and carry out covert paramilitary actions. While the presidents were loved as model democrats and men of courage, the intelligence world of covert action was the doppelgänger that had to do their dirty work for them. At the close of World War II the West was confronting a new enemy: Joseph Stalin. Nobody had studied him more intently than George Kennan. By then Hitler was finished but a new enemy, equally evil, had arrived, as Kennan explained in a 1996 interview on CNN:

We had accustomed ourselves, through our wartime experience, to having a great enemy before us who had to be considered capable and desirous of doing everything that was evil and bad for us. And as our attention shifted then from Hitler's Germany to what was now the other greatest military power in Europe, we began to attach these sorts of extremist views to Russia, too. We like to have our enemies in the singular, our friends, if you will, multiple. But the enemy must always be a center, he must be totally evil, he must wish all the terrible things that could happen to us—whether [that] made sense from his standpoint or not. . . . Carrying wartime extremisms into a period which was nominally one of peace . . . is one of the great fundamental causes of the Cold War.[19]

The narrative that the Soviets were evil incarnate and had to be met with all-out resistance, including paramilitary and covert action, would become the animating force behind the organization soon to be born with that exclusive purpose in mind—the Central Intelligence Agency. One among several intelligence agencies, the CIA would operate as a secret branch of the Pentagon, gathering information and conducting covert actions while the military-industrial complex would focus on the nuclear armaments race. Kennan's containment was understood, wrongly, essentially in military terms, as if "victory" for one's side was obtainable in the nuclear era. In a classical case of self-fulfilling prophecy, this would lead, in Kennan's own words, "to [the] 40 years of unnecessary, fearfully expensive and disoriented process of the Cold War."[20]

There was no room for a gray area: the Soviets were the paranoid bad guys; we Westerners were the good ones. Evil was written all over Stalin's reign of terror. We were wholly unlike him, but just in case Stalin thought otherwise, President Truman sent him an unmistakable message of what we were capable of ourselves by launching the nuclear attacks on Hiroshima and Nagasaki when Japan had all but surrendered. You must do anything to teach a lesson to the evil empire, including sacrificing randomly chosen cities with hundreds of thousands of innocent civilians. This was real war after all, not covert action or some other type of proxy warfare. Not surprisingly, Truman was uninterested in secret sabotage missions or intelligence operations. When Gen. William Donovan, the head of the wartime Office of Strategic Services (OSS), the forerunner of the CIA, visited Truman in May 1945 with the purpose of saving his spy network, the president listened to him for fifteen minutes and dismissed him. Before World War II, the United States lacked a secret foreign intelligence agency. Donovan had thought he could talk Truman into creating the CIA; instead, the president, for whom Donovan's plans looked like the Gestapo, fired him and ordered that the OSS be abolished. Six weeks earlier, Truman had dropped the atomic bomb. Who needs covert action when you are willing to wipe out entire cities in the name of freedom?

But nuclear dominance would not be forever, and soon the Soviets and the Americans were engaged in a dangerous armaments race (see next chapter). The prospect of a nuclear war appeared as the ultimate catastrophe. And if one compares them with weapons of mass destruction, covert action and subversion were seemingly patently lesser evils. Donovan might have been right after all. The CIA was formally established in June 1947. Unlike the nuclear bomb, that impressive invention of Western science and technology, subversion was a field in which the enemy held the advantages of history and experience. It was a matter of copying their secret tactics and dirty tricks. The Marshall Plan and what became known as the Truman Doctrine (a warning to Moscow not to engage in the subversion of foreign nations) were the public faces of American policy. The CIA became the secret army ready to fight the cold war as foreseen by Kennan. While having the ear of the president, the CIA would engage in political warfare in order to remake the map of the world in accord with U.S. interests.

The man in charge of covert action from the beginning was Frank Wisner. He opened forty-seven CIA stations in three years. In almost every post there were two station chiefs, one gathering intelligence, the other implementing covert action for Wisner—they would regularly double-cross one another. In April 1948 Italy was set for elections and the CIA warned the White House that, if the Communists won, a godless totalitarian police state might take over the cradle of Christian civilization and the site of the Holy See. War was preferable, thought Kennan. It was time for covert action modeled on the Communists' own methods. Millions of dollars were distributed to buy the good will of Italian politicians and priests. The Christian Democrats won comfortably. "The CIA's practice of purchasing elections and politicians with bags of cash was repeated in Italy—and many other nations—for the next twenty-five years."[21] All across Europe politicians, generals, publishers, religious groups, and cultural organizations began looking to the CIA for cash.

Stalin died in March 1953. What now? The CIA had no clue as to the thinking inside the Kremlin. "We have no plan. We are not even sure what difference his death makes," fumed President Eisenhower.[22] Fears about Soviet intentions did not diminish, but rather increased, with Stalin's death. His successor, Nikita Khrushchev, confessed that Stalin "trembled" at the thought of a global war with the United States. But the Americans were now scared to death that the ghost of the dead Stalin would return in the form of preemptive nuclear warfare. Eisenhower had to confront the Soviets, but without starting World War III. Allen Dulles, director of the agency since early 1953, gave a weekly briefing to the president and his cabinet on the world's hot spots, while discussing how to conduct the secret war. Nuclear bombs and covert action were the president's secret weapons.

One of the many countries that would be forever affected by America's secret crusade was Iran. This is a textbook case of how the CIA operated by creating a course of action that would become self-fulfilling in a long run. It is worth examining since Iran continues to this day to be a major stage for the theater of "terrorism." British intelligence had made a mess in Tehran and its friends in the CIA were asked to lend a helping hand. Winston Churchill had converted his coal-burning Royal Navy into oil-burning ships right before World War I; the British purchased the majority of the Anglo-Persian Oil Company in order to fuel the armada. Reza Khan had become the shah of Iran in 1925 and nationalist politicians soon discovered that the British oil company had systematically robbed their government of billions. Hatred for the British ran high and, in the 1930s, the Nazis made inroads. Churchill and Stalin invaded Iran in August 1941 and placed in power Mohammad Reza Shah Pahlavi after exiling his father, Reza Khan. The British were taking two-thirds of the revenues; the Iranians demanded a fifty-fifty split. The British said no and tried to bribe politicians and the media. Iranians responded by nationalizing their oil production in 1951. British warships were soon headed toward Iran in an attempt to overthrow Prime Minister Mohammed Mossadeq's government. The British organized an international boycott of Iran. Then Churchill, seventy-six, who had converted the Royal Navy to being fueled with oil forty years earlier, again became prime minister in 1951 and the British military made plans to seize Iran's oil fields. Mossadeq visited the White House and warned of triggering World War III. The United States would not back such an invasion, Truman told Churchill. But Churchill countered that this was the price for British support of the United States in the Korean War.

The Truman administration was in its final weeks; during the presidential transition the CIA could make policy by default and plans for a coup in Iran began to take shape. Thus, Operation Ajax was born. The CIA provided the guns and Iranian politicians, publishers, and the military were bribed with cash. Dulles aired the threat of a potential Soviet takeover of Iran and its oil fields, and warned that, should that happen, gasoline in the United States would have to be rationed. The new president, Dwight Eisenhower, did not believe a word of it. But the plot continued without presidential approval. Eisenhower then gave a speech declaring that no nation could dictate to others their form of government, which should be left to each country's choosing. The CIA's station chief in Tehran, Roger Goiran, echoed this position and argued that it would be a historic disaster for the United States to ally itself with British colonialism; Dulles recalled him to Washington and dismissed him. The U.S. ambassador to Iran objected to the British choice of the corrupt retired general Fazlollah Zahedi as the coup's front man. The plotters waited for the president's permission to proceed, which finally came in July 1953.

Street thugs paid by the CIA, posing as Communists, began attacking mullahs and defiling mosques. But Mossadeq outmaneuvered the plotters and the coup failed on August 14. The CIA tried to convince the world that it was Mossadeq who had staged a left-wing uprising and instructed the frightened shah to issue a broadcast to that effect before he flew to Rome. But the CIA was not in a mood to give in, and by the next morning it had produced a street mob of paid agitators, posing as Communists, to create chaos. The agency also sent emissaries to the supreme ayatollah of Iran asking him to declare a holy war. Days later, on August 19, a riot, assembled with CIA-paid tribesmen brought into Tehran in buses and trucks, took over the streets of the city, with the mob shouting slogans in favor of the shah and against Mossadeq. The crowd took over the building in which Mossadeq's cabinet was housed, sacked the headquarters, burned newspaper offices, and seized members of the government. One of the participants in the crowd was a fifty-one-year-old ayatollah by the name of Ruholla Musavi Khomeini. The CIA had engineered a future leader that, in a typical case of self-fulfilling prophecy, would one day return to haunt the United States.

The "coup," which, although successful, had gone awry in almost every detail and which was directed by operatives none of whom even knew Farsi, was still considered a great triumph for the CIA. Allen Dulles was ecstatic. An impression of the agency's omnipotence and tales of derring-do began to flourish—it was "the magic of covert action" in full force.[23] With the help of the CIA, the shah rigged the next election and tightened his control by imposing three years of martial law. He created a secret police trained by the agency, the infamous SAVAK. As would happen frequently in other countries as well, the CIA's station chief, not the ambassador, became the main U.S. spokesman vis-à-vis the shah, who was converted into the central figure of the Islamic world for the American agenda. It is hard to fathom who were blinder, the agency's believers in the magic of subversive action by hired street mobs on the ground or the politicians and commentators back in Washington who thought all of this was a great national victory. As generations of Iranians grew up with the knowledge of the CIA's meddling in their political life, a ticking time bomb was in the making. It exploded in the 1979 Iranian Revolution, led by the same Ayatollah Khomeini the CIA had brought to the streets of Tehran against Mossadeq. It would be followed the next year by the blowback effect of the American embassy's hostage crisis that followed the decision by President Carter to grant the shah entry into the United States. Ever since, Iran has figured prominently as a state "sponsor of terrorism." The seeds of the drama that would cost Carter his reelection had been planted by the CIA in the summer of 1953. In its latest incarnation, Iran resurfaces in George W. Bush's "axis of evil" and has become a major player in the ongoing War on Terror as Iraq's most influential neighbor. "Why do they hate us?" Bush asked candidly after 9/11.

And what about Iraq? Ali Saleh Sa'adi, the Iraqi interior minister in the 1960s, summed up the ascendancy of the Ba'ath Party: "We came to power on a CIA train."[24] And who was also riding it? Yes, someone by the name of Saddam Hussein. Another self-fulfilling prophecy was in the making.

The Iranian success story would lead directly to forty years of American involvement in subversive covert action in Central America and elsewhere.[25] It was all justified if you accepted the CIA's premise that a crusade against the evil of communism was imperative. And thus in country after country, in the name of freedom and democracy and against the proclaimed threat of godless communism, the CIA carried out sabotage and subversion against local governments by using cold cash and secret action, frequently imposing pro-American gangsterlike figures in the highest positions of power. That's how, for example, the Japanese political system was controlled by the CIA until the 1970s, in a clear case of "structural corruption." At times the agency would lend millions to support a leader, such as Egypt's Gamal Abdel Nasser, and then be surprised when he refused to remain bought. This led to plans to assassinate him and, when Eisenhower objected, to a long campaign of subversion as the alternative. In Hungary, seeing that the population was about to revolt against their Communist rulers, in the fall of 1956 Radio Free Europe urged the citizens to engage in sabotage and mortal conflict with the Soviets. But when the Soviets sent in their tanks, none of the promised help from the United States came and tens of thousands of insurgents were left to die.

There could be no neutrality in the black and white struggle against communism : thus Sukarno of Indonesia, who had declared himself neutral in the cold war, was not to be trusted, and the CIA planned to kill him. The 1958 attempt to overthrow his government "backfired so badly that it fueled the rise of the biggest communist party in the world outside of Russia and China. It would take a real war, in which hundreds of thousands died, to defeat that force."[26] At times, fighting evil simply demanded the elimination of foreign leaders, with direct orders to the CIA director from the president, as in the case of Patrice Lumumba, the freely elected prime minister of the Congo, or the repeated attempts against Fidel Castro for the better part of Kennedy's three years in power.[27]

Eisenhower launched 170 major CIA covert operations; President Kennedy, 163 in less than three years—an average of one per week. On July 30, 1962, Kennedy's tapes reveal his discussions with his ambassador to Brazil about spending millions to subvert the upcoming elections and to prepare for a military coup there—anything would be done in order to avoid another Cuba in the Western Hemisphere. On August 8, Kennedy was discussing with CIA director John McCone, a conservative California Republican and devout Catholic, a plan to drop hundreds of Chinese Nationalist soldiers into Mao Tse-tung's China, a dubious action he had already approved. On August 9, the plot at the White House centered on how to overthrow Haiti's dictator, Papa Doc Duvalier. On August 10, the Kennedy brothers, Defense Secretary Robert McNamara, Secretary of State Dean Rusk, and CIA director McCone were debating how "to liquidate top people in the Castro regime."[28] On August 15, McCone was back at the White House plotting the overthrow of Cheddi Jagan, the prime minister of British Guiana (next to Venezuela); Jagan had been twice reelected and a few months earlier had come to the White House to reassure Kennedy that Guiana would not become Communist, after which the president publicly proclaimed support for him and declared the right of every people to choose their form of government. At the same meeting the president was handed a document outlining covert operations in the following countries: Vietnam, Laos, Thailand, Iran, Pakistan, Bolivia, Colombia, the Dominican Republic, Ecuador, Guatemala, and Venezuela.[29] It was "a marvelous collection or dictionary of your crimes," McCone laughingly told the president. The zealous men with the mission to rid the world of the evil of communism were all educated at the top American universities, their lives were guided by Christian values, freedom and democracy were their stated political ideals, and they were willing to sacrifice everything on the altar of a burning patriotism. Their values and their *passage à l'acte* were not that different from the life-or-death commitments of the wave of underground insurgents willing to defy them in Latin America, Europe, Asia, and Africa. And so it goes.

During the cold war, the assumption was that covert action was the only alternative to nuclear war. By 1964, two-thirds of the CIA's budget, and 90 percent of its director's time, was devoted to covert action. This included not only cash and cunning; at some point real weapons had to be handed over to the CIA-trained paramilitaries. Eisenhower had created the Overseas Internal Security Program to police the world; by the time of Lyndon Johnson's presidency, the program, run by the CIA, the Pentagon, and the State Department, had "trained 771,217 foreign military and police officers in twenty-five nations."[30] The secret police of Cambodia, Colombia, Ecuador, El Salvador, Guatemala, Panama, Iran, Iraq, Laos, Peru, the Philippines, South Korea, South Vietnam, and Thailand were created with the CIA's help. A "bomb school" in Los Fresnos, Texas, trained the future leaders of death squads in Central and South America; that classroom opened the door to the torture chamber.

President Richard Nixon, who trusted nobody, despised the CIA. Nixon and Henry Kissinger reached an understanding that they would themselves conceive and run covert operations. The committee that had been created to oversee them under the CIA director, Richard Helms, "approved" dozens of operations without actually ever meeting once. Operating at a level of clandestinity even greater than that of the CIA, Nixon, already planning an antiballistic missile system, was outraged by the agency's arguments that the Soviets had neither the intention nor the capability of launching a nuclear first strike. Still, he used the CIA to subvert Soviet interests everywhere. One of those programs, code named Phoenix, was responsible for killing more than twenty thousand suspected Vietcong. In Western Europe the agency was secretly supporting politicians in Greece, Germany, France, and Italy, where $25 million were distributed not only to the Christian Democrats of Giulio Andreotti but also to the neofascists who attempted a failed coup in 1970 and used the financing for covert operations of their own, including terrorist bombings. But the one Kissingerian covert operation that will remain in infamy and that turned so many against the United States in the Americas and Western Europe was the military coup against Chilean president Salvador Allende.[31]

To what extent covert operations were part of the national fabric can be gathered from the fact that President Jimmy Carter, while considering the CIA to be a national disgrace, nevertheless ended up signing almost as many covert operation orders as his predecessors—only now in the name of human rights. They were aimed mostly at Moscow, Warsaw, and Prague, and they sought to subvert the control of publishing and the media by the pro-Soviet regimes. Carter also tried to change entrenched cold war foreign policies, in part by subverting the racist South African and Rhodesian regimes (Nelson Mandela had been arrested thanks in part to the CIA). Carter too had to protect the CIA's secrets; in Senator Patrick Moynihan's wry remark, "He's just discovered it's *his* CIA."[32] But it was with the 1979 hostage crisis of the American diplomats in Tehran that Carter would meet his nemesis; the seeds planted by the CIA's 1953 coup were about to yield their bitter harvest. The events that took place in Iran, including the hostage crisis, were still portrayed internationally as "a revolution," not as "terrorism." Carter would not be the last president to be damaged by the consequences of terrorism and counterterrorism. By the time he left the presidency, he himself had already planted in Afghanistan the seeds of the next terrorist nightmare. In July 1980, six months before the Soviet invasion, Carter had ordered covert action to help the mujahideen who were battling Kabul's pro-Soviet regime:[33] "His purpose—and that of his national security adviser, Zbigniew Brzezinski—was to provoke a full-scale Soviet military intervention"[34] or, in Brzezinski's words, "We now have the opportunity of giving to the USSR its Vietnam War."[35] It was a self-fulfilling prophecy; what the American officials ignored was that it was also a prophecy of al Qaeda and 9/11.

It was during the administration of Ronald Reagan, shortly before the collapse of the Soviet Union and the end of the cold war, that a new international enemy became the centerpiece of American foreign policy: "terrorism." As frequently stated, Reagan's administration conflated communism and terrorism, while itself engaging in all sorts of terroristic warfare in El Salvador, Nicaragua, Cuba, northern Africa, South Africa, and Lebanon.[36] In 1982, Beirut became a battleground for the United States after the CIA-supported strongman Bashir Gemayel was assassinated and the CIA's Maronite allies, backed by Israel, slaughtered seven hundred Palestinians. Imad Mughniyah, the bin Laden of the day, bombed the

American embassy in April 1983, killing sixty-three people, and in October his suicide terrorists managed to penetrate the American barracks
with a truck bomb, killing 241 Marines. Soon all American military forces
would leave Lebanon.

But the best-known case of counterterrorism by CIA director Casey
would be the Iran-contra affair, a masterpiece of covert-action nonsense
in which the profits made by illegally selling arms to the Iranians were
used to illegally arm the Nicaraguan contras. The United States had been
desperate to obtain the release of American hostages taken in Beirut; an
arms-for-hostages trade was conceived and approved by the CIA. The
Pentagon, under orders from Defense Secretary Caspar Weinberger and
his chief aide Colin Powell, would transfer missiles to the CIA for $3,469
per missile and then sell them to the Iranians for $10,000, with the net
profit going to the contras. When the illegal deal was made public, the
scandal almost derailed Reagan's presidency and the vice presidency of
the senior George Bush. The entire hostage-taking chapter had been
a classic example of self-fulfilling folly from the beginning: it started as
a case of international lawlessness when three Iranians diplomats and a
journalist were kidnapped and killed after their car, with diplomatic plates
and escorted by the police, was stopped by the Israeli-backed Christian
militia in Beirut in 1982. The incident, ignored by the local governments
and the United States, marked the genesis of hostage-taking in Lebanon.
When the United States struck the arms-for-hostages deal with the Iranians, there were four American captives being held in July 1986; there were
twelve six months later. It was a good policy for promoting the phenomenon, which led to the kidnapping of approximately 130 foreigners.

The more tragic case of self-fulfilling terrorism took place at the close
of Reagan's presidency, when the July 1988 downing "by mistake" of Iran
Air Flight 655 over the Persian Gulf by the U.S. guided-missile cruiser
USS Vincennes, with 290 passengers on board, was followed by the destruction of Pan Am 103 over Lockerbie, Scotland, with the loss of 259
lives in December. Contrary to the (later discredited) official version that
two Libyan officials were responsible for the Pan Am 103 crime, the widely
shared assumption among the experts was that it was an act of revenge by
Iranian leaders for the earlier downing of their airliner and that it was one
of those acts that "might be better understood as manifestations of blood
feuding."[37] The West applied to Pan Am 103 the discourse of "terrorism"
and, indeed, it is this ultimate instance of the killing of civilians to send an
ulterior message to a wider public that is the textbook definition of the

phenomenon. The anomaly is rather that it is the downing of the Iranian flight that does not figure in any terrorism database. This simply points to some of the foundational premises of counterterrorism: acts of terror perpetrated by Western states are assumed to have a legal and ethical ground. After the fact, they are covered by the rules of war and international law, or else are tragic accidents that should be dismissed as "errors"; if they happen, no link can be established between them and future acts of blowback or revenge. Such parsing of one aspect of the continuum as utterly unprovoked and arbitrary violence, while ignoring one's own culpability, is a key dimension of the circular nature of terrorism. The history of the CIA—our actions are justified because we are fighting evil; they are godless Communists—is a prime example of this very self-fulfilling process.

From the Cold War to the War on Terror

The global policy of containment evolved in the 1960s into its almost inevitable extension: the war in Vietnam. It was the culmination of what the most committed American statesmen and generals and editors and secret agents had believed during the cold war— communism was the Evil that had to be fought if Christianity was to prevail. Those same cold warriors would later wonder what the crusade was all about. Even George Kennan, the architect of the cold war policy of containment, having recognized that the struggle "will lead to no total victory for one side or the other," ended up renouncing the cornerstone of the Pax Americana he had designed: "I should make it clear that I'm wholly and emphatically rejecting any and all messianic concepts of America's role in the world, rejecting, that is, an image of ourselves as teachers and redeemers to the rest of humanity, rejecting the illusions of unique and supreme virtue on our part, the prattle about Manifest Destiny or the 'American Century.' "[38] What that meant was "a policy far less pretentious in word and deed than the ones we have been following in recent years."[39] Had the cold war been but a delusional pas de deux between the two superpowers?

The end of the cold war marked for the West the end of the *evil empire*. Without its foundational foe, it was also the death knell for the CIA's war against godless communism . The Soviet enemy had provided the West with a sense of purpose, a vocation, even a crusade. Now what? Mikhail Gorbachev had become a hero of historic proportions in the West, adoringly received by enthusiastic Americans when he visited Washington in

1987; only the CIA could not grasp the prospect that the cold war was over. Gorbachev had famously declared a period of *perestroika* (restructuring) and *glasnost* (openness) when he became the secretary general of the Communist Party in early 1985. Both watchwords implied a radical change in the politics of the Soviet Union. But the CIA would not see it that way; more than three years later, on December 1, 1988, the CIA still opined in a report that the Gorbachev reforms had not changed the basic elements of Soviet defense policy and practice. A week later, at the United Nations Gorbachev offered a unilateral reduction of half a million troops from the Soviet armed forces. Gorbachev continued with one bold initiative after another regarding arms control, cutbacks in defense spending, the withdrawal of the Soviet navy from the Mediterranean and the Indian Ocean. The CIA failed to anticipate any of these changes. In fact, as the Soviet Union was imploding, the CIA reported that its economy was growing. The agency was implicitly pleading not to be deprived of its enemy, its raison d'être. The CIA needed the Soviet Union for its very subsistence. If, by a quirk of history, its historical foe was going to disappear, a new adversary became an urgent necessity: "It was easy, once upon a time, for the CIA to be unique and mystical. It was not an institution. It was a mission. And the mission was a crusade. Then you took the Soviet Union away from us and there wasn't anything else. We don't have a history. We don't have a hero. Even our medals are secret. And now the mission is over. *Fini.*"[40] The Soviets understood that their system, based on secrecy, was terminal; the CIA could not grasp that the game was over. But what was out there with sufficiently high stakes to justify secret warfare and the flaunting of all legality? But yes, there was something still out there—something that might rekindle the fight against "the axis of evil" and even require another Vietnam—perhaps another cold war: "Terrorism."

The first Bush presidency marked the end of the cold war and the collapse of the Soviet Union. Was the defeat of communism going to signal as well the end of Reagan-era terrorism? It might seem so, even if, while the Soviet Union was imploding in the 1980s, counterterrorist experts such as Brian Jenkins were prophesizing that "we could see a doubling of terrorism by the end of the decade."[41] If during 1980–85 there had been seventeen terrorist murders, during the seven years from 1986 to 1992 there was not a single fatality caused by terrorism in the United States.[42] Yet over four of those same years, from 1989 to 1992, American libraries catalogued over fifteen hundred new book titles under the rubric "terrorism" and 121 books under "terrorist." The obvious question at the time was:

How could the counterterrorism industry portray itself as the ultimate guardian of civilization from a presumed threat that at the time was statistically almost nonexistent?

We might be unable to cite a single case of the seventeen "terrorist" murders that took place in the United States during the happy 1980s, yet it was also the decade in which the Reagan administration labeled terrorism as the major international problem. At one time more than 80 percent of Americans came to regard terrorism as an "extreme" danger. In April 1986, a national survey showed that terrorism was "the number one concern"[43] for Americans. The true reality had to wait until 1993 and the bombing of the World Trade Center. For the first time the United States was vulnerable to foreign terrorists. In 1995, the Oklahoma City bombing further dispelled any doubts as to whether terrorism in America was now for real. The experts had been prescient all along. Who could dispute the cold murderous facts?

What such a "reality effect" fails to take into account is an analysis of the extent to which Sheikh Omar Abdel Rahman, Osama bin Laden, or Timothy McVeigh could have been partly the self-fulfilling products of counterterrorism practices. Regarding the lone McVeigh, not only do his acts fail to fit any classical definition of terrorism (typically, a member of an armed group practicing psychological terror for the sake of furthering some political agenda), but, more important, the basic references of his plot were all provided by the dominant terrorism discourse in the United States: his shooting practice targets while a soldier were "terrorist"; his action plan was scripted by William Pierce's right-wing *The Turner Diaries* (itself inspired by the apocalyptic novel *The John Franklin Letters* in which America falls under a global Soviet conspiracy); his alias was "T. Tuttle," the name of the superterrorist hero in the Hollywood movie *Brazil*; the day chosen for the explosion was April 19, the second anniversary of the Waco tragedy, a cause célèbre for militias angered by the government's violent response to the apocalyptic Branch Davidians. Was a McVeigh possible without the culture of counterterrorism?

As the cold war was over, the anticipation that Russian plutonium would fall into the hands of terrorists created much fear. Sure enough, by May 18, 1995, there were reports that the German police had twice seized samples of radioactive material. There were rumors that the smugglers were negotiating with Iran or Iraq. But then it was determined that the operation had been concocted by the secret agencies in unison with the politicians to save the jobs of thousands of German spies who had been left with no enemy and no purpose. In short, this was one more case of self-fulfilling prophecy, one in which "those who are fighting this market are those who created it."[44] That very same day Osama bin Laden was expelled from Sudan. By then the blind sheikh Omar Abdel Rahman had been incarcerated and was awaiting a sentence of life in prison. September 11 was in the making.

As soon as Clinton became president, he ordered dozens of covert-action operations overseas. If during the Reagan years terrorism had turned into a substitute for communism and other strategic interests having to do with the cold war, during the Clinton years terrorism had become a significant structural reality of American foreign policy capable of prompting military attacks against Sudan and Afghanistan. After 9/11 the counterterrorist War on Terror emerged for the Bush administration as the seemingly only U.S. domestic and international politics. How did we get here?

The Banality of Evil and Its Terrorist Version

After Hitler, the embodiment of evil, was vanquished and gone, Stalin became evil itself. Arthur Miller reflected on the times: "The Germans clearly were to be our new friends, and the savior-Russians the enemy, an ignoble thing. . . . It seemed to me in later years that this wrenching shift, this ripping off of Good and Evil labels from one nation and pasting them onto another, had done something to wither the very notion of a world even theoretically moral. If last month's friend could so quickly become this month's enemy, what depth of reality could good and evil have?"[45] The crusade against communism had been served and, as related by Frances Stonor Saunders,[46] some of the best minds became passionately engaged in an epic struggle in the defense of freedom. At the end of the Cold War, as the Soviet Union dissolved and the evil empire collapsed, the remaining superpower was left with no clear evil enemy in sight.

But could a heavily militarized empire hold together without an enemy? By some accounts, the U.S. military budget "is an amount larger than all other defense budgets on Earth combined."[47] Fifty percent of all U.S. governmental discretionary spending was absorbed by defense between 2003 and 2007. Not surprisingly, this can be seen as a Keynesian war economy leading to constant wars, heavily dependent on "the kindness of strangers" (mostly China and Japan's central banks) "willing to support our illusions,"[48] while ominously clouded by a staggering national debt that threatens national bankruptcy. Gore Vidal lists 201 overseas military interventions since the end of World War II until 9/11.[49]

The Soviets lost the cold war and had to change their thinking and policies. They became aware that a system based on secrecy could not compete with Western open societies. The game was up. But could the remaining superpower change its thinking and do without an enemy? Initially the CIA refused to recognize that the Soviet system had changed. But it soon became obvious, after the fall of the Berlin wall and the collapse of the Soviet Union, that the dreaded cold war enemy was no more. So what now? Wasn't there anywhere a new mythology identifying some cosmic evil to maintain the struggle? There was still something out there beyond the "rogue states"—enter terrorism.

Terrorism is the new evil in the current political discourse. "We are in a conflict between good and evil, and America will call evil by its name" (June 1, 2002), President Bush declared; evil "is real," he has insisted; "[O]ur responsibility to history is already clear: to answer these attacks and rid the world of evil" (September 14, 2001).[50] Modern thought hasn't dismissed the concept of evil, but its understanding is poles apart from the satanic notion of evil of former times. In Immanuel Kant's ethical revolution, for example, the modern subject's freedom is autonomous and does not derive from abiding by some preestablished prohibition; both the tendency toward evil, as well as moral law, are deemed to be part of human nature and necessary. But even much earlier, in Saint Augustine's well-known formulation, evil has no positive substance of its own but is merely an *absence* of good and good an *absence* of evil. This has led Zizek to the conclusion that, "The difference between Good and Evil is thus a parallax"[51]—that is, a shift in perspective. Alain Badiou recognizes the existence of evil but only as a possible dimension of a truth-process and of the subject that embodies such a process;[52] Nazism, for example, was a political sequence based not directly on an exterior and substantive evil but on a worldview that integrated the word "Jew" in a manner that made the extermination of the Jews possible. In short, there is a world of difference between seeing evil as the parallax effect of our own desire and the inability to follow the symbolic norms necessary for the social order, and seeing it as a mystical force that must be vanquished from the face of the earth once and for all. This last view is premodern, even pre-Christian, and is closer to a witchcraft type of thought in which power acts secretly and almost mystically, as if by contagion.[53]

The neoconservative warriors grounded the War on Terror against "the axis of evil" in a very specific historical analogy: they were fighting Hitler. Paul Wolfowitz, in particular, believed that the policy of containment of Saddam Hussein during the Clinton administration was immoral. He frequently compared it with an attempt to "contain" Hitler rather than remove him. Having lost his extended family in the Holocaust, "this orientation towards Nazism would prove central to his thinking on Iraq"[54] and granted him an instant advantage over more cautious critics. When being considered as Rumsfeld's deputy, Wolfowitz admitted that he favored getting rid of Saddam Hussein, a position that initially would place him in a minority within the Bush administration. After 9/11, Wolfowitz, Richard Perle, Douglas Feith, and others had an opening to make the case that the blind "realism" of US foreign policy amounted in fact to "accommodation with evil."[55] Wolfowitz advocated toppling Hussein as the president and his national security team met to discuss the response to 9/11. The State of the Union address in January 2002 brought what was clearly a declaration of war against Iraq, Iran, North Korea, "and their terrorists allies," which constituted "an axis of evil." The following month, Wolfowitz and Senator Joe Lieberman went to Munich for an annual conference on security issues and received moralizing responses from top German and French officials contemptuous of their preemptive intentions against the "axis of evil." It all seemed to be a morality play. In the final analysis, was the Nazi analogy, and the subsequent comparisons with Neville Chamberlain and Winston Churchill, in fact helpful? Or did it rather confuse historical realities and confound thinking, as James Fallows argued?[56] Is it our intellectual task to see Hitlers everywhere, or is it rather to examine the creation of new singular formations of evil, including our own involvement in it?

Hannah Arendt produced "a report on the banality of evil" with her book *Eichmann in Jerusalem*. Yes, what the Nazis did was evil, but their inability to transcend orders and instead think for themselves made their crimes *banal* as well. With terrorism, a new dimension of the banalization of evil has taken place. It begins by categorizing the enemy one wants to destroy as equivalent to Hitler. Amos Oz replied thus to his prime minister, Menachem Begin, when he stated that destroying Arafat's headquarters in Beirut was like sending the Israeli Defense Forces to Berlin to eliminate Hitler: "Hitler is already dead, my dear Prime Minister. . . . Again and again, Mr. Begin, you reveal to the public eye a strange urge to resuscitate Hitler in order to kill him every day in the guise of terrorists."[57] Much the same could be said of the Bush administration's "axis of evil" as the excuse for starting a calamitous war that has resulted in the deaths of hundreds of thousands—a banality that diminishes the nature of true historic evil, while excusing one's own participation in the evil of a war of choice. The least possible thought in such a worldview is Hegel's point: the eye that sees evil is also part of evil.

Dual Sovereignty: Never Let Your Left Hand Know What Your Right Hand Is Doing

One of the standard dichotomies used to differentiate Western societies from the rest is the open/closed axis: non-Western societies are described as "closed" systems whose flow of information and decision making are controlled by the existing nondemocratic powers. A corollary to the openness of Western democracies, it is said, is their disadvantage in protecting people from the risks and vulnerabilities imposed by their own freedoms. During the cold war, this meant that the enemy had recourse to secret ways of acting that were antithetical to the openness of free societies. The challenge was therefore how to preserve the Western lifestyle while fending off the dangers emanating from the totalitarian Communist agenda.

The CIA's mandate was to be the president's covert army while protecting him from being held accountable for anything illegal or immoral. It was given the tasks of collecting, coordinating, and disseminating intelligence, plus a vague order to perform functions and duties that affected the national security—this entailed having to engage in covert action without any declaration of war by the Congress. Senator Frank Church, chairman of the 1975 Senate Select Committee to Study Governmental Operations with Respect to Intelligence Activities, produced this definition of "covert action": "semantic disguise for murder, coercion, blackmail, bribery, the spreading of lies, and consorting with known torturers and international terrorists."[58] It was essential that the covert action be conducted in such a way that its source went undetected. By 1954, Senator Mike Mansfield could state that "[s]ecrecy now beclouds everything about the CIA—its cost, its efficiency, its successes, its failures."[59] The list of CIA failures was in fact daunting. A major reason for secrecy was to maintain the myth of the agency's omnipotence. It wasn't only that the left hand did not know what the right hand was doing; frequently neither hand had a clue of what was going on.

In the post-Watergate period Senator Church's Senate committee conducted the investigation into the CIA's secret activities. Was this a sincere
effort to clean up past excesses and shift the agency to a higher moral
ground, or was it an exercise in hypocrisy? It was clearly the latter for
former CIA director Richard Helms. Asked by Church how the agency
could engage in such activities without explicit written orders from the
president, Helms was more than once tempted to fire back: "Senator, how
can you be so goddamned dumb? You don't put an order like that in *writing*."[60] Helms was of course convinced that all the senators knew who gave
the final orders and how these actions are carried out, "and yet Church
affected not to know."[61] Helms had been asked about assassinations in
the past as well, including by Dean Rusk in 1963, but he "had no right
to a candid answer" even if he was the secretary of state. Assassinations
were secrets that should stay secret to anyone except the president; when
President Johnson asked Helms the same question in a direct and explicit
manner, he was the one man who had the right to an honest reply.

Even if unhelpful for foreseeing upcoming events or unrelated to a final
"truth," the creation and possession of secrets was in the end the symbolic capital by which the agency's worth was measured. Upon his arrest
in November 1961, it was revealed that the double agent Heinz Felfe, the
CIA's West German chief of counterintelligence, had passed to the Soviets
"some fifteen thousand secrets."[62] The breach of secrecy would violate the
president's direct orders and the agency's charter. From Eisenhower on, as
stated in his secretary's notes, measures to guarantee secrecy were paramount: "The great problem is leakage and security. . . . Everyone must be
prepared to swear that he had not heard of it. . . . Our hand should not
show in anything that is done."[63] Above all, no covert action should lead to
the president. As Kennedy's national security adviser, McGeorge Bundy,
the former dean of arts and sciences at Harvard University, wrote to Ambassador Henry Cabot Lodge in Saigon, "They [the Vietnamese after their
president, Ngo Dinh Diem, had been assassinated in coup promoted by
the CIA] should be left under no illusion that political assassination is easily accepted here." Strict secrecy was required because "assassination was
too sensitive a matter to be discussed in official meetings or to be recorded
in official memos and minutes."[64] The agency would frequently hide the
secrets from the chief executive himself in the name of national security.
The bond of secrecy and the risks of survival went both ways: on the one
hand, the CIA had been rebuked for its incompetence by Presidents Kennedy, Johnson, Nixon, Gerald Ford, and Carter, and, as Ford told his clos-

est officials, "the CIA would be destroyed" if its secrets were disclosed. On the other hand, it was also President Ford who, at a luncheon for the editors and the publisher of the *New York Times*, shockingly admitted that "the reputation of every president since Harry Truman could be ruined if the deepest secrets [were] spilled. Like what? an editor asked. Like assassinations! Ford said."[65]

Lying was imperative in order to preserve the secrets, but even so it was difficult to keep them completely out of the public eye. Eisenhower had to bite the bullet and deny that American pilots had anything to do with a plot to overthrow Sukarno in 1957. It happened again after the downing of the U-2 in central Russia, but the CIA's cover story soon blew up and the president was made out to be a liar. There was no longer plausible deniability. Kennedy also had his moment of truth with the Bay of Pigs fiasco. The lies based on fake intelligence regarding Vietnam would haunt Presidents Johnson and Nixon. President Reagan lied to a joint session of Congress to protect the CIA's covert operations in the Iran-contra affair. The White House passed the blame to the CIA and its director, William Casey, who, in turn, lied about the matter, thereby becoming guilty of contempt to Congress. Casey had to lie even to his own deputy director, Adm. Bobby Ray Inman, who subsequently resigned. The lies about the Iraq War followed the same pattern.

In the end, crucially, the CIA's game of deception would include *fooling itself* and thereby becoming incapable of sorting out true information from self-deception. Already in the mid-1950s, an internal report regarding widespread frustration in the agency came to the conclusion that its young officers saw that the intelligence service "was lying to itself."[66] Or, as Bobby Kennedy thought after the Bay of Pigs disaster, "We had been deceived by Khrushchev, but we had also fooled ourselves."[67] One dangerous development was the hiring of a large number of double agents who did untold damage to the agency. There were also cases of Russian defectors, such as Yuri Nosenco, who, despite telling the truth, was not believed by Angleton, which resulted in catastrophic consequences. "Rather than being disinformed by the enemy, we are deluding ourselves,"[68] a senior Soviet Division officer wrote regarding the paranoid Angletonian mind-set. Truman Capote *knew* when his murderers were lying to him. CIA agents, caught in their professional game of deception, did not have the same luxury of subjective knowledge.

The end result of the culture of deception was that the agency itself was unable to know whether or not it was in fact delivering misinformation to the White House. The case of Aldrich Ames proves the case. He was arrested in 1994 after having spied for the Soviets for nearly nine years and given away the identities of hundreds of his fellow CIA officers. During the years 1986–94, senior officers at the CIA knew that some of their sources were contaminated and compromised by Russian intelligence. Still, "The agency knowingly gave the White House information manipulated by Moscow—and deliberately concealed the fact."[69] Some of these warped reports, regarding the key military and political developments in Moscow at the end of the cold war, went directly to the president. It was an individual agent of deception, Ames, who knew the truth, but not the agency. It thereby became itself a source of disinformation. The result of such "lying" to the White House was that the agency could no longer be trusted. The events leading up to 9/11 would repeat the pattern whereby individual agents knew the facts, yet the agency was ignorant. The inability to read through Saddam Hussein's rhetorical obfuscation regarding his alleged possession of weapons of mass destruction, as well as the patent lies of the Iraqi defector known as Curveball, was similarly catastrophic. The CIA was manipulated by Vice President Cheney and his colleagues first into self-deception and then into deceiving Colin Powell to unknowingly lie to the American public.

"Admit nothing. Deny everything"—that has been the official policy regarding the secrets of the state. Lying became an imperative sworn under oath (the oath implied one *had* to lie), even if in the end presidential lies undermined the power of secrecy. Nixon's fall brought the realization that some noble lies were no longer acceptable in a democracy—which is why there was nothing more destructive to the agency's morale than Carter's post-Nixon morality with its pledge never to lie to the American public. Even his own CIA director, Adm. Stansfield Turner, a devout Christian Scientist who would not even drink coffee or tea, let alone the whisky of the good old boys, had problems with Carter's moral allergy to deceit—the quintessence of a secret intelligence service. Carter's naïve aversion to deception and secret action was simply a radical dismissal of the sort of *dual sovereignty* on which American politics was predicated throughout the cold war: there was the open political process based on the three branches of government and the rule of law; and there was the covert political process based on secrecy and unaccountability and that could go beyond the rule of law with total impunity. Both sovereignties required de facto mutual reinforcement. This required that when necessary the agency applied one of its basic rules, namely, lying even to the president in order to fulfill its true mission.

Counterterrorism is besieged by covert action's legal and moral dilemmas: how to honestly employ dishonesty, how to respect the law by flouting it if required. The premise, believed by Nixon, Reagan's CIA director William Casey, and many in the intelligence community, is that *if it's secret, it's legal.* In other words, covert action, with its secrets and risks, considered as the only workable path in the no-man's-land between war and diplomacy, and restricted to exceptional situations, ends up acting as if it has its own law and moral legitimacy beyond ordinary law. Various CIA directors did contemplate the possibility of having to go to jail to protect the agency's secrets. The antithesis of a CIA director and a direct threat to its survival was a man such as Judge William Webster, a man of moral conviction who was brought in to clean up the mess left by Casey. He simply ignored the very raison d'être of the agency: "All of his training as a lawyer and a judge was that you didn't do illegal things. He could never accept that this is *exactly* what the CIA does when it operates abroad. We break the laws of their countries. It's how we collect information. It's why we're in business."[70] Also at home, the CIA could be used to spy on Americans or to sabotage federal institutions.

James Angleton, when asked why he had refused to destroy the stockpile of poisons as requested by the White House, put it in these terms: "It is unconceivable that a secret arm of the government has to comply with all the overt orders of the government."[71] Nor is it surprising that a public official such as Henry Kissinger should be the architect of American policy during the Nixon and Ford administrations and yet, by having headed the dual sovereignty of illegal covert action, should also be pursued for his alleged crimes in the courts of various countries. Anthropologists have recorded many cases of "dual sovereignty" in societies in which there was opposition and complementarity between the jural/administrative power of the chiefs and the mystical authority of priests and sorcerers. "Given that it is a premise of a culture that men are subject to the power of unseen forces and personages," premodern societies have taken for granted the existence of a "collective localization of the mystical"[72] that had to be coped with and mediated by specialists in the spirit world. Edward Evans-Pritchard's study of the Shilluk is a classic case: their divine kingship can only be understood by distinguishing the existence of judicial and administrative power, on the one hand, and the ritual office of a sacerdotal kind, embodied by the king, on the other.[73] The relationship between the open political process and secret covert action in our own society evokes a similar dual sovereignty by which legal authority is complemented with a different type of power that finds its legitimacy in the elusive principle of national security. If overt politics is based on the rule of law, covert politics is grounded in the magic of secret action and the mysticism of evil powers that must be confronted without legal restraints.

CHAPTER SEVEN

Dr. Strangelove Meets the Terrorist

On Political Madness

The risk of nuclear terrorism is the final apocalyptic fear in current political discourse. Such ultimate taboo of the terrorist madman was a decisive element in granting credibility to President Bush's doctrine of "the axis of evil" and in justifying going to war against Saddam Hussein. He announced it solemnly in his 2002 State of the Union address: "States like these [Iran, Iraq, and North Korea], and their terrorist allies, constitute the "axis of evil," arming to threaten the peace of the world. By seeking weapons of mass destruction, these regimes pose a grave and growing danger. They could provide these arms to terrorists, giving them the means to match their hatred." The symbiotic relationship between nuclear power and terrorism could not be stated more forcefully.

John Mueller has shown convincingly how "overblown" the threat of terrorism is; he writes that the likelihood of dying from terrorism is about the same as dying from the impact of an asteroid on the Earth or from an allergic reaction to peanuts.[1] The actual capacity for terrorists to develop a nuclear device is considered by the experts to be extremely low.[2] The technological sophistication of the 9/11 attacks rested on box cutters. But such healthy factualness does not address key components of the terrorist phenomenon—those having to do with the imaginative and subjective aspects of the threat. They constitute the context of *madness* in which both nuclear proliferation and the feared nemesis of its terrorist displacement transpire.

What accounts for the self-righteousness of a preventive *just war* in the nuclear era? It is presented as legitimate on the grounds that other countries, such as Iraq under Saddam Hussein, desire the weapons of mass destruction of which we already possess mountains of stockpiles. The war in Iraq is not only the frontline of the War on Terror; it also marks, as the testing ground for the complicity between nuclearism and terrorism, a radical change in nuclear nonproliferation—it was no longer a matter of eliminating nuclear arsenals but evil regimes.[3] It is in this war that WMDs and the figure of the Terrorist emerged as systemically linked and in full force. Nuclear nonproliferation was no longer an end in itself but part of the War on Terror. The only problem with nonproliferation was suddenly not the very existence of the nuclear arsenals and the foot-dragging to fulfil the promises to dismantle them, let alone the double standard of a policy by which the United States determines who has the right to possess nuclear weapons and who does not, but the existence of rogue states and their potential links to terrorist groups. Much as for the earlier cold warriors there were "good" and "bad" atomic bombs, for the new counterterrorists the real issue is no longer the obscenity of the tens of thousands of nuclear warheads ready to be used and a renewed armaments race that could lead to the collapse of nonproliferation, but the terrorists' *desire* to have them.

Remember the mantra: "It is not *if*, but *when*." What such ominous prediction does is to concentrate the danger of nuclearism in the tabooed figure of the terrorist to the exclusion of its historical context and current nonproliferation issues. Even liberal authors such as Michael Walzer have come to differentiate categorically between the aerial bombing of German cities during World War II (wars as such are not in principle immoral) and terrorist suicide bombings that are in principle and always evil.[4] Remove that figure of madness, the Terrorist, and the entire crusade ("the defining issue of our times") collapses. Remove the fatalistic prophecy that nuclear terrorism is a certainty waiting to happen and the entire armaments race appears for what it is—madness. Such blindness to history and common sense is the precondition for the prophecy to become self-fulfilling.

The Terrorist Madman

The terrorist is haunted by madness in that madmen are solitary people who cannot share in the basic rituals and flow of communal life. They are underground, cast away from society, living at the margins of morality and legality. That which is "truth" for them is "madness" for the world at large. Various forms of contemporary terrorism are expressions of such madness. In the case of jihadist terrorism, it is madness that frightens and elicits a pause. In the case of the Basque ETA, it is madness that smacks of impotent, irrelevant anachronism, and which can be summed up in the obvious paradox that ending the cease-fire implied at the same time ruining its own political goals.[5]

But madness is not only political exclusion, it is also a domain of knowledge; Lacan characterizes it as "a fault, a point of rupture in the structure of the external world that finds itself patched over by fantasy."[6] The unending paradox of desire advocates imaginary solutions at the fantasy level. The fascination with madness as a form of experience and knowledge goes back in Europe to the beginning of the Middle Ages. Concerned that "modern man no longer communicates with the madman," Foucault made a point of asking how "can we determine the realm in which the man of madness and the man of reason, moving apart, are not yet distinct."[7] By the end of the Middle Ages madness—in its ambiguity, menace, mockery—had become a major factor in European culture. It even becomes a sign of wisdom praised by Desiderius Erasmus and painted by Hieronymus Bosch and Pieter Brueghel. As Foucault explains:

> What does it presage, this wisdom of fools? Doubtless, since it is forbidden wisdom, it presages both the reign of Satan and the end of the world; ultimate bliss and supreme punishment; omnipotence on earth and the infernal fall. The Ship of Fools sails through a landscape of delights, where all is offered to desire, a sort of renewed paradise. . . . This false happiness is the diabolical triumph of the Antichrist; it is the End, already at hand. . . . The end has no value as passage and promise; it is the advent of a night in which the world's old reason is engulfed. . . . The world sinks into universal Fury. Victory is neither God's nor the Devil's; it belongs to Madness.[8]

What other contemporary figure can better embody the madman than the Terrorist?

Two days before they killed themselves and three thousand others, Mohamed Atta and his companions went to a strip club to drink, enjoy lap dances, and celebrate amid laughter the pending massacre. Like madmen in former times, they embodied "the mockery of madness" that "replaces death and its solemnity" and by which "death's annihilation is no longer anything because it was already everything, because life itself was only futility, vain words, a squabble of cap and bells. The head that will become a skull is already empty. Madness is the *déjà-là* [already there] of death."[9] The madman's laughter is the laughter of death; he disarms death by anticipating it in the form of lunacy. As Capote knew well from his protagonists, the murderers typically laugh after committing the murder or when confronted with it—as if, except for crying or laughing, any other communication or verbal explanation is radically silenced by the mute madness of the act.

"I who am thinking cannot be mad"[10] is the Cartesian position of Western thought. I who am a democrat cannot be a terrorist is a political axiom of counterterrorism discourse. But the boundaries of both madness and terror are not that clear. The decisive moment in which Western reason thought it had expelled madness, argues Foucault, was the Cartesian cogito. René Decartes asks: "And how shall I deny that these hands and this body are mine? Unless perhaps I were to compare myself to those lunatics. . . . But then, they are madmen, and I would hardly be less demented if I followed their example."[11] Madness is excluded from the realm of thought. But this Cartesian move was not an innocent one; it was rather "symptomatic of the oppressive order, of the monarchic and bourgeois regime which was at that time being organized in France."[12] It anticipated the "great internment" of six thousand people—madmen, drunks, tramps, paupers—and the creation of the General Hospital, an institution that worked alongside the law and the police and had the power to convict and execute people. While madness had earlier been something tragic and mysterious, now it was totally desacraclized and politicized.

If madness is exclusion from society, terrorism is the outside of politics. When terrorist violence is normalized in a society, madness becomes internal to the system. Suicide is also excluded—except when, as in Iraq, blowing oneself up in a suicidal attack becomes the expected and the normal. They seem to be saying: "Yes, we know this is crazy, immoral, illegal, mad . . . so? Is there anything else we can do? In fact, this is not suicide; this is martyrdom. We know this makes no sense to you, but we still prefer to be mad, we desperately need you to know we are mad." Who owns their madness and who controls the horror of their bodies turned into a bomb? Are they perhaps going mad because of our power and our wars, or is it simply their caprice? The bodies of American soldiers are also burned and maimed horribly. But the suicidal sacrifice of those categorized as "terrorists" is quite different—self-willed, seemingly demonic, mad. Yet are they mad-crazy or just mad-angry at us?

Western thought reduced madness to nonbeing just when the "great internment" of thousands of madmen was being contemplated. Similarly, "terror" is ruled out of Western political discourse as the ultimate taboo just when the West is engaged in producing the most terrifying weapons of mass destruction in human history—as if to blind itself to the obvious. By positioning itself in a deadly struggle against terrorism, the West would like to believe that terror is excluded from its political culture. By depriving terrorist madness of any tragic connotation, the West protects itself from any political interpelation provoked by "terrorist" desperation.

Blindness to itself is what typifies madness. And belief in reason, as in the logic of the nuclear armanents race, can be a form of madness. Francisco José de Goya, who painted "the monsters of reason," knew this well. "Reason and madness are . . . inextricably linked," writes Shosahana Felman; "madness is essentially a phenomenon of thought."[13] Madness transpires among thoughts in conflict, in self-reflection—calls into question the very essence of thought. What concerns us here is the relationship between terror and politics. Is terrorism to politics what madness is to thought? Is our belief in political reason in the era of nuclear deterrence another form of terror?

The madman doesn't make sense, cannot communicate, is often silent. The terrorist, too, usually feels compelled to refuse talk, explanation, persuasion. Were he to be listened to, any insurgent labeled "terrorist" would argue that the separate category of terrorism is built on a basic misunderstanding of the role of terror in politics in general. But the terrorist knows the only true expression left to him is action, gesture, pathos, the body in flames. He has given up argument, theory; he knows he is never right or despairs of being deemed so. His persistence can only be madness. He needs no language, no reason, no truth. Why does he give up so much so readily? The terrorist confronts us with a text that, to the extent that it springs from the political unconscious, is unreadable in the manner of a political treatise. The very silence of the plotters, their failure to narrate, adds to the terror and grants the story its specific character—its unconsciousness. Enough of consciousness—the terrorists seem to be saying, as if they had realized that conscious purpose, too, like language, is too fickle.

Commenting on Foucault and Derrida, Felman argues that literature *includes* the madness that philosophy excludes by definition; thus literature is in a posture of "excess." Similarly, we might say that it is the surplus of madness that characterizes terrorism in relation to politics. Paraphrasing what Foucault wrote about the history of madness, we could say that terrorism is pathos itself—that it not only connotes it, but *participates* in it.[14] Derrida objected to Foucault's absence of a guiding definition of madness; one reason that definitional clarity regarding terrorism is conspicuously absent must derive, in part, from its participation in madness. Of terrorism, too, it can be said that its proper meaning is that it has no proper meaning—that, like madness, it is a "false concept." As for madness, it can be said that the question underlying terrorism "cannot be asked" because "language is not capable of asking it"; that the very formulation does in fact exclude an actual interrogation, it being an affirmation of the contrary; that it remains alive and active by the act of writing itself; and that we are unable to locate it, "because it questions *somewhere else*: somewhere at the point of silence where it is no longer we who speak, but where, in our absence, we are *spoken*."[15] Counterterrorism refuses to confront terrorist subjectivity by suppressing the unconscious component of his or her actions. Its goal is to situate the terrorist outside of politics. By reserving exclusively for the terrorist the tabooed "excess" component of political madness, the counterterrorist feels secure in denying any of it to his or her own polity.

Maddening States

A key arena that breeds terrorist madness is the modern nation-state. The literature has long identified the struggle against the liberal state as a major historical perspective of the entire phenomenon of terrorism.[16] Historically, the political radicalness and paradoxes of nationalist groups such as ETA and the IRA need to be situated in the larger labyrinthine conundrums of the nation-state. In the context of this chapter, are substate nationalities confronted with a "maddening" situation? This is Aretxaga's position when she observes that recourse to self-defeating violence by groups such as ETA "might be an expression of something intrinsically mad, or maddening, in the nation-state form itself. I would argue that something is profoundly at odds in the hegemonic form of the modern polity that engenders a constant tension between the logic of nationhood as a utopian, fraternal community sustained by imaginary acts of identification, and the practice of statehood as a force of law sustained by multiple relations of power."[17] Recourse to the "madness" of terrorism is one way of expressing the inability to overcome the conflicting demands of a stateless national identity experienced as intrinsically incomplete and with no apparent solution in the future.

The state form can be described from a multiplicity of perspectives and disciplines. If, on the one hand, the neoliberal logic of globalization has clearly eroded the traditional functions of the Weberian state, on the other hand more and more states are being created and, stimulated in part by globalization, the desire for statehood continues to be as intense as ever. But it is the rethinking of the state as a field of contradictory practices that confronts us directly, not only regarding the state's services, culture, economy, security, and so on, but also with the question of what can be labeled as "the subjectivity of the state"[18] emanating from the identifications and unconscious desires of state officials and citizens, as well as from public performances, representations, discourses, narratives, and fantasies that anchor the idea of the state. In this regard, the state is a reified idea, a collective illusion, a network of power relations masked as a single public interest, and not necessarily a unified political subject. Such "magic of the state"[19] is grounded ultimately in "the power of a fiction" that mystifies the unequal power relations among the various classes and national groups. For anthropologists in particular, this fictional character of the statist ideology works as a powerful *fetish*. When the fantasy of the state is oversaturated "with the force of law without signification," it acquires "the capacity to drive people mad."[20]

The weakening of the European state and the loss of competitiveness of European firms vis-à-vis those of the United States and Japan gave impetus to the project of Europeanization. It is important to note, however, that the goal, rather than a supranational federal entity, was the reconstruction of state power at a European level.[21]

The contradictions regarding the state's loss and recuperation of sovereign power directly affect the political aspirations of substate peripheral nationalisms in various European countries.[22] The constitutional compromise had to reconcile those in favor of a federal state and those in favor of a centralized one. This resulted in constitutional ambiguities, the consequences of which are again at the center of the current political debate in Spain. They concern the demands of several Spanish autonomies, notably the Basques and the Catalans, for reconfiguring their statutes. Article 2 is at the core of these ambiguities: "The Constitution is based on the indissoluble unity of the Spanish Nation, the common and indivisible

country of all Spaniards; it recognizes and guarantees the right to autonomy of the nationalities and regions of which it is composed, and solidarity amongst them all." It is thus a legally unitary but politically composite
state; it affirms the "unity of the Spanish Nation," yet it affirms the existence of other "nationalities" by way of recognizing, in the Catalan and
Basque cases, the existence of their "Historic Rights." In short, the propo-
nents of the unitary state, as well as those of a plurinational federal one,
can draw their antagonistic arguments from the same text.[23]

But who is sovereign here? "National sovereignty is vested in the Spanish people, from whom emanate the powers of the state," says Article 1.2.
The unity of the state expresses the unity of the sovereignty that is rooted
solely in the Spanish people. A different approach by the Catalans and the
Basques during the constitutional debates fostered the view that Spanish
sovereignty resulted from a voluntary transfer of the original sovereign
authorities by the different peoples of Spain to a central government, but
without giving it up definitively and irrevocably. They also called for the
notion of "shared sovereignty." This federal approach to sovereignty was
defeated. There is thus a dual scenario in which the issue of sovereignty is
being played out in European states such as Spain. On the one hand, it is
with the substate regions that states have to affirm and share their sovereign power; on the other, substantial functions of sovereignty have to be
delegated by the states to the supra-state European Union. Threatened at
both the infra- and supra-state levels, the European states have reacted by
entrenching themselves with a notion of sovereignty that makes the European Union dysfunctional.[24] The central government is caught in a bind:
confronted with demands for greater autonomy, its negative response fos-
ters increased secessionist attitudes. The entrenched state, a shadow of its
former self in a globalized world, yet invested with the magical force of
sovereignty, clings to the belief that it still dictates the course of history.
This maddening paradox affects the historical nationalities that reside
within the state in Spain and elsewhere.[25]

The irony for actual nation-sates or for nationalisms that dream of having one is that a globalized world has become, in Michael Keating's word,
"post-sovereign." The final paradox of sovereignty in these postsovereign
times is that, in order to have it at all, you must surrender it, at least in
part, to the interdependencies of new economic and political structures.

In short, various interpretations of the Spanish Constitution may lead
toward the view of a unitary authority, or else that of federal systems of
authority that are neither fully sovereign nor superior to one another. This

guarantees that the central Spanish state and the peripheral nationalities will remain in an endless state of warfare. The current challenge posed by the historical nationalities is the replacement of its centralist view with a federal one. The linking of intrinsic sovereignty to the state is in itself problematic. The final result is a labyrinthine and maddening situation with no political solution in sight. This is the perfect soil for terrorism.

Nuclear Deterrence and Its Terrorist Displacements

It is no accident that nuclear power and terrorism emerged simultaneously during the second part of the twentieth century as the two types of warfare that made conventional wars practically obsolete. What we fear most about the terrorists, their ultimate sin, is their evil intentionality, their desire—if only they had a nuclear or biological weapon, if only they could wipe out one of our cities. The unbearable threat is that they could one day have what we now have. What defines the counterterrorist position is that their desire is far more dangerous than our actual possession of the dreadful Thing. Our wisdom consists in anticipating the evil possibility of what they *might do*, never in stating the reality of what we already *did*.

What is the role of the ominous prophecy *not if, but when* in such a context? It replicates the fatalistic thinking of the nonfeedback or "purposeless" nature of the terrorist's suicidal action. A parallel process has been described by Derrida as the law of "auto-immunitary process," namely, "that strange behavior where a living being, in quasi-*suicidal* fashion, 'itself' works to destroy its own protection, to immunize itself *against* its own immunity"[26]—a modern disorder that in his view threatens the life of participatory democracy and the legal system. Such "protecting itself against its self-protection by destroying its own immune system"[27] is what the suicide terrorist and the armaments race deploy as their ultimate lethality. If what is most "unacceptable" about jihadist terrorism is that "such actions and such discourse *open into no future and, in my view, have no future*,"[28] the traumatic *future* of counterterrorism (the "waiting for terror") and the nuclear armaments race replicates unconscionably the very perverted terrorist temporality. Suddenly it is as if there is nothing to be done about nuclear stockplies or nonproliferation; as if there is no time for change in the coordinates of the status quo; as if all the political madness of nuclearism is concentrated on the tabooed desire of the Terrorist. It is by forgetting the historical facts that led to the armaments race and the perversion of temporality they entail that counterterrorism's "not if, but when" adopts all the ominous traits of a self-fulfilling prophecy.

Albert Einstein, the man who symbolizes Western science and rationality, regretted that he had signed the letter urging President Roosevelt to build an atomic bomb—he called it the one mistake of his life. The letter had been premised on the assumption that the Nazis might be working on a similar bomb (they were, although the project was abandoned in 1942). The scientists had justified their good intentions by projecting onto the evil enemy the very Thing they themselves were about to create. When the truth was made clear at Hiroshima and Nagasaki, after Germany had already surrendered, it was harder to still maintain the fiction of our goodness versus their evil. The scientists thought that a test somewhere in the desert could demonstrate to the world our capability. But the politicians knew better: what matters, what projects frightening power, is not merely the technical capacity, but the *will* for mass murder. Terrorists don't have the capacity for a nuclear attack, but they have the will, or at least so we believe. Dr. Strangelove understands this perfectly: the terrorists have the main component.

Horrified by their invention—"Little Boy" they called it, as if to show how much it was their child and a labor of love—Einstein, Leo Szilard, Robert Oppenheimer, and the other scientists tried to come to terms with the moral implications of their Faustian gamble. But the military and the politicians knew better than to have moral qualms. Even though they had already vanquished Japan, they had given a lesson to Stalin. President Truman, in possession of his bomb, was soon all for disarmament and by June 1946 his representative, Bernard Baruch, was arguing passionately for it at the United Nations. The U.S. plan called for the establishment of an international authority to control the spread of nuclear weapons that would ensure that no other nation could build the bomb; the United States would guarantee the destruction of its nuclear weapons *afterwards*. Stalin asked that Washington should disarm *prior* to other states signing onto the plan. But Truman would not compromise. Prominent Americans thought at the time that the United States should keep a nuclear monopoly; the secretary of state used the bomb as a trump card in his meeting with the Soviets. When the Soviets exploded their bomb, Truman went for the hydrogen bomb, which even many of those responsible for the initial bomb opposed because they thought it was a weapon of genocide. The Soviets quickly replicated and the arms race was on.

"[I]nsane, inmoral, militarily unncecessary and destructive of the non-proliferation regime," that is how Robert McNamara, who knows something about nuclear weaponry and its potential for apocalypse, recently judged the U.S. and NATO's continued possession of large nuclear arsenals. The nuclear powers possess twenty-seven thousand atomic bombs, almost all of them by the United States and Russia, each one capable of destroying a city. Eight or nine states actually have the bomb, but forty could build it. A recent book by Joseph Cirincione,[29] who was director of nonproliferation at the Carnegie Endowment for International Peace, as well as serving on the staff of the House Armed Services Committee, warns that there is a real possibility that the nuclear nonproliferation regime that was established in 1968 might collapse. The reason is that the nuclear powers themselves refuse to abide by Article 6 of the Nuclear Non-Proliferation Treaty, which calls for complete nuclear disarmement under international control; hence, "It is difficult to convince other states to give up their nuclear weapons ambitions or adhere to nonproliferation norms when immensely powerful nuclear weapons states reassert the importance of [these] weapons to their own security."[30]

Nothing is more tragically telling of the madness of scientific military rationality than the history of nuclearism and its current status quo. After the United States and the Soviets, Great Britain and France developed their atomic weapons—the great civilized powers had to fend off the barbarian threat. Unwilling to endure the menace of its former Soviet ally, China tested its own bomb by 1964. Subsequently, no responsible Indian leader could rule out its possession and the country had its "peaceful nuclear explosive" by 1974. And if India, then Pakistan also must have the bomb, even if, as Prime Minister Ali Bhutto put it, they had to eat grass to stave off hunger. The rationale is clear: if your enemy develops a weapon, can a responsible leader not reply in kind? The *rational* policy, of course, is that you must defend your country by whatever means are necessary.

The Nuclear Non-Proliferation Treaty was signed and reaffirmed indefinitely in 1995 by 188 countries. Only India, Pakistan, and Israel declined to sign; North Korea later withdrew. Under the treaty, only the first five states—United States, Russia, Great Britain, France, and China—are allowed to own the weapons but may not transfer them. The other states must agree not to develop nuclear weapons. There is an additional clause, however: the five nuclear powers must dismantle their arsenals under a *future* agreement. But the nuclear powers, the United States in particular, refuse such a general agreement and continue to pursue new advances in nuclear technology. Here is where the nuclear powers, the bastions of science and civilization, espouse "madness" as a show of their military and political superiority.

The self-righteousness of these powers evokes the temptation of in-nocence *a la Abraham*—sacrifice what you most love, the life of your son and all future generations, to the *credo quia absurdum* in the big Other of your national security. This, as if the recent history of the twentieth century—Stalin, Hitler, the Holocaust, Hiroshima, the Cuban missile crisis—had taught us nothing. Jason Epstein, evoking Freud's universal death drive, comments: "Our common sense has failed us once again. Rather than dread these suicidal weapons, nations embrace them as symbols of strength, imagining future conflicts in which their enemies but not themselves are vaporized, a flight from reality that would be shocking were it not so deeply embedded in human behavior."[31] The "maddening states" become truly so when, to their premise of absolute sovereignty, is added the capacity for nuclear weapons. The combined logics of national sovereignty and national security make it imperative that, vis-à-vis a neighboring nuclear enemy (following Carl Schmitt's classical definition that politics is a matter of friends and enemies), arming yourself with nuclear destructiveness is the reasonable decision. Why should you not defend yourself with the Thing itself when others have It with the intent of threatening you and potentially using it against you? Thus, no other alternative is left: either the folly of pacifism or the madness of nuclearism.

But, if anything, madness is blind to itself. Hence we watch the obscene spectacle of these very same nuclear powers preaching disarmament to other nations while they obstinately and illegitimately hold on to their stockpiles. Should the other nations acquiesce to such colonialist hypocricy and agree to the militarily imposed unequal status between friends and foes of the West? The premise under which President Bush followed the neoconservative agenda of removing not only nuclear and biological weapons from rogue nations but the regimes themselves was that "the US could determine which countries [should] have nuclear weapons and which [should] not. American power, not multilateral treaties, would enforce this judgment."[32] For a country such as Iran, with its nuclear sites under threat of being bombed, the alternative appears to be either act as Iraq did under Saddam Hussein (namely, abandon its nuclear weapons in the context of a substantial military defeat) or act like North Korea (whose leader is reviled in the West as a "madman," but whose development of nuclear weapons in defiance of the West did not result in the fate of a nonnuclear Iraq). This is one more aspect of the self-fulfilling prophecy.

Still, what really worries the nuclear powers is not primarily the dishonest reneging on their own nonproliferation commitments, with the likelihood that it will lead to the unraveling of the nonproliferation regime, let alone the sheer madness of their suicidal arsenals. Neither is it the delusion that other nations should accept an unequal status imposed categorically by a nuclear hegemony, according to which certain nations have the right to possess weapons of mass destruction while it is taboo for others to even desire them. No, the real threat is of course the Terrorist. It is the possibility that one day the Terrorist bogeyman may possess one of those tens of thousands of nuclear warheads that the West *responsibly* possesses. There is enough material today, shared by some fifty nations, to build three hundred thousand nuclear bombs. To this the nuclear powers react with a strategy: first, to pursue further nuclear weapons technology in an unconcealed attempt to gain advantage over nuclear competitors; second, to bind the nonnuclear nations to disarmament with promises they themselves are unwilling to fulfill; and third, to raise the specter of the Terrorist in relentless pursuit of nuclear weapons as the real danger about which we should all be concerned.

The general public by and large realizes the folly of nuclear armaments and is overwhelmingly against possessing them; 66 percent of Americans believe they should not be allowed and only 13 percent think that the United States and its allies should hold a monopoly on them. Yet the latter is the basic policy of the United States. As an example, prior to the Islamic Republic, when the ruler was the shah, Iran was encouraged by the United States to pursue nuclear power and was even provided with its first reactor in the late 1960s, but the continuation of these plans by the subsequent Islamic regime was and is anathema. The function of the Terrorist is to create the overwhelming perception that "we are being attacked" before engaging ourselves in full-fledged war. The 9/11 attacks provided evidence that such perceptions were for real. But this is reality long anticipated and feared in a Beckettian waiting for terror and couched in the tabooed discourse of the terrorist madman. It is the assertive presence of the suicide terrorist's madness, turned into the nemesis of the Western hegemonic madness, that became so terrifying in 9/11.

With nuclear weapons off the table as a usable arsenal, and conventional warfare antiquated, low-intensity warfare and terrorism became more relevant than ever during the second half of the twentieth century.

The war in Iraq is the primary ground for testing the complicity between nuclearism and terrorism. This war is not only the frontline of the War on Terror, it is also the test of a *radically new approach to nuclear non-proliferation* that consists not in eliminating arsenals but in eliminating evil regimes. That is when and where the systemic relationship between weapons of mass destruction and the figure of the Terrorist emerged in full force after 9/11. Proliferation was now part of the global struggle in the War on Terror, which was concentrated on a few evil states and their real or potential links to terrorist groups such as al Qaeda. Suddenly, in a radical reversal of decades-long policy whereby nonproliferation was an end in itself, "the most significant and direct application of the new approach to nonproliferation was the war with Iraq."[33] And Iraq is, we have been reminded every day, the main theater of the war against terrorism. In short, the figure of the Terrorist is critical to justifying the subversion of the nonproliferation regime.

In conclusion, fear of the Terrorist serves as a *displacement* for the nuclear threat and the double standard of the exisiting system. A 2005 report by the Carnegie Endowment for International Peace advocating a comprehensive approach was entitled *Universal Compliance*. Universality is indeed the principle of the law of justice; such a global and holistic perspective should be an undisputed and necessary condition regarding issues of survival such as nonproliferation. The current two-tier system, which allows certain countries to have nuclear weapons but not others, is not equitable. The terrorist threat serves as displacement for this lack of universal justice in the very powers who boast of being bastions of civilization and democracy.

In the end, terrorist desire is so alarming because of the potential for terrorist madness. But the unthinkable for the West is that the madness of such terrorist desire reflects the logic of what Hannah Arendt described as "the weird suicidal development of modern weapons."[34] The unbearable thought is that terrorist madness is in a nutshell the *nemesis* of Western nuclearized madness—the Greek goddess who demanded retribution for human hubris. Dr. Strangelove, please meet the Terrorist.

CHAPTER EIGHT

9/11 and the Iraq War as Self-Fulfilling Prophecies

Terrorism news in 1995 was dominated by the trial of the blind Sheikh Omar Abdel Rahman after the first attack on the World Trade Center. He was charged under the seditious conspiracy statute for providing the green light for the 1993 attack. The main witness against Sheikh Rahman was a shadowy police informer named Emad Salem, who was rewarded by the government with $1.5 million for his testimony. The *New York Times* reported that Salem "began his testimony by admitting that he had lied to just about everybody he ever met," that he was "always ready with another believe-it-or-not exploit," and that his testimony sounded "like sheer fantasy."[1] An editorial by the same newspaper gave a sense of the type of evidence used to indict the blind sheikh: "[it] only required [the government] to prove *the intention* to wage a terror campaign." And it concluded that "only the sketchiest connections [were] established between Sheik Omar Abdul-Rahman and the alleged mastermind of that crime, Ramzi Ahmed Yousef."[2] But the U.S. public was understandably relieved. His friend Osama bin Laden had not yet emerged as the leading anti-American jihadist. The "evidence" had proven that the Islamic plotters had been finally caught red-handed. They had been taught their lesson—end of the story. Or so thought counterterrorism.

For a detective-like enquirer or a writer of Capote's skills things could not have appeared more ominous as the sheikh was imprisoned for life. If the trial was a sham for the *New York Times*, just think how the travesty must have appeared to the Muslims who revered their spiritual leader. In particular, one imagines the enormity of the injustice in the eyes of someone who had been intimately close to the sheikh, someone who had paid his living expenses while he was in the United States—Osama bin Laden.[3] Bin Laden had been known as a fund-raiser for the Afghan war against the Soviet occupation. Like Sheikh Omar Abdel Rahman, he had worked side by side with the CIA in President Reagan's crusade against the Soviets. Now his friend and spiritual leader was in jail for life, humiliated as the scum of the earth, after enduring a mock trial in the alleged land of freedom and human rights. Soon, by January 1996, President Clinton would sign off on a CIA finding establishing that bin Laden was a threat to national security. "The group was small—only ninety-three members at the time—but . . . [t]he possibilities of contagion were great."[4] A new terrorist enemy had been created.

Once again, the former close ally was going to transmogrify into the archterrorist nemesis. As a result of the trial of the blind sheik, William Douglass and I were forced to add to our 1996 book *Terror and Taboo* an "Epilogue as Prologue: The Apotheosis of Terrorism Foretold." The old cast of terrorist characters appeared by then moribund, we stated, and then added:

> Yet there is suddenly a new promised land for terrorism—the United States. Its major networks now dispatch their reporters to London to determine how civilized Europe adjusted to mindless terrorism. They send back the sobering warning that Americans better get used to it. . . .
>
> We were once astonished that the politicians and the media could confidently include under the same 'terrorist' rubric such disparate characters as Sheik Omar, Mr. McVeigh, the Unabomber, and the Chechen Dudayev. From now on our real surprise will be if the counterterrorism crusade does not increasingly regale the American public with a new 'war' game and all sorts of 'successes' against terrorism. We assume that the reality-making power of terrorism discourse is by now almost unstoppable. All that is necessary to produce the loathsome thing is some CIA-trained 'rebels' turned against their mentors (as with Sheik Omar and his followers) or a military 'error' (as in the shooting down of the Iranian passenger flight that preceded Pan Am 103) or a disgruntled, Rambo-esque army veteran (such as Timothy McVeigh) or some uncontrolled arm smuggler in the thriving post–Cold War arms bazaar (as in plutoniumgate). This emerging terrorism 'reality' appears to be already a blooming, self-fulfilling prophecy in the United States.[5]

The Iraq War would become the final apotheosis of terrorism, as Dipak Gupta comments: "[T]he focus of the US and its allies became distracted by the war in Iraq. Once again, as has happened many times in history, an unwise policy in the pursuit of the so-called 'global war on terror' . . . provided a fertile ground for future terrorism."[6] The danger of being beholden to terrorism as a reality-making discourse is not only the perversion of culture implied by the fatalistic waiting for terror. It is also that such mythology becomes a major hindrance to the prime security requirement of preventing acts of terrorism such as 9/11. To the question of how the U.S. counterterrorism agencies failed so dismally to uncover the 9/11 plot we must add the analytical question: To what extent is the counterterrorist episteme complicit in *not* preventing acts of terror and thus in unwittingly promoting them? Why couldn't it figure out that Hussein was *bluffing*?

Ghost Wars in a Haunted Afghanistan

Inspired by the Iranian Revolution led by Ayatollah Khomeini, in the spring of 1979 a mutiny erupted in Herat, Afghanistan; the recently installed Marxist government in Kabul, led by Nur Mohammed Taraki, was pressing for secular reforms such as making the education of girls compulsory. If the KGB, led by Yuri Andropov, had seen in the Iranian chaos of 1979 an opportunity to undermine the United States, the CIA was about to find in the Afghan revolt a way to retaliate. Zbigniew Brzezinski, Carter's national security adviser, recommended to the president that he endorse covert CIA action in support of the Afghan rebellion. Carter authorized support for the rebels, although not weapons. Andropov and the Politburo's inner circle became convinced that the CIA was plotting in Kabul and came to the fateful conclusion that only drastic measures such as invading Afghanistan could succeed in saving the regime. "Brzezinski and his colleagues knew nothing about the KGB's fears of CIA plotting. They interpreted the invasion as a desperate act of support for the Afghan communists and as a possible thrust toward the Persian Gulf."[7] Convinced that the Soviets had encountered their Vietnam, Brzezinski sketched a new policy of helping the Afghan resistance and forging a close alliance with Pakistan. The CIA and the Pakistani secret service, the Inter-Services Intelligence, or ISI, were soon the closest of allies.

The Saudis had their own secret service, the General Intelligence Department, or GID, headed by Prince Turki al-Faisal. His chief of staff,

Ahmed Badeeb, had studied at an American college and had been a teacher. One of his students and later close friend was Osama bin Laden. In July 1980 Turki reached an agreement with the CIA that the Saudis would match U.S. funding to the Afghan insurgents. "In spy lexicon, each of the major intelligence agencies working the Afghan jihad—GID, ISI, and CIA—began to 'compartment' their work, even as all three collaborated with one another through formal liaisons. Working together they purchased and shipped to the Afghan rebels tens of thousands of tons of weapons and ammunition."[8] Since bin Laden operated within the Saudi compartment, he did not have direct contact with the CIA. Badeeb recognized that the relationship between bin Laden and GID was active and operational, and he worked as a semiofficial liaison between GID and the leading Afghan Islamist commanders. Bin Laden met regularly with Prince Turki and the Saudi minister of the interior, Prince Naif, "who liked and appreciated him." Turki described bin Laden as "very shy, soft spoken." As for Badeeb, "I loved Osama," he admitted. "We were happy with him. He was our man. He was doing all what we ask him."[9]

Covert action was proving cost effective. CIA director Bill Casey briefed President Reagan that by January 1984 seventeen thousand Soviet soldiers had been killed or wounded in Afghanistan; the Soviets had lost about four hundred aircraft, 2,750 tanks and armored personnel carriers, and eight thousand trucks and other vehicles—all at a cost of only $200 million to U.S. taxpayers, a figure matched by the Saudi GID. "Casey was among the most ardent of the jihad's true believers."[10] Having become its "champion," he more than doubled its spending from 1981 to the end of 1984. But soon he was involved in something else: taking the jihad into the Soviet Union itself. Having discovered the anti-Soviet potential of Islam, the CIA began to print Qurans in the languages of the Soviet Union's Islamic minorities and hand them out for free to rebels who were secretly crossing into Soviet territory. The ISI was in charge of organizing small teams to mount violent attacks inside the Soviet Union, but it was Casey who first urged such cross-border incursions: "We should take the books [Qurans] and try to raise the local population against them, and you can also think of sending arms and ammunition if possible."[11] Books and swords for jihad, Casey urged. These propaganda and sabotage operations were against U.S. law, but Casey, a devout Catholic whose mansion was filled with statues of the Virgin Mary, was fighting against a power that Reagan had declared to be "the evil empire." The alliance he had forged for conducting the "Afghan jihad" between Saudi intelligence, the Pakistani army and secret service, and the CIA was "not merely statecraft" but "an important front in a worldwide struggle between communist atheism and God's community of believers."[12] Casey's deputy, Robert Gates, confirmed that the cross-border attacks took place with Casey's encouragement because ultimately "Bill Casey came to the CIA primarily to wage war against the Soviet Union."[13] In Casey's "giant vision" of a global anti-Soviet struggle, "Afghanistan was a little part of it."[14] Casey and Reagan were obviously on the same page, even if Reagan confessed to William F. Buckley that he could not understand what the mumbling Casey was saying in the meetings. In short, the Islamist mujahideen and the Reagan/Casey CIA were soul mates engaged in the same jihad against the same evil empire, using the same violent methods and sharing the same fundamentalist ideology. As a crusader, Casey wept tears of joy when he visited Afghanistan and saw the freedom fighters using antiaircraft guns against Soviet aircraft. Counterterrorism was once again *promoting* the very thing that would soon come back to haunt the United States as its terrorist archenemy.

Issues of what constituted "terrorism" and what constituted "assassination" periodically emerged. "Every time a mujahedin rebel kills a Soviet rifleman, are we engaged in assassination?" Casey asked, and replied: "This is a rough business. If we're afraid to hit the terrorists because somebody's going to yell 'assassination,' it'll never stop. The terrorists will own the world."[15] In short, the bottom line was that terrorism discourse allows for any enemy soldier to be cast potentially as a terrorist and thus deserving of elimination. This mentality dovetailed perfectly with the jihad mentality of the radical Sayyid Qutb, who justified violence against nonbelievers, and who became the intellectual father of the Muslim Brotherhood. Zawahiri was a student of Qutb, who was a great influence on bin Laden. The use of the word "assassination" by the mujahideen was strictly prohibited, though, particularly during visits by members of the U.S. Congress. President Ford had banned assassinations after the exposure of CIA plots during the 1960s, but now it was time to revisit the issue since preventive killings when faced with the prospect of a terrorist attack should not be considered assassinations. What about targeting a Soviet commander with a sniper rifle, a killing that is described as "shooting ducks in a barrel"? What makes the Soviet soldier a "terrorist" and the sniper a "freedom fighter"? Certain killings ("nonbelievers" for fundamentalist Islamists, "terrorists" for counterterrorists) are not assassinations because, conceptually and morally, those being killed belong to a sort of subhuman species. In this categorical definition of what constituted legitimate killing, the CIA and the jihad were on the same page.

There was one significant battleground development in the Afghan war: the supply of Stinger portable antiaircraft missiles by the CIA. After 1986 Afghan rebels downed scores of Soviet helicopters and planes with these missiles. The only problem was that the Stingers might fall into the hands of terrorists who might use them against U.S. civilian or military aircraft. Indeed, hundreds of the two thousand to twenty-five hundred Stinger missiles given to the Afghan rebels would fall into the hands of anti-American radical Islamists. Characteristically, counterterrorism was helping promote the terrorist agenda.

The Soviets had given the United States a good cause for a fight and for once the Americans were helping the freedom fighters. When Soviet foreign minister Eduard Shevardnadze called U.S. secretary of state George Shultz to inform him that the Soviets were going to leave Afghanistan, "Shultz was so struck by the significance of the news that it half-panicked him. He feared that if he told the right-wingers in Reagan's Cabinet what Shevardnadze had said, and endorsed the disclosure as sincere, he would be accused of going soft on Moscow. He kept the conversation to himself for weeks."[16] In the global struggle between the superpowers, Afghanistan had been a godsend to the United States. But now the Soviets had decided to leave it and began to warn the Americans about the dangers of Islamic radicalism; it was the last thing Americans wanted to hear. Mikhail Gorbachev pleaded with President Reagan and Vice President Bush to cut off aid to the Afghan rebels in exchange for withdrawal, but he was told that was impossible.

The State Department and the CIA disagreed on how to wage the Afghan war. After the withdrawal of the Soviets, the purpose of covert action was to obtain "self-determination" for the Afghan people; this required, in the eyes of the special envoy, Ed McWilliams, that the CIA cut its ties to Pakistani intelligence. He thought that it was the Islamist agenda, ISI included, that was the greatest danger, not communism. The CIA favored ties with the Pakistani intelligence agency. CIA officers embarked on establishing clandestine communications for the rebels, as well as building bunkers and caves for storing munitions in Tora Bora, the area where the rebel commanders were for the most part loyal to the ruthless Gulbuddin Hekmatyar, a friend of Osama bin Laden and a favorite of the CIA. Bin Laden's training camp was thirty miles to the south of Tora Bora; "he had a military following, but it was not remotely as hardened or violent in 1989 as Hekmatyar."[17] McWilliams was followed by ambassador Peter Tomsen who, in early 1990, devised a two-track policy of allowing the continuation of the CIA-led military track, while sidelining "extremists" such as Hekmatyar, and opening talks on an Afghan political settlement at the United Nations with the Soviets, Pakistani president Benazir Bhutto, and with the exiled Afghan king, Zahir Shah. But Tomsen was outflanked by the CIA and told not to go to Rome to talk to the exiled king because that would be the end of the Islamist mujahideens' fight. If Tomsen's goal had been to isolate the Islamists, the CIA needed them for its war even after the Soviets had withdrawn. "By appealing to Zahir Shah as a symbolic ruler, the State Department hoped to create space in Afghanistan for federal, traditional politics. . . . The alternative—the international Islamism of the Muslim Brotherhood, enforced by Pakistani military power—promised only continuing war and instability, Tomsen and his allies at State believed.

CIA analysts, on the other hand, tended to view Afghanistan pessimistically. They believed that peace was beyond reach anytime soon."[18] The only thing that mattered to the CIA and Pakistani intelligence was the fall of Kabul's Najibullah communist government. The CIA backed Hekmatyar, and so did the ISI, which had a plan to install him as the new ruler in Kabul. But there was a third key component supporting the anti-American and extremist Hekmatyar: "The CIA's informants reported that a wealthy fundamentalist Saudi sheikh, Osama bin Laden, was providing millions of dollars to support ISI's new plan for Hekmatyar. The Islamabad station transmitted these reports about bin Laden to Langley."[19] In short, the CIA, ISI, and bin Laden were the backbone of the Islamist movement in Afghanistan in the early 1990s. To give an idea of who Hekmatyar was, in October 1990 there was a report that he planned to crush Kabul with forty thousand long-range rockets that had been brought across the border from Pakistan; their use could have caused an estimated two to three hundred thousand civilian casualties. Only after the intervention of ambassador Robert Oakley, opposing the plan in the strongest terms, did Pakistani intelligence decide to call off the assault. The head of the Islamabad CIA station knew and approved of the operation, according to people at the State Department; in fact, "in the two previous years [to the fall of Kabul] the agency had facilitated massive arms transfers to Hekmatyar and some to Massoud."[20] The legendary Ahmed Shah Massoud, a tolerant Afghan nationalist and the most charismatic and internationally respected rebel leader, did not enjoy the level of CIA support his rival Hekmatyar did;

Massoud was not only a military genius but he had also been willing to cut a deal with the Soviets in 1983, an act of betrayal the CIA would never forget.

The final cutoff of support by the Soviets and the Americans would not come until January 1, 1992—twelve years after the Soviets committed military forces to Afghanistan, and twelve years and two months after Brzezinski presented President Carter with a plan for covert CIA anti-communist action. The superpowers had waged their war in a pawn country, and it was now time to retire. By then Afghanistan was enmeshed in an unending war. There was no American policy on Afghanistan; after the war Afghanistan would be a mess and this was something for the Pakistanis to handle. Indifference is the best term to describe the American attitude toward Afghanistan. There was only one concern: how to buy back the Stingers provided to the rebels that had now turned into feared weapons in the hands of anti-American jihadists; President George H. W. Bush and President Bill Clinton authorized a secret program to that end. By the mid-1990s the cash spent in retrieving the Stingers was the equivalent of the cash given to Afghanistan for humanitarian assistance during those years. It was counterterrorism biting its own tail. Otherwise, there was utter indifference to the country's political or economic fate. During the first Bush presidency, according to CIA officers who met with him, the president seemed barely aware that there was a war going on: "Is that thing still going on?" he asked when Milt Bearden, the former CIA chief in Islamabad, mentioned the Afghan war in passing.

If only history could be forgotten like that. If only Americans, championing a jihad with people such as Hekmatyar, had listened to the secular-minded exiled Afghans who warned them that "for God's sake, you're financing your own assassins."[21] Massoud, among others, saw all along that "American policy was profoundly misguided, and [by the late 1990s] he could not understand why it was so slow to change."[22] Even Pervez Musharraf, the Pakistani military strongman and U.S. ally, warned the Americans of their ignorance of the Taliban, saying that "they had adopted a certain approach towards the Taliban without really understanding what the Taliban was all about" and that the United States "had ended up with a self-fulfilling prophecy."[23] In September 1990, Gary Schroen, the CIA station chief in Islamabad, met face to face with Massoud. Schroen told him that "the United States is becoming more and more interested in Afghanistan."[24] How so? The Afghans had been abandoned by the United States in their brutal war; but now they needed military and political support against the Taliban, who were helped by bin Laden, and the only thing that concerned Schroen was the Stingers. And there was something else: "One concern in particular was now rising: terrorism."[25] A self-fulfilling prophecy, indeed.

Terrorists and Counterterrorists Plotting Together: Please, Give Us a Fatwa

Let us return to the events surrounding the blind Sheikh Omar Abdel Rahman in the early 1990s. While living in New Jersey, he had been arrested in the company of the 1993 World Trade Center plotters. The plotters had all been under close police surveillance since 1989, when they were photographed by the FBI on four successive weekends on Long Island while taking target practice. The blind sheikh was arrested as their spiritual leader and mastermind of the entire conspiracy. This was about to become another instance of yesterday's friend turned into today's terrorist archenemy. The sheikh had been a recruiter and spiritual guide for the Islamic anti-Soviet guerrillas in Afghanistan. After the Soviets left Afghanistan, he participated with the CIA in the campaign to set up several jihad offices across the United States to recruit for the guerrillas trying to overthrow the pro-Soviet Najibullah regime that the Soviets left behind. The most important was called Al Khifa (Arabic for "the struggle") and was established in Brooklyn where the sheikh had settled after repeatedly traveling to the United States with visas provided by the CIA.[26] After examining the evidence, Robert Friedman concluded that the CIA's involvement with the first attack on the World Trade Center was "far greater" than was known to the general public and that "the CIA has inadvertently managed to do something that America's enemies have been unable to: give terrorism a foothold in the United States."[27]

John Miller and Michael Stone document the extent to which counterterrorists and future terrorists worked hand in hand at times in the events that led up to the 1993 attack on the World Trade Center.[28] A key figure was the shadowy informer Salem, who would later become the main witness in the bomb conspiracy trial against the sheikh. According to Miller and Stone, once he infiltrated Abdel Rahman's group, "Salem was offering to restart the paramilitary training that had lapsed in the year since Nosair's [Alkifah's former leader] arrest."[29] True to his calling, Salem was soon securing for his fellow plotters "a warehouse in which to build bombs."[30] In other words, nothing was going on in Abdel Rahman's circle and the FBI actually planted someone in order to activate illegal paramilitary activities, including renting a warehouse for them to start making bombs. Another undercover agent named "Wilson" had been given on "loan" (and later retracted) to train Abdel Rahman's close circle. Not surprisingly, there was concern within the FBI that "the Bureau was training potential terrorists, holy warriors who may not be breaking the law now, but who might one day turn the skills they were acquiring against the U.S."[31] They were aware of "the heat the Bureau would take if it turned out it had assisted a future terrorist," but still "the subjects were going to get training whether or not the FBI provided it" and "if you weren't willing to get close to the action, to get your hands dirty now and then, how would you ever know what he's [the blind sheikh] plotting to do?"[32] In other words, since they were going to be terrorists anyway, let us be complicit and push them into action and find out how far they are willing to go. This is how the 1993 plot began. This is no longer a self-fulfilling *prophecy*, it is rather self-fulfilling *action*, for we are dealing with a plot hatched by counterterrorism itself by playing with the *desire* of potential terrorists and seducing them into a course of monitored action in order to catch them.

Later, in April 1993, two months after the first World Trade Center explosion (and before Abdel Rahman and others had been arrested), Salem warned the FBI that Abdel Rahman's circle was planning a simultaneous bombing of the Lincoln and Holland tunnels, the United Nations, and the New York offices of the FBI. Once again, since the plotters allegedly needed a safe house in which to build the bombs, "*Salem offered to find one*," and then the co-conspirators "accepted the offer."[33] So who took the initiative? Was it the counterterrorist informant who "offered" to find a place to build bombs or the terrorists who "accepted?" The counterterrorist is *playing terrorist* in order to catch the *real terrorists*. But in the *deep play* that is the terrorist *passage à l'acte* both senses of "play" (by the terrorist and the counterterrorist) get inextricably linked.

There was something else that Salem's handlers wanted from him: Abdel Rahman's blessing on tape for the plotters' murderous intentions—that is, a fatwa. Despite Salem's insistent questioning, the sheikh was unresponsive or kept putting him off with the argument that such acts of violence would work against the Muslims. In short, counterterrorists were paying an informer to entrap the blind sheikh, who in the past had been a major U.S. ally and had come to this country with visas repeatedly issued by the CIA, into issuing a fatwa condoning terrorism so that he could be arrested and put in jail for life. Once you accept counterterrorism's basic tenets, this is *normal* behavior, and so it seemed to the American justice system, the Clinton administration, and the media.

But counterterrorism had triumphed not only with the arrest of the blind sheikh. Soon an FBI SWAT team would foil "the second terrorist plot" in the safe house set up by Salem, their own informant, to great media fanfare. The public was relieved by the impression of efficiency given by the security agencies. Counterterrorists could be proud of what they had achieved: they had sent to life in prison the plot's alleged mastermind *and* had averted another round of terrorist plots.

Although less known to the public, counterterrorism was also aware of something else: the wretched plotters were dupes who could be easily manipulated. The potential terrorists were after all people the counterterrorists knew intimately, who had been their associates in the past, who had been under their surveillance, who could be infiltrated by informers willing to testify about anything they wanted in exchange for money. Then there were bizarre events such as the case of Mohammed Salameh who, after the 1993 attacks against the Twin Towers, repeatedly went back to the rental agency to reclaim the $400 deposit for the van that carried the explosives. How stupid could they be? In short, counterterrorists could reasonably assume that they were in control of an enemy they had in part created and who in the process had provided themselves a heroic status and the funding to be the guardians of a free society. Thus, as the impending events involving bin Laden would soon show, there was another side to the mythology of the terrorist monster acting outside any realm of law or morality: namely, the complacent counterterrorist fiction of its superior intelligence and technological control.

Blind Law and Blind Rage: Welcome to the Real

Yes, there would be a fatwa. On May 26, 1998, bin Laden and his deputy, Ayman al-Zawahiri, gave a press conference in Afghanistan to announce the creation of the International Islamic Front to carry out a jihad against the West. Present at the press conference were the blind sheikh Omar Abdel Rahman's two sons. They were distributing plastic-laminated cards containing their father's picture and his written "will":

THE FATWA OF THE PRISONER SHEIKH DOCTOR OMAR ABDEL RAHMAN

America is in the process of eliminating the *ulema* [clergy] who are speaking the truth. And America has suggested to its clients in Saudi [Arabia] to imprison Sheikh Safar al Hawali and Sheikh Salman al Awdah, and all the other[s] who speak the truth, just as Egypt had done. . . .

And the Koran has made a decree upon these Jews and Christians, which we have forgotten or allowed to be forgotten:

Allah said, "If they could, they will continue to kill you until they make you turn away from your religion."

And so to Muslims everywhere.

Cut off all relations with [the Americans, Christians, and Jews], tear them to pieces, destroy their economies, burn their corporations, destroy their peace, sink their ships, shoot down the planes and kill them on air, sea, and land. And kill them wherever you find them, ambush them, take them hostage, and destroy their observatories. Kill these Infidels. Until they witness your harshness. Fight them, and God will torture them through your hands, and he will disgrace them and make you victorious over them, and the nation of the believers is on the verge of creation, and the rage will go from them.

Your brother Omar Abdel Rahman from inside American prisons.[34]

The fatwa was widely distributed at al Qaeda's training camps. In the words of journalist Peter Bergen, who interviewed bin Laden and many other al Qaeda jihadists, and who obtained a copy of the "colorful" card containing the blind sheikh's will through other journalists who had attended bin Laden's press conference, the card "is a key to understanding why some three thousand Americans lost their lives on the morning of September 11, 2001."[35]

Was counterterrorism aware of what it had achieved? Rahman had long been the spiritual guide of Egypt's two most radical Islamist violent groups whose members, such as bin Laden's deputy, Ayman al-Zawahiri, and the group's three successive military commanders, were most prominent in al Qaeda. Key to Rahman's authority is that he holds a doctorate in Islamic law from al-Azhar University in Cairo, the top university in Islamic scholarship. Thus, he is one representative of the highest spiritual and legal authority to Islamists in general and the highest authority to al Qaeda militants in particular. The fatwa is the ultimate expression of that unique power—"Sheikh Rahman's fatwas are the nearest equivalent that al Qaeda has to an ex cathedra statement by the Pope. . . . [He] was able for the first time in al Qaeda's history to rule that it was legally permissible, and even desirable, to carry out attacks against American planes and corporations, exactly the type of attacks that took place on 9/11."[36]

A key aspect of the counterterrorist mind-set is that terrorists everywhere have no sense of moral law. The truth is that Islam is a religion of strict laws and that violence in the name of Islam cannot make sense to its followers unless sanctioned by legal authority. This is what had been provided by the blind sheikh's fatwa. Until 1998 al Qaeda had refrained from attacks on civilians; bin Laden had nothing to do with the World Trade Center attack of 1993. When the blind sheikh was arrested, for example, al Qaeda members debated a plan to bomb the U.S. Embassy in Saudi Arabia but it was rejected because civilians could be injured. We might not know whether it was the blind sheikh himself who wrote the fatwa or some al Qaeda leader, but there is no question that he did communicate with the followers through his family and lawyers. His fatwa was the ultimate legal cover al Qaeda needed to engage in the killing of American civilians. It was no longer lawlessness; it was now a moral and legal imperative to attack American interests. It was blind law and blind rage coming from the blind sheikh.

Previously, on February 22, 1998, bin Laden, Zawahiri, and three other leaders had issued "the following fatwa to all Muslims: The ruling to kill the Americans and their allies—civilians and military—is an individual duty for every Muslim who can do it in any country in which it is possible to do it, in order to liberate the al-Aqsa mosque [in Jerusalem] and the holy mosque [in Mecca] from their grip."[37] Bin Laden's biographer, Hamid Mir, asked him about the legitimacy of this fatwa: "The Koran says that the blood of an innocent non-Muslim is equal to the blood of a Muslim. If you are killing an innocent non-Muslim Christian who is an American citizen, if you are killing an innocent non-Muslim Jew, this is the violation of Koranic teachings." Bin Laden replied: "Actually, this is not my fatwa. Actually, the fatwa is issued by some very big Islamic scholars. I am just following that fatwa."[38] It was the jailed sheikh who provided the real moral sanction for 9/11. Mir observes that up until 1998 bin Laden was against attacking ordinary Americans but that Sheikh Rahman's language was 'very, very strong' and that it was Rahman's long-time Egyptian comrade Zawahiri who was most affected by his leader's humiliation and who "is against every American."[39]

It was in February 1998 that al Qaeda first declared war against the United States; bin Laden explained as a reason for the war that the "holy warrior" Sheikh Rahman had been arrested. In a 1997 CNN interview bin Laden spoke of his arrest as "the kind of injustice that is adopted by the U.S. A baseless case was fabricated against him even though he is a blind old man."[40] In September 2000 Al Jazeera broadcast footage of a convention to support Sheikh Rahman, with bin Laden vowing "to work with all our power to free our brother" while one of his sons shouted "Forward with blood!"[41] And in case there was any doubt about the pivotal relevance of Sheikh Rahman's imprisonment as a cause of the 9/11 attacks, in the spring of 2001 al Qaeda released a two-hour propaganda video in which "reasons" are given why a holy war against the United States is necessary. A picture of the blind sheikh is shown while bin Laden explains: "He is a hostage in an American jail. We hear he is sick and the Americans are treating him badly. . . . We consider the American government directly responsible . . . for holding Sheikh Abdel Rahman, whom we consider one of the great scholars of Islam, who is now languishing in jail."[42]

Journalists who have interviewed bin Laden insist on the religious motivation at the core of his jihad to avenge the deep sense of humiliation of Muslims worldwide. He hated secularist politicians such as Yasir Arafat and Saddam Hussein. He told the journalist Abdel Mari Atwan that "he wanted to kick him [Saddam Hussein] out of Iraq, as he considered the Ba'ath (Iraqi socialist) regime [to be an] atheist regime. He considered Saddam Hussein as an atheist, and he hates an atheist."[43] His hatred against the United States was rooted, as he repeated in all his interviews, in its permanent military presence "in the holy land of Arabia." Explaining his declaration of war against the United States, he told Peter Arnett in a May 10, 1997, CNN interview that "we have focused our declaration on striking at the soldiers in the country of the Two Holy Places [Saudi Arabia]. The country of the Two Holy Places has in our religion a peculiarity of its own over the other Muslim countries. In our religion, it is not permissible for any non-Muslim to stay in our country. Therefore, even though American civilians are not targeted in our plan, they must leave."[44] The February 22, 1998, fatwa issued by him, Zawahiri, and three other leaders called for killing every American; the first reason adduced was that "for over seven years the United States has been occupying the lands of Islam in the holiest of places, the Arabian Peninsula, plundering its riches, dictating to its rulers, humiliating its people."[45] Michael Scheuer, a senior U.S. intelligence officer with almost two decades of experience who is credited with knowing bin Laden "more than anyone in America,"[46] explained that "bin Laden and most militant Islamists, therefore, can be said to be motivated by their love for Allah and their hatred for a few, specific U.S. policies and actions they believe are damaging—and threatening to destroy—the things they love. Theirs is a specific target for specific, limited purposes."[47] And who is bin Laden? He is "a combination of Robin Hood and St. Francis of Assisi," Scheuer said, "a pious, charismatic, gentle, generous, talented, and personally courageous Muslim who is blessed with sound strategic and tactical judgment, able lieutenants, a reluctant but indispensable bloody-mindedness, and extraordinary patience."[48] Bergen saw bin Laden as someone who "comported himself like a cleric" and who "believes that today Muslims are still being humiliated whether it is in Kashmir or Palestine or in Iraq. As far as he is concerned, his war is about humiliation and reclaiming Muslim pride."[49] In a tape discovered by CNN after the fall of the Taliban, bin Laden concludes his speech about the formation of the International Islamic Front with these words: "We hope to lift the shame from the face of the Muslims."[50]

Did the Clinton administration, the media, and the general public have a sense of the Muslim outrage around the world? The CNN interview with bin Laden did not get much reaction. When the journalist John Miller was told by bin Laden that "I am declaring war on the United States. I'm going to attack your country," a skeptical Miller echoed the thought of most viewers, "Yeah, you and what army?"[51] But most of all, as Bergen comments, "the intense interest that al Qaeda has taken in the fate of Sheikh Rahman may come as something of a surprise to most Americans."[52] Indeed, who should care about the burly cleric dressed in religious robes and wearing dark glasses, portrayed by the media as the mastermind of the 1993 attack on the World Trade Center and convicted as a wretched terrorist? Such disregard for the consequences of the ignorance and humiliation of one's "enemy," while assuming the legal and moral superiority of one's own, typifies counterterrorist culture. At the core of this culture reigns the mythology of the terrorist Other's essential lawlessness while allowing oneself to dispense with the rule of law, as shown ad nauseam by Abu Ghraib and Guantánamo. The blind sheikh's indictment and conviction on the testimony of a shadowy paid informer who had to admit "he had lied to just about everybody he ever met," a testimony that according to the *New York Times* sounded "like sheer fantasy," was good enough for the self-righteous passion for ignorance of counterterrorist culture. Rifi'a Ahmed Taha, a leader of Egypt's Islamic Group and one of the signatories of bin Laden's 1998 declaration of war against the United States, released the following statement in 2000: "Regarding the case of Omar Abdel Rahman, the Islamic Group's spiritual leader who is detained in a U.S. jail, the policy of talking and making threats is over. We will address the United States in a language that it understands."[53] Welcome to the Real.

The System Refuses to Know

After the Soviets' defeat in Afghanistan, in 1990 bin Laden returned home to Saudi Arabia as a war hero and initially went back to work for his family's construction company. But Iraq's invasion of Kuwait moved him once again. He offered to recruit a Muslim army to drive the Iraqis out of Kuwait. The Saudis turned instead to a U.S.-led coalition, which became a defining event for bin Laden. Once the Iraqis were driven out of Kuwait, he declared jihad against the communist regime in South Yemen. None of this sat well with the Saudis, who placed him under virtual house arrest and soon expelled him "by convincing bin Laden that the U.S. forces stationed in Saudi Arabia had been tasked by the CIA to kill him."[54] By the summer of 1992, he had moved to Sudan with an army of three hundred al Qaeda recruits.

Bin Laden was outraged that U.S. troops had not pulled out of Saudi Arabia as promised after the Gulf War, thereby prolonging a Western presence—tantamount to the Soviet occupation in Afghanistan—but this time in Islam's holiest land and bin Laden's homeland. This was against his core religious beliefs and politically intolerable. Still, in mid-1993 he opposed a plan to bomb the U.S. embassy in Riyadh because it endangered civilians. He wasn't a "terrorist" yet. But by then he was convinced that the United States was "a snake" in need of beheading. In 1994 the blind sheikh was in jail awaiting trial; it was also the year in which bin Laden's assets were frozen and the Saudis tried to assassinate him.

Al Qaeda terror would begin in August 1998 with the simultaneous embassy bombings in Kenya and Tanzania, which killed 221 people and injured some 4,500. Earlier that year, bin Laden had told the journalist John Miller that there was no longer any difference between military and civilian targets.[55] By then the U.S. government was treating al Qaeda as a global terror network.

Meanwhile, Sheikh Omar Abdel Rahman's son, Saif Rahman, was recruiting al Qaeda members in Afghanistan. A defector told Miller in 1999 about a specific bin Laden plan: "The target was a commercial airliner.

The objective was to hijack a plane that was carrying a U.S. senator or ambassador and then try and use the dignitary as the bargaining chip to demand the release of the blind sheikh from American prison."[56] This was consistent with a report by the CIA that was provided to President Bush a month before the September 11 events, and which said that "bin Laden's organization had plans to hijack a plane and use the hostages to spring Sheikh Omar Abdel Rahman from U.S. federal prison."[57] Only a bold action might free him. The hijacking of planes had been tried many times before by terrorist groups. It could be used as a bargaining chip for the freeing of Sheikh Omar Abdel Rahman. Or perhaps it was already too late to engage the enemy in an exchange of prisoners. Perhaps what the enemy needed most was a lesson, even if an apocalyptic one.

The final chapters of the *9/11 Commission Report* are devoted to how to fight terrorism, preceded by the U.S. failures revealed in the 9/11 attacks. The first of the failures concentrates on "imagination." Hijacking planes to crash against emblematic buildings had been repeatedly imagined. By 1998 there were reports of plans by al Qaeda to hijack a plane in an operation to free the blind sheikh. One of the reports mentioned flying an aircraft filled with explosives into a U.S. city. Another source mentioned a plot by a group of Libyans to fly a plane into the World Trade Center. A group of Algerians did hijack an airliner in 1994, intending possibly to crash it into the Eiffel Tower. A private plane did crash on the south lawn of the White House in 1994. An accomplice of Ramzi Yousef told Philippine authorities about their discussions to fly a plane into CIA headquarters. The 1996 Atlanta Olympics had issued an alert regarding the possibility of aircraft attacks. There was the crash of Egypt Air Flight 990, in late 1999, the final explanation being that most plausibly the pilot had flown it into the sea. The Counterterrorism Security Group had devoted a meeting to airplane hijacking in 2000. The Office of Civil Aviation Security reviewed all the hijacking threats in August 1999, including a "suicide hijacking operation," but judged the operation unlikely.

In short, "the possibility was imaginable, and imagined."[58] What is missing from the picture is not the capacity to imagine that it could happen, but an assessment of the possible *will* of the terrorists. What the counterterrorists ignored, as observed earlier in bin Laden's changes, was the capacity for decision of humiliated people, including the willingness for self-immolation. It was ignorance of their enraged political subjectivities that proved to be so calamitous. A total disdain and loathing of the tabooed subject is far simpler and more self-righteously satisfying. The authors of the Report whimsically observe: "Analysts could have shed some light on what kind of 'opportunity for dialogue' al Qaeda desired."[59] But this is the exception to the very counterterrorist discourse espoused by the Report. Once the enemy is defined as terrorist, dialogue with him? This is simply anathema ruled out by the sanctimonious mantra: "We don't negotiate with terrorists."

The drumbeat of threats became a crescendo throughout the spring and summer of 2001. By the summer of 2001, in CIA director George Tenet's words, "the system was blinking red." The Report details many warnings from sources about prospects for "spectacular" attacks—which makes it even more puzzling that the counterterrorism agencies should dismiss the leads that they had regarding the actual plotters. Nineteen months before September 11, one of the 9/11 plotters, Nawaf al Hazmi, who was in the plane that struck the Pentagon, had flown to Los Angeles and had been identified by the CIA as a member of al Qaeda. He had been photographed at an al Qaeda meeting in Kuala Lumpur, Malaysia, in January 2000. A few days later the CIA followed his tracks from Malaysia to Los Angeles. Another participant in the Kuala Lumpur meeting, Khalid al Mihdhar, was with him. Inexplicably, the CIA did nothing with this information; it warned neither the authorities in Los Angeles nor the FBI or the State Department; repeatedly, following a pattern of infighting between the agency and the bureau, the CIA was asked but refused to provide the information.[60] Hazmi and Mihdhar did not even change their names in San Diego when they opened bank accounts and obtained driver's licenses. They attended flight training schools during the year and eight months before September 11. When Mihdhar's visa expired, the State Department issued a new one in June 2001, even though by then the CIA had linked him with one of the suspects that had planted a bomb on the *USS Cole* in October 2000. Having photographed the participants of the Kuala Lumpur meeting and warned the CIA about it, Malaysia's police could not understand the U.S. intelligence services' disinterest. The Report concludes: "We believe that if more resources had been applied and a significantly different approach taken, Mihdhar and Hazmi might have been found."[61] A different approach—meaning that all that was needed to catch them was to look in San Diego's telephone directory for Hazmi's name. The two future hijackers were frequently in the company of the rest of the September 11 plotters, who thus could have all been detained.[62]

Individual agents from the CIA knew that al Qaeda associates were in the United States and that they might be taking flying lessons in order to hijack planes. A report made public on August 21, 2007, stated that fifty to sixty CIA officers knew of the presence of al Hazmi and Mihdhar in the United States.[63] There was also the famous "Phoenix memo" sent to FBI headquarters and to two New York international terrorism squad members by the FBI agent Kenneth Williams in July 2001, advising of the possibility that bin Laden was sending students to the United States to enroll in civil aviation schools; the agent had found an "inordinate number of individuals of investigative interest" attending them in Arizona.[64] He recommended compilation of a list of such schools and establishing contacts with them to seek information on the applicants—yet his recommendations were ignored. The Minneapolis office of the FBI even arrested Zacarias Moussaoui, who had begun flight training in Oklahoma and who later planned to continue his studies in Minnesota. The agent who interviewed him learned about his jihadist beliefs and his $32,000 bank account, and came to the conclusion that he was preparing some radical action that was related to his flight training. But not even this was enough to trigger suspicion that an al Qaeda plot was in the making. Moussaoui had overstayed his visa, was arrested, and a deportation order was signed on August 17. On August 24, the CIA finally described Moussaoui as a potential "suicide hijacker."[65] When the FBI sent a teletype on September 4 to various U.S. agencies with the known facts about Moussaoui, it did not report the agent's assessment that he might be planning to hijack an airplane; such a "complete report" by the Minneapolis agents was unwanted at FBI headquarters. The Minnesotans were instructed then not to share it. When the Minneapolis supervisor argued that they were "trying to keep someone from taking a plane and crashing into the World Trade Center," the agent from headquarters replied that this would not happen.[66] CIA director Tenet, briefed about the case, was "told that Moussaoui wanted to learn to fly a 747, paid for his training in cash, was interested to learn the doors do not open in flight, and wanted to fly a simulated flight from London to New York."[67] Yet no possible al Qaeda link apparently crossed the CIA director's mind, even if, in his own words, "the system was blinking red."

As if these leads weren't enough, the Report identifies further information that was in the system and that, had it been made available, could have uncovered the plot. First, by 2001 the terrorist Ahmed Ressam had identified Moussaoui as someone who had been in al Qaeda's training camps in Afghanistan. This information would have been sufficient to link him to the organization's feared "imminent attacks." Second, the British government also had information regarding Moussaoui's links to al Qaeda, which was not passed to Washington until September 13, 2001. "Either the British information or the Ressam identification," concludes the Report, "would have broken the logjam."[68] There was also the opportunity provided by the information regarding Khalid Sheikh Mohammed; on June 12, 2001, a CIA report stated that he was actively recruiting people to go to the United States, where others were waiting to meet them to carry out terrorist actions.

"If . . . a significantly different approach [had been] taken," the terrorists might have been arrested before 9/11. But this implies an entirely different mind-set. This is "not so much a failure of sources or observation of data as a structural inadequacy of the system itself to make a conceptual leap from chessboard to hurricane," as Gary Sick put it, summing up the Carter administration's inability to deal with terrorism.[69] A different approach required that the counterterrorist turned into a detective able to read the terrorist's desire by the abundant signs he has left in the open. It needed a Capote able to project his own madness into that of the murderer.

Counterterrorism as Terrorism's Best Ally

Why such blindness? Why this "bizarre trend in the U.S. Government to hide information from the people who most needed it?"[70] *The information was in the system, yet the system refused to read and act on it*. The specific information was known to fifty to sixty agents, yet collectively the system failed to discern the plot. How are we to explain that the same surveillance agencies that, frustrated by the lack of concrete planning of terrorist acts by Sheikh Rahman's circles, and willing to go so far as to plant an agent provocateur to prompt the criminal activities,[71] were now, when confronted with verifiable information from several sources, so unwilling to act during the planning phase of September 11? In fact, U.S. intelligence services had not only known of Sheikh Rahman's son's plan to hijack a plane, but "a Congressional inquiry into intelligence activities before Sept. 11 found twelve reports over a seven-year period suggesting that terrorists might use airplanes as weapons."[72] Doesn't such oversight suggest that there is, at some level, unconscious but systemic complicity between terrorists and counterterrorists?

That is to say, both the hunter and the hunted have been on each other's radar for so long that a mind-set emerges in which they assume they know one another's thoughts and plots. In such an imaginary relationship of mutual dependence, the other can scarcely act without one's knowledge. It is as if the counterterrorist system had to reassure its operatives that, despite the threats, the waiting, and the red flags, they were still in control. President Bush's former counterterrorism czar Richard Clarke wrote a book corroborating the existence in the administration of a mind-set, before and after 9/11, that was the product of the cold war and obsessed with Iraq.[73] The result was that, in the words of the Report's chairman, Thomas Kean, and vice chairman Lee H. Hamilton, "evidence gathered by their panel showed the attacks could probably have been prevented."[74]

In other words, even if it didn't know specifically the day and place, the system knew of the upcoming plot in general terms but it wasn't aware that it knew. What is the genesis of such a seeming anomaly? It is in good part due to the organizational ways in which intelligence agencies protect their information by compartmentalizing knowledge, so that the potential damage caused by an agent can be minimized and tracked down.[75] But the question points partly at something else that is at the heart of our argument: the myopia inherent in ignoring the terrorist's political and unconscious subjectivity. Counterterrorism knew that Islamists were plotting hijackings, yet the system decided to ignore the signs. How? By not linking the evidence to the humiliations, desires, decisions, and the potential for madness and suicide of the despised enemy. And why? To begin with, the tabooed terrorist enemies are denied political subjectivity. Were they even capable of intelligent decision or were they like Salameh, the terrorist who was captured after returning repeatedly to claim the $400 truck rental deposit after the vehicle had been used to blow up the World Trade Center? Could they form an effective terrorist organization? All that was required to destroy the suspicious group around the blind sheikh was simply buying an informant and agent provocateur and using the legal system to land him in jail for life. And do they have the will to sacrifice themselves? They are not heroes, they are simply ignorant fanatics—cowards in essence, thinks counterterrorism. Furthermore, they are so gullible as to be easily manipulated—treated as allies when convenient and kicked to the curb when not. They are pathetic dupes, losers who have neither the knowledge nor the will to win, both their logic and emotions are inferior to ours, as is their humanity. In short, while we alarm the public with impending threats, deep down we know better—the terrorists simply don't have what it would take to pose a real threat to us.

Hence the crucial question: To what extent does counterterrorism actually *promote* the very thing it purports to fight? Or, in John Mueller's words, "Which is the greater threat: terrorism, or our reaction against it?"[76] Isn't counterterrorism, with its historical and militant complicities with terrorism, as well as with its lack of action regarding intelligence and ignorance regarding subjectivity, a pivotal component for sustaining and expanding the entire phenomenon? In short, how does counterterrorism become a self-fulfilling prophecy?

Even authors who are opposed to the idea that the 9/11 attacks resulted from previous involvement with Islamic fighters admit that "[t]he global Salafi jihad is without doubt an indirect consequence of U.S. involvement in that Afghan-Soviet war."[77] As for the Iraq War, it has become conventional wisdom, believed by a majority in public opinion polls, that, far from combating terror, it is planting the seeds of al Qaeda's second generation. Hence the critical question of whether counterterrorism discourse and practice in fact promotes terrorism.

The issue has to do with counterterrorism's impasses as an ideology and as a mind-set. I alluded to them in the distinction I made between the proverbially dumb policeman and the detective. The policeman reads evidence literally while the astute detective concentrates on the inner workings of the suspect's subjectivity. The narration of the above failures is less startling if we hypothesize the premise of the "dumb policeman" who is unable to read the evidence that for a detective is right there, in front of his eyes. For starters, there is the ironic chapter of pro-American jihadists turned anti-American terrorists. Khomeini, Saddam Hussein, the blind sheikh, and bin Laden are instances of former allies suddenly turned into archterrorist enemies. Robert Friedman's conclusion in an article entitled "The CIA's *Jihad*" leaves little doubt.[78] But the crucial case for this discussion is the decision to go to war against Saddam Hussein: as was widely reported in the media, he appears to have been bluffing in his pretences that he had or was seeking WMDs. Counterterrorism's basic epistemic problem is summed up in such inability to distinguish a bluff from a real threat, a wink from a blink.

Unlike the detective, the policeman has no clue that a locked-room type of paradox is involved in the murder. Merely sifting through the "evidence" is not enough for the detective; he has to find a way to look as well into the *zero* object, the internal limit of the locked room that *closes* the series and which will finally solve the case. By dismissing the premise that the evidence is there to be interpreted, the policeman and the terrorism expert are essentially mustering measurable and verifiable data to confirm their presumption of terrorist guilt. But desire produces evidence that may *not* be measurable, such as the effects of the charisma of a leader over his followers, or the suicidal "death drive" of a humiliated subject. One result of failing to effect such a reading is that al Qaeda was much underestimated before 9/11.[79] The last thing in the counterterrorist's agenda is a willingness to take the tabooed terrorist subject at face value by listening to what he has to say. This leads to the irony that the terrorists' own interpretation of their actions are dismissed out of hand. The detective, on the contrary, has to look at the workings of desire whereby lack becomes excess and humiliation turns into madness. The detective can only do this through the intervention of his or her own subjectivity, *by taking desire literally* in a Lacanian fashion.[80]

This latter intellectual strategy is the polar opposite of the norm in most of the counterterrorism literature, namely, the tabooing of the terrorist subject as utterly anomalous and wholly unlike us. Nevertheless, the blind sheikh and bin Laden were not so unlike us when we used them as allies against the Soviets. But now that the taboo is in force, it requires that we forbid ourselves to listen to their words, or, heaven forbid, try to engage them subjectively in order to understand their motives. Indeed, when bin Laden issues his latest message it is scrutinized in detail by the policeman for "clues" as to its authenticity, its precise date, even the quality of its author's voice as an indication of the state of his health—anything but his expressed desire. In short, any physical contact or psychological transference with the dreadful terrorist is strictly forbidden. In the Guantánamo era "confessions" from terrorists are elicited basically under torture. The consequences of abiding by the taboo are that we deprive ourselves of true comprehension of the subjective conditions under which the terrorist operates.

Capote, "the discoverer of death," knew better. He understood his shared culture with his murderous subjects. He reported in detail Perry's thoughts regarding how to commit suicide. Some of Capote' best friends had attempted or committed it. He himself contemplated suicide during many periods of his life. Far from the skepticism elicited in the FBI headquarters, Capote would have had no problem taking seriously rumors that the enraged followers of the blind sheikh might engage in a suicide assault to revenge their leader. He would have found it to be only too "normal" that militants, trapped in the paradox of how to avenge the humiliation of their religion, would seize upon suicide. What the counterterrorism system ignored in the end was the subject formations of the terrorists and their willlingness for self-immolation. It was terrorist desire and will that the system could not face. The very subjectivity of the terrorist had to be avoided, denied, tabooed.

The War in Iraq: The Empire's Self-Fulfilling Secrets

The ultimate catastrophic self-fulfilling prophecy of the War on Terror should be by now obvious to everyone: the war in Iraq. It will remain a textbook case of a war premised on self-deception and willful ignorance.

Intelligence, shrouded in secrecy, is the central currency of counterterrorist politics. Forty percent of the U.S. military budget is secret,[81] as are the budgets of the intelligence agencies. If anything, the Bush administration, particularly in its decision to go to war against Iraq, had become known for its pervasive culture of secrecy. There was a good reason for secrecy: in reality the administration essentially knew nothing about Iraq's weapons of mass destruction. As reported by a Senate committee, the U.S. intelligence community did not have in Iraq a single human intelligence source collecting data about its weapons of mass destruction.[82] Yet, in a speech to the Veterans of Foreign Wars, Vice President Cheney had "no doubt that Saddam Hussein now has weapons of mass destruction"; behind him sat Gen. Anthony Zinni, the man in charge of the policy of containment of Iraq after the 1991 war until his retirement in 2001. Even after his retirement, Zinni was privy to top-secret information and could not believe what he was hearing from the vice president. There was simply no evidence to support his certitude. During his tenure, all Zinni had observed in Hussein's army was "a decaying force."[83] But if there were critics, Cheney challenged them to prove him wrong while reminding them that they had not "seen all the intelligence that we have seen." It was the law of secrecy pure and simple.

Gen. Richard Myers, the chairman of the Joint Chiefs of Staff, played the same trick with secret intelligence that couldn't be revealed even after Secretary of State Colin Powell had aired the fabrications about Iraq's WMD at the United Nations. The media could not dispute the allegations. Senator Robert Byrd puzzled, weeks before going to war, that Congress was "ominously, dreadfully silent. . . . We stand passively mute in the United States Senate, paralyzed by our own uncertainty."[84] Mohamed ElBaradei, director of the nuclear watchdog office of the International Atomic Energy Agency, had reported earlier to the United Nations that there was no evidence of nuclear activities in Iraq. Even senior Bush's closest advisers, such as James Baker and Brent Scowcroft, suspected that the intelligence was being fabricated, that of course there was no evidence to tie Hussein to terrorist groups and to 9/11, and that attacking him could turn the region into a nightmare and undermine the war on terrorism. Why did the son's administration not apply the same *standard of evidence* that was in force during the father's term? Because a different type of reality, having to do with the Terrorist, and a different type of information—its absence turned into apocalyptic dread, its lack into the ultimate secret—had taken ahold of Washington politics.

What is the meaning and value of "information" in such a crisis situation and in the presence of a community of believers? Information becomes suspect at best when it contradicts the premises of those who are "supposed to know" and who claim secret information. The frequent visits by Cheney to the intelligence community are well documented; essentially the community did not know what it was asked to know regarding Iraq and the War on Terror. Knowledge had to be *created* by tying together the bits and pieces of scattered information while adding inferences and guesswork in order to come up with a plausible scenario. This required that a new intelligence unit be formed at the Pentagon. Reportedly, only six senators read the classified intelligence about Iraq prior to authorizing war. Who cares about intelligence once the decision has been made that the enemy is Hitler? When belief drives knowledge, the ordinary standards of factual evidence are supplemented with untested premises; nothing that might help unveil the secret of the evildoer should be discarded. And, as is always the case with the true believers, if information is provided that countermands the belief system, better to reject it. As an informant told Thomas Ricks about Wolfowitz, "you have this know-it-all who won't believe the intelligence community."[85] The "know-it-all" has essentially secret knowledge having to do with the realization that the world is confronting evil. This is not a matter of ordinary "information"; it has as much to do with holding a different view of the world and a willingness to transform it. Once you "know" that Saddam Hussein stands for the apocalyptic combination of terrorism and weapons of mass destruction, wouldn't that even justify falsifying facts if that was what was needed to go to war against evil and ultimate danger? And still, the same informant liked Wolfowitz because, of the two types of villains existing in Washington, hacks and fools, he is not a hack. The only problem was that "[h]e's deeply misguided, *he's impervious to evidence*"[86]—including the evidence of lack of evidence.

Faced with the War on Terror, the leadership of the military abandoned the accumulated knowledge of its profession and was driven into ignoring the basic ways of fighting a counterinsurgency. Rumsfeld and the civilian leadership, arguing that this was a different type of war and that new technology had rendered obsolete traditional modes of action, were simply contemptuous of the military profession's basic tenets in the preparation and conduct of war. The initial plan for the war put forward by Rumsfeld called for fewer than ten thousand combat troops. This was obviously the antithesis of the Colin Powell doctrine of overwhelming force put in practice during the Gulf War. But why should the experience of the Colin Powells, the Norman Schwarzkopfs, the Anthony Zinnis, the Eric Shinsekis, and other eminent military leaders count? For people like Wolfowitz who, according to the Central Command's deputy chief planner, Col. John Agoglia, suffered from a "complete and total lack of understanding" of what was needed for the invasion of Iraq,[87] this war was an altogether new type of war and the knowledge that mattered was not primarily professional or technical—a moral vision and a commitment of will were no less relevant. Above all, what mattered was to root out evil itself—Saddam Hussein. What if, as a result, the entire region turns into a cauldron? General Zinni paraphrased the leadership thinking as follows: "Who cares? I mean, we've taken out Saddam. We've asserted our strength in the Middle East. We're changing the dynamic. We're now off the peace process as the centerpiece and we're not putting any pressure on Israel." Zinni added: "I think—and this is just my opinion—that the neocons didn't really give a shit what happened in Iraq and the aftermath."[88] General Shinseki, army chief of staff, argued to the last minute against Wolfowitz that we were not adequately prepared for the war, but the administration was not interested in the military's worries. The president did not even hear their advice. Why this willful ignorance of what the military already knew? The answer is that when confronting the Terrorist the ordinary standards of evidence, information, and knowledge no longer apply. With such an enemy before you, once you have rock-hard certainty that he embodies evil itself, you already *know* what has to be done. From then on, thinks the crusader, let all evidence against the premise vanish, let all historical sequence be abolished—only a self-fulfilling prophecy of blind determination will do justice to the timeless stakes at hand.

Only such zealous "thoughtfulness" by people confronting evil can explain Judith Miller's role at the *New York Times* in reporting utter fabrications by "an Iraqi defector." The paper thereby carried misinformation

crucial to gaining the public's support for the war in Iraq. This demonstrates the assimilation of the culture of counterterrorism even by the
liberal media—a culture for which "information" is subservient to the final
secret of the enemy's incomprehensible evil and the duty to fight it by
any means. As Dan Rather, an icon of American journalism, confessed
publicly, "George Bush is the president. . . . [If] he wants me to line up,
just tell me where." In short, with a president given a blank check by the
Congress to use dictatorial powers and the overwhelming support of the
American public, the ascendancy of the War on Terror as the single hegemonic agenda of U.S. policy cannot be blamed on the administration
alone; one has to unmask the self-righteous fictions of the very culture of
counterterrorism that allowed for such massive deception.

The task has to begin by questioning why there was a stark inability
to read the evidence at hand and a systemic manipulation of intelligence,
why there was the belief in unproven information and skepticism regarding accessible and obvious inconvenient facts. One has to start by asking
whether such disarray and the leadership's lack of confidence in its own
information from the intelligence community, and its own knowledge by
the political class and the media, do not derive from the paralyzing force of
a phenomenon defined by the premodern categories of utter exceptionality, untouchable taboo, and ultimately unknowable evil.

The political and military failures in responding adequately to the new
reality of suicide bombing against U.S. targets were premised on the intellectual failures of counterterrorism. These are the same failures that
evoke a witchcraftlike conception of malevolent omnipotence, leaving
no room for decisions informed primarily by professional knowledge, as
in the case of military expertise trampled upon by zealous counterterrorists, and opting for moralistic responses that, eschewing pragmatic
approaches that rely on testing hypotheses, are based on belief and secret
knowledge. It is simply the apotheosis of the passion for ignorance, of
the desire not to know, turned into the central political program of the
land and believed even by the liberal media. As an officer of the Joint
Chiefs put it, bothered by Powell's presentation on WMDs to the United
Nations, but casting aside such doubts, "If he believes it, I believe it,
because I put a lot of stock in what he says. And I figured out that people above me had information I didn't have access to."[89] It was belief,
it was inevitable, it was all written in the media, it was by now self-
producing. Not if, but when. If the fiasco of the Vietnam War was the inevitable result of the cold war policy of containment, the Iraq War sums up

the follies of a War on Terror that is interminable and unwinnable, self-fulfilling and self-defeating.

Learning to Eat Soup with a Knife: Bremer vs. Petraeus

Leaving aside any judgment on the disastrous decision to go to war and turning now to its actual conduct, nothing could be more revealing of the conceptual bankrupcy of counterterrorism and its catastrophic consequences than to compare Paul Bremer and David Petraeus.

Bremer became the head of the Coalition Provisional Authority in Iraq in the weeks after the invasion. Having replaced Gen. Jay Garner, Bremer began his tenure with the disastrous decision to fire five hundred thousand Iraqi state workers, most of them soldiers but also doctors, nurses, and teachers. Garner had opposed such a move, but the counterterrorists in the Bush administration knew better. Faced with the alternative of whether to keep former state workers, who had been part of Saddam Husseim's old regime, or to start over from scratch, what would counterterrorism (in which Bremer had been schooled for decades) recommend? It is not difficult to guess if one takes into account that, much like in witchcraft, *association by contagion* seems to operate in the tabooed discourse of counterterrorism: anything touched by Hussein was forever polluted and hence anathema.

Bremer had been the Ambassador-at-Large for Counterterrorism from 1986 to 1989. In his speeches he recycled findings from counterterrorism experts such as Jerrold Post, who for decades has claimed to be conversant (among other areas of expertise) with Basque terrorism. As discussed elsewhere,[90] Post's facts regarding the Basques are persistently and grossly erroneous but still valuable for Bremer. Having recently served on the National Committee on Terrorism, in May 2003 Bremer was appointed by President Bush to serve as chief administrator in Iraq after the invasion. Bremer brought his counterterrorism credentials and mind-set to Iraq. There is now little doubt that his initial decisions to fire the Iraqi army and to get rid of the Baathist leadership were historic blunders for the future of the war. The "true believers" in the Bush administration, as they were called, led by Cheney and Rumsfeld, wanted the shock therapy of the clean beginning associated with Bremer. Anything coming from the old regime had to be eradicated. This is how counterterrorist "true believers" mask with "expertise" their ignorance of the realities at hand.

The counterterrorist stance masks itself as the high moral ground: "You don't negotiate with Hitler, you don't compromise with evil." Anyone touched by the old regime's institutions—soldiers, doctors, teachers—was, in the final analysis of counterterrorist thinking, contaminated. But in fact the counterterrorist Bremer had forgotten what his predecessor cold warriors had done in Wisner's times with support from the German allies: "Many of Hitler's industrialists, scientists, administrators, and even high-ranking officers, were . . . quietly reinstated by the allied powers in a desperate effort to keep Germany from collapsing."[91] Garner and the CIA station chief in Baghdad were appalled with Bremer's decision, but he replied that he had his instructions from Washington. Bremer's approach had been discussed with Rumsfeld and others at the Pentagon. The CIA warned Bremer of the obvious: his policy would drive tens of thousands of Baathists and soldiers underground to fight the invasion. Bremer the counterterrorist was unmoved. The value of the military's experience on the ground and the intelligence community's information was not to be disputed when you are fighting a conventional war; but, for the counterterrorist, such knowledge was essentially of no value because it was now a qualitatively different fight—against terrorism. The military leadership was astonished that the Coalition Provisional Authority, led by Bremer, was designing plans without even discussing them with the commanders on the ground.

If Bremer acted against the recommendations of the military and the intelligence community, then on the basis of what knowledge did he make his decisions? One has to assume that he acted according to his instructions from Washington. But that doesn't seem to be the case either. According to former deputy secretary of state Richard Armitage, Bremer's decisions "were not the decisions that the administration had reached."[92] Wolfowitz and Bremer did not get along; Wolfowitz complained that Bremer "ignored my suggestions. He ignored Rumsfeld's instructions."[93] There did not even seem to be clarity at the top of the chain of command either. At one meeting at the White House, the national security adviser, Condoleezza Rice, reminded Secretary of Defense Rumsfeld that Bremer "works for you, Don," to which Rumsfeld responded, incorrectly, "No, he doesn't."[94] If we take the perspective of "dual sovereignty" sketched earlier, and assume that counterterrorism belongs to the covert type of power ultimately unaccountable to Congress's open political process, it was very hazy whom, if anyone, Bremer should report to in Washington.

A starkly different mind-set, with very different results, was brought to the Iraq War in January 2007 by Gen. David Petraeus. He was one of the generals who opposed Bremer's decision to carry out de-Baathification as a "de-Nazification-type campaign."[95] In September 2005 Petraeus returned from Iraq and for fifteen months devoted most of his time to writing a counterinsurgency manual. He did so in collaboration with other military writers such as Lt. Col. John Nagl, the author of *Learning to Eat Soup with a Knife.*[96] The cornerstone of counterinsurgency was political legitimacy, they concluded: if an insurgency was legitimate, there was not much that could be done to defeat it. But wasn't the issue "terrorism"? The military knew that labeling "terrorist" an insurgency viewed as legitimate was self-delusion. But they went further and saw certain "paradoxes" unknown to counterterrorism such as that "use of force can generate more insurgents."[97] Not surprisingly, this approach was criticized as "too soft" by some experts and it was corrected to "*sometimes*, the more force is used, the less effective it is" and "*some* of the best weapons for counterinsurgents do not shoot."[98] The manual pointed out that legitimacy was enhanced above all by "an understanding of the population's sentiment and the culture."[99] In January 2006 Petraeus had published an article entitled "Learning Counterinsurgency," whose fourteen "observations" are a stark rebuttal of the thinking of counterterrorists such as Bremer.[100] We are told in the first recommendation that "[e]mpowering Iraqis to do the jobs themselves has, in fact, become the essence of our strategy."[101] The following quote gives an indication of Petraeus's thinking:

Observation Number 9, cultural awareness is a force multiplier, reflects our recognition that knowledge of the cultural "terrain" can be as important as, and sometimes even more important than, knowledge of the geographic terrain. This observation acknowledges that the *people are, in many respects, the decisive terrain*, and that we must study that terrain in the same way that we have always studied the geographic terrain.

Working in another culture is enormously difficult if one doesn't understand the ethnic groups, tribes, religious elements, political parties, and other social groupings—and their respective viewpoints; the relationships among the various groups; governmental structures and processes; local and regional history; and, of course, local and national leaders. Understanding of such cultural aspects is essential if one is to help the people build stable political, social, and economic institutions. Indeed, this is as much a matter of common sense as operational necessity. Beyond the intellectual need for the specific knowledge about the environment in which one is working, it is also clear that people, in general, are more likely to cooperate if those who have power over them respect the culture that gives them a sense of identity and self-worth.[102]

The view that the success of the entire war depended in the end on local leaders, on understanding local culture, and on the political environment is obviously a polar opposite from Bremer's counterterrorist thinking by which everything touched by Hussein had been irredeemably contaminated. Petraeus and his partner, Ambassador Ryan Crocker, successfully urged that the de-Baathification law be revised to allow former regime members to take part in the political reconciliation process.

A cornerstone of counterterrorist thinking is that you should never negotiate with the terrorists. Nothing could have been further from Petraeus's approach. Petraeus avoided an all-out confrontation with Muqtada al-Sadr and tried dialogue with the moderate members of his group. Another counterterrorist premise is that the forces of terrorist evil must be vanquished by whatever means. To this Petraeus opposed the view that "[t]he official goal was not a classic military defeat of the enemy but rather a negotiated settlement—in fact, a series of them."[103] In the end, Petraeus even committed what is the cardinal sin for counterterrorists: through one of his subordinates, he was "collaborating with an illegal group of armed men, some of whom until very recently had been insurgents fighting the Iraqi and U.S. forces."[104] And an alliance was forged with Abu Abid's Sunni militia. It was the beginning of the success of the "surge." Soon "[t]he Americans were offering them [the Sunni insurgents] a new option instead of treating them as the enemy."[105] What had happened to the evil Terrorist?

There is no greater repudiation of the follies of the War on Terror than the success of the strategy led by Petraeus following the lessons of classic military science. It proves that it is counterterrorist thinking itself, as put into practice by Bremer, that becomes critically dangerous by helping *create* the very thing it abominates.

"Not If, but When": Witchcraft, Oracles, and the Perversion of Time

The comparison between Bremer and Petraeus is, for an anthropologically informed writer, starkly reminiscent of issues concerning the nature of "reality" and "intelligibility" brought about by the study of witchcraft and other similarly mystical powers in primitive societies. "We're an empire now, and when we act, we create our own reality,"[106] an anonymous presidential aide who sounded like Karl Rove bragged to Ron Suskind, while scorning journalists for being mere commentators about a reality already fabricated for them. The remark goes to the heart of the political culture of the cold war and attempts to perpetuate it as the War on Terror. Ever since the declaration of "Mission Accomplished," the unveiling of the false pretenses for going to war and the inept implementation of the occupation in Iraq, critics in Congress and the media constantly decried the administration's unwillingness to face "reality"—a charge that was met with disdain by the "true believers" in the War on Terror.

What was the background, the information, the consensus informing counterterrorism's most fateful decisions, at times even contradicting the military and the intelligence communities? They are reminiscent of secret oracle consultations among the Azande as famously described by Edward Evans-Pritchard, as summed up by Peter Winch:

> Oracular revelations are not treated as hypotheses and, since their sense derives from the way they are treated in their context, they therefore *are not* hypotheses. They are not a matter of intellectual interest but the main way in which Azande decide how they should act. If the oracle reveals that a proposed course of action is fraught with mystical dangers from witchcraft or sorcery, that course of action will not be carried out; and then the question of refutation or confirmation just does not arise. We might say that the revelation has the logical status of an unfulfilled hypothetical.[107]

Hypotheticals are premised with the conditional "if"—"*if* A, *then* B." What characterizes basic counterterrorist knowledge about the next impending attack is that *it will happen*. This is captured by the oft-repeated formula "not if, but when." Much as does Azande witchcraft, the counterterrorist axiom of "not if" rules out mere hypotheses. The revelations are *unfulfilled* hypotheticals that will become real with time. Counterterrorist projections become thus *oracular certainties*—the horror will happen no matter what. So does it matter if we decide to do A or B? Terrorism is going to happen anyway and we will not be responsible for something that is already written in the books. What matters, therefore, is that we can divine what the course of action will be. As President Eisenhower made clear to Allen Dulles, "*divining* the intentions of the Soviets through espionage was more important to him than discovering details about their military capabilities."[108]

On the other hand, since we have the certainty that, no matter what, evil *will* happen, in the fatalistic manner that the Azande know that witchcraft will happen, and attribute guilt by recourse to an oracle, we need to act *preemptively now* against events that are to happen *in the future*. The rationale for nuclear deterrence used to be that developing armaments now, ready to strike at the push of a button, guaranteed that they would not be used in the future. Many commentators saw in such logic the quintessence of technological madness. But that was not enough. As discussed earlier, Western powers now seem intent on turning the madness of nuclear deterrence into a self-fulfilling prophecy by categorically establishing the counterterrorist axiom of "not if, but when" regarding terrorists' nuclear desires and the alleged certainty that one day it will happen.

Whose "reality" are we dealing with in such a counterterrorist culture? One way to look at it is through comparison with the culture-based reality shared by belief communities, whose sense can only be grasped in the way anthropologists have deciphered primitive societies. Generations of historians and anthropologists have struggled to grasp the cultural premises by which the very *reality* of, say, witchcraft—the "mystical" power possessed by certain individuals to harm others—can be made intelligible in modern times. Philosophers joined the debate by discussing "the criteria of intelligibility" by which we can say that such beliefs and ritual practices are "rational." The ethnographer describes the pragmatic ways in which witchcraft functions as a social idiom in cultures all over the world; the philosopher rejects it as illogical because it fails modern criteria for rationality. Such beliefs are notoriously unfalsifiable for those holding them. Still, after having paid close attention to the social and existential contexts in which they take place, the anthropologist claims to grasp the cultural meaning of beliefs and practices—taboos, rituals, norms—that she does not share. Similarly, modes of believing in witchcraft and Christianity that were taken as "normal" and unquestionable in medieval Europe (divine predestination, the antimonies of omnipotent good versus satanic evil) later became obsolete and gave way to skepticism—the historical context made earlier forms outdated. The anthropological explanation of concepts alien to modern thought may help us to understand not only the transition from medieval types of belief to contemporary skepticism but also the existence in the twenty-first century of true believers in political modes of thinking that might be deemed medieval.

Belief in witchcraft is based on "mystical notions" that are "patterns of thought that attribute to phenomena supra-sensible qualities which . . . are not derived from observation or cannot be logically inferred from it, and which they do not possess." [109] The Western mind keeps asking "why [the] Azande do not perceive the futility of their magic,"[110] and the anthropologist provides an array of twenty-two "reasons."[111] It is not that the Azande do not observe the phenomena like Westerners do, "but their observations are always subordinated to their beliefs"; and any argument against their belief system, "if it were translated into Azande modes of thought it would serve to support their entire structure of belief. For their mystical notions are eminently coherent."[112] Similarly, at issue between the believers in and the skeptics about the War on Terror is the coherence of the very premises of counterterrorism culture—notions such as "war," "terrorism," "insurgency," "evil," "secrecy," "victory," as well as the very character of the oppositions between just war and terrorism, conventional and unconventional violence, guilt versus innocence, "them" versus "us."

The need to consult oracles concerning witchcraft is not an idle matter but springs from the intellectual urge to know the causation of unfortunate events: "Witchcraft explains *why* events are harmful to man and not *how* they happen."[113] How they happen is perceived by the senses; why they happen is what magical thinking is all about.[114] This is where revelations by oracles become essential to Azande thought. The spirit of consulting an oracle is obviously very unlike a scientist's experiments.

But it is the play with the axis of *time* that is revelatory of the typical manipulations of associative magic as well as of counterterrorist thinking. The oracle reveals whether witchcraft has transpired and whether its danger looms ahead. Through the axiom of "not if, but when," counterterrorism hinges on the waiting for terror that creates a fatalistic temporality. This is temporality that in the final analysis becomes *self-fulfilling*. No more chilling example can be found than in Bremer being told by knowledgeable people on the ground that his decision would drive tens of thousands of disaffected Iraqi soldiers into terrorism—and yet he didn't give a damn. It is as if counterterrorism was daring the Iraqis to become terrorists, as if it needed to constitute the evil enemy first in order to destroy it, as if the self-fulfilling crusade *needed* terrorists to show the victorious powers of the armies of good.

The terrorist threat thus creates the temporality of *waiting*. Actual historical temporality becomes subservient to the feared future. The "waiting for Terror" becomes "a prolonged moment of suspension and anxiety, of terror transformed into spectacle, of terror that is also a thrill, of terror that focuses and binds into a new sense of patriotic affect."[115] Such ominous foreboding, intensely imagined and feared for decades, had been waiting for 9/11. Terrorism foretold thus became prophecy fulfilled at some point. The army of public officials, agents, experts, journalists, and academics who orchestrate the doom of terrorist futurology were thus vindicated.

This waiting for terrorism results in a politics whose reality is to be decided by the experience of what could happen in the future (the imagined horrors of a nuclear attack on a U.S. city) as much as by what is happening in the present; by alleged plots as much as by real ones; by what does not happen as by what does. It is the dispute between the temporality of real historical events and real deaths versus the traumatic temporality of waiting, of possible events becoming more real than actual ones. Such perverted temporality is anchored in the typically oracular mentality of mystical powers and secret consultations displayed by witchcraft societies. In the end, the counterterrorist waiting replicates the temporality of the suicide activist for whom true time resides solely in upcoming explosive action. The great victory of the suicide bombers is that they imposed on U.S. politics their own suicidal temporality of waiting and a culture grounded on the oracular knowledge of secret intelligence, which then justified the War on Terror. It is time for the war and its sustaining mythology to end.

The Passion for Ignorance
and Its Catch-22

The title of Joseph Heller's novel *Catch-22* refers to an army regulation of inescapable contradiction by which, if a man wants to fly missions in the circumstances of the novel, he is so crazy that he must not be allowed to fly, whereas if he does not want to fly missions, he is sane and must fly.[1] A further injunction states that no one can question the validity of the regulation. This is a typical case of what Gregory Bateson theorized as a "double bind,"[2] and which he applied to play, schizophrenia, communication, and learning in general. In Heller's novel it is the chronological structure that expresses the absurdity of the situation: one sequence moves forward and backward as seen from the perspective of the psychological time of one protagonist, whereas its countersequence viewed through a second protagonist moves directly forward in the manner of nineteenth-century fiction. "Independently, each chronology is valid and logical; together, the two time-schemes are impossible."[3] Counterterrorism's self-fulfilling narratives display a similarly double temporal axis: a linear temporality of the ongoing political events combined with the logical/psychological primacy of *future* developments ("not if, but when") mixed with *past* ones (fighting terrorists or Saddam Hussein is equivalent to fighting Hitler; in Iraq Cheney was "stuck in a time warp, still fighting Watergate."[4]). The schizophrenic double plot of the novel (the struggle for power of the aggressors and the hero's struggle to live) finds a parallel in counterterrorism's well-known capacity to simultaneously produce *both* the hero and the antihero, and to transform the ally into the archterrorist.

A Catch-22 between the Past and the Future

As pointed out previously, what is common to the careers of Ayatollah Ruhollah Khomeini, Saddam Hussein, Muammar Qaddafi, Sheikh Omar Abdel Rahman, and Osama bin Laden is that at one point they all were tied to the U.S. intelligence services. They were close allies only to then become U.S. nemeses. It is the Catch-22 logic by which both plots, the one of the ally and the one of the terrorist, are generated *by the same process* in apparent simultaneity. Switching sides regarding which countries are sponsors of terrorism is another aspect of the same split dynamics; the most recent case was North Korea when, in October 2008, it was removed from the list of sponsors of terrorism. What needs to be grasped is that this split simultaneity, this Catch-22, is an "edge" that separates and links the two surfaces at once, but both terms are not complementary in their opposition; the duality happens by the very structure of this split and thus expresses the *real* of terrorism. The terrorism/counterterrorism duality is in this regard a Lacanian "nonrelationship" that is constituted by its very impossibility.[5]

The war in Iraq, with the attempt by its promoters to root out Hitler and prevent future terrorist attacks while currently spreading democracy, provides a paradigmatic instance of Catch-22's paradoxical temporalities. This is the situation in which the very chaos in which the action is enmeshed typically *reproduces* the very enemy it is fighting against: there was no al Qaeda inside the country when the United States invaded Iraq; it was the invasion that created a thriving al Qaeda in Iraq. This was also the sense of Amos Oz's remark addressed to the Israeli prime minister: "Again and again, Mr. Begin, you reveal to the public eye a strange urge to resuscitate Hitler in order to kill him every day in the guise of terrorists."[6] It recalls a person caught defensively in a double-binding situation in which the individual is unable to discriminate between metaphoric and literal expressions, distinguish jokes from factual statements, real threats from bluff, real war from rhetorical war, and thus perpetuates endlessly the initial crisis. The war in Iraq, from its fraudulent inception to the creation of the insurgency, from the promotion of al Qaeda to the later humanitarian fiasco, is the clearest illustration of such self-fulfilling Catch-22 logic at all levels.

"In the beginning, we knew nothing,"[7] observed former CIA director Richard Helms, a sentence that could be applied to the decision to go to war in Iraq and the declaration of the War on Terror. The current situation is reminiscent of President Truman who, having ordered the Office of Strategic Services to disband in 1945 and while resisting the pressure to create the CIA, was told that "he had to choose between knowledge and ignorance."[8] If, in Eisenhower's expression, the CIA had already produced "a legacy of ashes," by 2004, with improved technology but growing all the more myopic, for George W. Bush the counterterrorist agency was "just guessing." "For sixty years tens of thousands of clandestine service officers have gathered only the barest threads of truly important intelligence—and that is the CIA's deepest secret."[9] The history of the agency is a narrative in which "failure is routine." The litany of failures includes not foreseeing the explosion of an atomic bomb by the Soviet Union in 1949, the invasion of South Korea in 1950, the Hungarian uprising in 1956, the installation of Soviet missiles in Cuba in 1962, the 1973 Arab-Israeli War, the Iranian revolution of 1979, the Soviet invasion of Afghanistan in 1979, the fall of the Soviet Union in 1989, the invasion of Kuwait by Iraq in 1990, or the explosion of a nuclear bomb by Pakistan in 1998.[10] The agency's wrong assessment on Iraq's weapons of mass destruction in 2002 was only the latest failure.

Mirroring the current counterterrorism system, the history of the agency dwells in its proverbial ignorance of the languages, cultures, and histories of the countries it was trying to subvert in the name of American interests. Vietnam was a good case: as Helms put it regarding the failure to penetrate the North Vietnamese, at root it was "our national ignorance of Vietnamese history, society, and language. . . . The great sadness was our ignorance—or innocence, if you like—which led us to mis-assess, not comprehend, and make a lot of wrong decisions."[11] The more information they gathered, the more they knew they did not know. The agency's state of ignorance made it vulnerable to being manipulated on the basis of ideological premises.[12] There was hardly any oversight by the White House, the Pentagon, or the State Department. By 1961, more than three hundred major covert operations had taken place and nobody in power knew about them. It was as if nobody watched and nobody cared; such institutional carelessness and tradition of arrogance and denial were later blamed for the "systemic failure" of the Aldrich Ames case. The pattern would repeat itself with al Qaeda: by the late 1990s, with talk of "aerial terrorism" as a potential threat, you could count with the fingers of one hand the people in the intelligence community who could understand Arabic.

One egregious case of manipulated intelligence was the way CIA director William Casey convinced President Reagan, against the advice of intelligence analysts, that Nicaragua was a threat to the United States by raising the scarecrow that leftists could come from Central America to Texas. He selected as mission leader Duane Clarridge, who spoke no Spanish and knew nothing about the region, and ordered him to "take a month or two and basically figure out what to do about Central America."[13] Clarridge came up with a dual strategy: "Make war in Nicaragua and start killing Cubans. This was exactly what Casey wanted to hear and he said, 'Okay, go ahead and do it.'"[14] This was the level of ignorance and hubris informing covert actions. Other similar sentences could serve as illustrations—in Cuba, East Germany, Lebanon, Grenada, Somalia, Afghanistan, the Middle East. At the end of the cold war, while refusing to recognize the historic changes taking place in the Soviet Union, the agency lacked spies there; its best thinkers, like Robert Gates, had never been in the Soviet Union. The wrong call on Iraqi weapons of mass destruction and the inability to trace down bin Laden in Afghanistan are but recent examples. The pattern is clearly not one of using intelligence to avoid wars but creating the evidence that will justify going to war. Spy satellites can pick up billions of words but they have no meaning when, to begin with, almost none of the officers can read or speak Arabic, Hindi, Chinese, or Farsi.

But what stands out in the history of the intelligence agencies and in current counterterrorism is that the ignorance is *willful*. Most of the CIA's directors considered intelligence gathering secondary to the thing that really mattered—covert action. And much of such action was better left secret, particularly if it had to do with explosive events such as assassinations. The agency had to take its orders from the president, but nothing on paper, please; nothing should even be discussed in any official setting. As Helms told the Church Committee, "I just think we all had the feeling that we're hired out to keep these things out of the Oval Office," because "nobody wants to embarrass a President of the United States by discussing the assassination of foreign leaders in his presence."[15] In other words, the president should ignore his own orders. Pressed by the Church Committee, what Helms found hypocritical was that officials working for the U.S. government were pretending to actually ignore what should have been obvious to anyone—that the events being asked about were covered by an *official ignorance* that extended to the entire administration, beginning with the president himself. Helms himself did not oppose the idea of murder, but his precondition was that it had to be kept secret; if it was going to be outed, then it was not worth it. As the hearings focused on the issue of presidential authorization and Helms insisted that the presidents "jolly well knew" what was going on, with the lifting of the veil of official secrecy "several different men, in fact, showed dramatic signs of psychological stress in discussing this point."[16] There are situations in which the left hand simply shouldn't know what the right hand is doing.

The demand to produce the intelligence needed to justify a preconceived policy finds a historical case in the nonexistent North Vietnamese attack in the Gulf of Tonkin—the excuse President Johnson was looking for to start bombing North Vietnam. Intelligence was purposefully skewed to support the idea that U.S. Navy ships had been attacked so that the Congress would authorize the war in Vietnam—the house voted 416–0 and the Senate 88–2 to go to war. The 2003 decision to go to war against Iraq was a repeat of the same logic of producing fake intelligence to conform to a previous political decision. Yet, the puzzling fact, both in Vietnam and in Iraq, is that the secret agencies *knew* that the war could not be won. A book-length study sent to the president and his top aides by the CIA in 1966 had concluded that the Vietnamese enemy could not be defeated. Similarly, then Secretary of Defense Dick Cheney knew during the Gulf War in 1991 that occupying Baghdad would be ruinous—for all the reasons that later transpired after the 2003 invasion—yet he pushed for it after 9/11. Why did they decide to ignore what they abundantly knew? It is a case of the Lacanian principle of the *passion for ignorance*, the imperative for *not* knowing when knowledge would be too disturbing.

Such pattern of willful ignorance to fit a president's preconceived policies can be documented in the CIA's history under every director. Nixon and Kissinger rarely even read the intelligence reports; Schlesinger complained that seven thousand CIA analysts were bogged down in detailed data and could therefore not come up with the larger patterns. President Reagan had already decided to substitute international terrorism for Carter's human rights campaign as the number-one U.S. concern. It was his premise that the Soviets were secretly orchestrating terrorism, and he ordered the CIA to prove the assertion. At other times, the CIA would produce a study stating that a disaster was about to happen in some third world country only to be ignored by the president. Under President Clinton the warning that half a million Rwandans might die was studiously dismissed. But the crisis in knowledge affects primarily not the quantity but the quality of intelligence; when President George W. Bush pledged to increase by 50 percent the people at the agency, it deserved these comments from a former CIA officer and assistant secretary of state for intelligence: "Fifty percent more operators and fifty percent more analysts equals fifty percent more hot air."[17]

What the operatives and analysts would never be able to overcome was their own ideological investment in a discourse that deliberately taboos and ignores the worldviews and intentions of the enemy. They are therefore utterly unable to know, in the manner of Truman Capote, the subjective truth behind either the terrorist suicide killers or the double agents among themselves. When the cold war links between the CIA and some prominent foundations and publications were revealed, the list of those who knew was long, but many claimed ignorance: "Everyone knew except, apparently, those who worked for it. Isn't that odd?" Or, "They knew, and they knew as much as they wanted to know, and if they knew any more, they knew they would have to get out, so they refused to know."[18] Something similar would happen inside the agency, as when former director William Webster remarked about Robert Gates regarding what was going on at the agency during Casey's tenure: "Bob's approach had been that he did not want to know."[19] When news of al Qaeda emerged, Webster said that for years "we walked away from it. We should not have walked away."[20] In December 2004 the job of director of the CIA would be abolished by a new law that established a director of national intelligence as recommended by the 9/11 Commission; President Bush filled the post with John Negroponte, a diplomat who, although he had been involved in covert operations, had not worked one day in intelligence.

At the close of the cold war there was someone who *knew* about the inflated claims of turning the Soviet Union into a growing threat against the United States. He was the traitor Aldrich Ames. As the chief of counterintelligence for the Soviet Union and Eastern Europe, he remembered thinking, "I know what the Soviet Union is really all about, and I know what's best for foreign policy and national security."[21] But, since ignorance of the actual facts regarding the Soviets was the ideological imperative, it was as if *he could know the truth only by an act of betrayal.* This follows the Christian implicit logic by which Jesus needed Judas in order to fulfill his high mission of saving the world; according to Judas's apocryphal story, he was the beloved apostle, the only one who was willing to go to the final consequences of shouldering eternal damnation by obeying the Master's order: "Betray me if you really love me." Perpetuating the perverse logic by which Jesus *needed* a Judas to be able to fulfill his redemptive mission, the ignorant cold warrior required a traitor in order to be himself a hero. Something similar happens with counterterrorism: it is only by betraying the belief in its very premises that one can abandon its misplaced heroics and see a glimpse of the truth—that the Empire *requires* a global, perpetual, evil enemy.

In the end, after the demise of the cold war, 9/11, and the war in Iraq, counterterrorism's state of ignorance regarding even the basics of what is labeled the War on Terror became increasingly glaring in the eyes of the general public. Such "passion for ignorance" starts by categorically confusing the very terms "war" and "terror" in the way they relate to actual events. When we talk of "the war on drugs" or "the war on crime" we know we are using "war" metaphorically, but when the counterterrorist says "War on Terror" he means it literally. In actions that are labeled "threat," "bluff," "risk," "play," "ritual," "deceit," and the like, what the actions denote and what they in fact are belong to categorically different frames. In a playful fight a dog may *pretend* to be biting in order to avoid a real bite. The cold war is filled with instances in which the two superpowers faked military tests to impress the enemy that were believed by the other side; the inability to distinguish the simple tests and "war games" from actual war at times came very close to provoking a nuclear catastrophe.[22] It is that type of categorical breakdown, a huge trompe l'oeil, that is taking place by the generalized use of the labile frames "this is war" or "this is terrorism"—the misplaced *literal* reading ("war," "terrorism") of messages that might better be situated under "threat" or "risk" or "ritual" or "bluff" or "rhetorics." After all, let us not forget that the United States went to war in Iraq essentially because counterterrorism could not figure out that Saddam Hussein was *bluffing* to keep his enemies at bay while pretending that he had or was after the WMD.

Traumatized by 9/11, and caught by the Catch-22 whereby not responding to the attack would imply defenselessness and replying might make things worse, the alternative is between a regression to more elementary communication in a premodern mind-set or else an increased understanding of what its causes are as well as creative thinking regarding how to avoid its repetition. It is by now painfully obvious that the reactions to 9/11 were along the path of the first alternative—a movement toward more mechanical and noncorrective responses within an unchanging pattern of action-reaction consistent with premodern, medieval types of thinking that have already proven tragic.

Kicking Ass, Going Medieval

"I want you all to understand that we are at war and we will stay at war until this is done. Nothing else matters. Everything is available for the pursuit of this war. Any barriers in your way, they are gone"—these were the words addressed by President Bush to the members of his Emergency Operations Center on the evening of September 11, 2001. When Rumsfeld noted that prevention, not retribution, was all that international law allowed for, Bush replied: "No, I don't care what the international lawyers say, we are going to kick some ass."[23] As Rumsfeld ordered his subordinates to "take the gloves off," the first victims were being interrogated under torture, a crime according to international law, and their reponses were being faxed to the Pentagon. If up until the War on Terror anyone under U.S. jurisdiction had rights, suddenly a radical change had taken place: terrorists, actual or suspected, were *torturables* with no rights.

Rumsfeld approved many of the techniques of torture and humiliation; Gen. Richard Myers was personally involved in establishing a regime of mistreatment at Guantánamo and in Iraq; Gen. Ricardo Sanchez, the commander of U.S. forces in Iraq, authorized twenty-nine interrogation "methods." Some of these were classic, such as "waterboarding," a much feared and favorite of Spanish torturers under Franco during my youth. Other forms of psychological abuse and humiliation were invented for the occasion, such as insulting the prisoners' religious beliefs by smearing them with fake menstrual blood or allowing females in underwear to grab and kick their genitals. There were other abuses using dogs and the stressful positions shown in the Abu Ghraib photographs. At the same time back in the United States, in the wake of 9/11, the administration had rounded up thousands of Arabs and other Muslim foreigners, incarcerating them in secret, beating them, while the courts had done nothing. Yet not a single one of these victims had any links with the attacks; the Supreme Court refused to even consider the legality of the arrests.

It is commonplace knowledge that torture is not a reliable source of information; the tortured individual will confess to anything in order to stop the ordeal. In fact, there are reports that Guantánamo has not helped to prevent a single terrorist attack.[24] So why the torture despite all the bad press? One answer seems to be: to demonstrate America's unrestrained *sovereignty* by disregarding international laws and conventions. Such unrestrained power leads to the type of self-righteous thinking typical of medieval inquisitors: if the victim is guilty, he deserves punishment;

if he is not, his body will burn in the bonfire but his soul will be saved in the afterworld and ultimately justice will be served. Justifying torture is the decisive test of the inquisitorial mind-set and the state's dictatorial power as well. The "terrorists" have suceeded in turning the emperor into a vengeful tyrant. All it needed was that the emperor *ignores* what the entire world has known for centuries—that waterboarding is torture.

Invoking the European witch-craze in order to understand current counterterrorism might not be as far-fetched as it might seem. The historian Hugh Trevor-Roper has established a close correlation between the entire grotesque phenomenon and the use of judicial torture: "When we consider all these facts, and when we note that the rise and decline of the European witch-craze corresponds generally with the rise and decline of judicial torture in Europe, we may easily conclude that the two processes are interdependent: that the Dark Ages knew no witch-mania because they lacked judicial torture and that the decline and disappearance of witch-beliefs in the eighteenth century is due to the discredit and gradual abolition of torture in Europe."[25] Torture alone cannot explain the perplexing credulity of so many learned Renaissance men duped into superstition, yet it underpinned the entire phenomenon and turned the bizarre demonology into a self-generating, worldwide conspiracy.

One recent example of such normalization of torture was Khalid Shaikh Mohammed's "confession" that made it onto the front page of the *New York Times*.[26] Mohammed was praised by his interrogators because he could endure "waterboarding" for two and a half minutes before being willing to confess. If the rise and decline of the witch-craze of the sixteenth and seventeenth centuries largely corresponded with the rise and decline of torture, we can safely assume that its obscene legitimation in contemporary public discourse is one more casualty of the War on Terror, not to mention a return to medieval forms of thinking. It ignores anything we have learned from such mass delusions and plunges the public discourse into a process of moral corruption. Nothing provides more steel to the backbone of "terrorist" insurgents than seeing the corruption of tyrannical power embodied in the humiliating horrors of torture. Lawrence Wright recounts how, according to one line of thinking, "America's tragedy on September 11 was born in the prisons of Egypt . . . [where] torture created an appetite for revenge, first in Sayyid Qutb and later in his acolytes, including Ayman al-Zawahiri,"[27] a revenge that was primarily aimed at the Egyptian government but also at its Western enablers. Whether dealing with witchcraft or terrorism (despite their vast differences in culture and motivation and goals), if you wish to make them self-perpetuating and self-fulfilling, just legitimize and defend the use of torture. Incredibly, this has been the U.S. response to the 9/11 attacks, thus handing al Qaeda the greatest possible victory—whether of the moral variety or the pragmatic one of facilitating its efforts to recruit new activists/martyrs.

By projecting the eschatological battle between good and evil, the believer knows in advance that the forces of good will ultimately prevail. This must have been one reason why American leaders were so convinced that their troops would be welcomed as liberators in Baghdad. Or that by accelerating its capture, while bypassing rather than eliminating the enemy, the army believed that regime removal was itself tantamount to winning the war and changing the country. In theory this was all part of the War on Terror, but the Pentagon seemed to have lost sight of even the very type of warfare it was getting into, having all but forgotten that it might have to face a subsequent insurgency—a reality that, even if officially denied for months, soon became the news of the day. In such warfare one thing is axiomatic: it does not end with a military defeat, not even when one side proclaims "Mission Accomplished" and declares that "major combat operations in Iraq have ended," as did President Bush after landing as top gun on a navy aircraft carrier, once again confusing *future* events with *past* ones.

That was true enough in the temporality of conventional warfare, the only problem being that he had mistaken the type of war that he had involved his army in. It had won the combat operations in the conventional phase of a war that would prove anything but conventional. The very fact that the defeated Iraqis did not agree that the war was over and continued to fight, a very likely scenario about which some experienced military commanders had issued warnings, took the civilian military leadership in Washington by surprise. This was simply the beginning of the counterterrorists' inability to get in touch with basic reality. For once you know in advance that the forces of evil will be defeated in the ongoing War on Terror, should you really care about the day-to-day setbacks on the ground? The Coalition Provisional Authority's bureaucracy was so dysfunctional that it took months before the Iraqi security forces, trained by the U.S. Army, even had flak jackets and other basic equipment. So what? We are going to win anyway.

A fateful consequence of such moralization of politics is the stark inability to see the evidence at hand while fabricating substitute evidence that suits one's beliefs. Such regression to a premodern type of thinking explains the obstinate unwillingness to see contrarian evidence in the months leading up to the war in Iraq and the delusional credulity on any fabrication to support one's assumptions. Soon the point is reached when the very presence of unwanted "facts" on the ground is no longer recognized. This was in line with the prewar "rollback fantasy" of people such as Wolfowitz and Richard Perle, as it was called in an article in *Foreign Affairs* by three authors from three mainstream national security institutions. It advocated moving from containment to rollback in Iraq; without knowledge of the military issues, these officials thought that a small force could bring down Saddam Hussein's regime and thus install democracy and change the dynamics of the region once and for all. The State Department and the CIA knew that Ahmed Chalabi's fictions were not to be trusted and opposed him. Yet the powers that be, as well as journalists such as Judith Miller, opted for the *evidence* of the converted who had seen quintessential evil. Anything that would distract from the overwhelming reality that Saddam was Hitler had to be discarded.

There is now agreement that the United States went to Iraq with perhaps the worst war plan in its history. Once there, the U.S. Army was convinced that the Iraqi army had poison gas that would be used against them, a belief that refrained the advancing forces from detonating Iraqi bunkers filled with conventional weaponry for fear that they contained WMDs, thus helping the future insurgency. In short, when the overwhelming "fact" is a nonexistent reality, such as Iraqi WMDs, and while thousands of experts and U.S. personnel were looking for them after the invasion, the real facts of an Iraqi insurgency being organized with conventional weapons were simply ignored. No matter how overwhelming the U.S. military force, such fantasy war would soon have to face the realities of a military occupation. Even the fact that this was an "occupation" was denied for months and no routine measures of occupying powers, such as the imposition of curfews and other means of control, had to be taken. This was rather a "liberation," a joyful historic moment for democracy.

What about the costs? Wolfowitz and others predicted that the Iraqi reconstruction would be largely "self-financed" by Iraqi oil wealth. Economists Linda Bilmes and the Nobel Prize winner Joseph Stiglitz have estimated that the costs of the war in Iraq will come to about $2 trillion. As to costs of the War on Terror since 9/11, they also run in the hundreds of billions if we only take into account the $50 billion annual budget of the Department of Homeland Security.

When confronted with the looting of fifteen thousand items from National Archeological Museum in Baghdad, a unique legacy of ancient

Mesopotamia, Rumsfeld had a cool reply: "Stuff happens." But do such "facts" really matter when the single important thing is to engage in a War on Terror to remove a Hitler from power?

Is This War? The Unknown Knowns

Was 9/11 "an act of war" understood as an armed conflict between warring parties or a heinous crime? It all depends on how one defines the various components of the armed conflict and, even more important, on the decision to declare a given situation that is murky and undefined as "war." The primary and most deceptive statement about the War on Terror is the assumption that *it is a war*. There are of course various types of warfare. One point of consensus in the literature on terrorism is that it uses the economy of symbolic warfare—the strike against the one is meant to provoke fear in the many. It is never an insntrumental type of warfare of the conventional kind, in which terrorist groups would be vastly outnumbered and outmaneuvered by a regular military; rather it is closer to a *ritual type of warfare*, which is functionally impractical but efficient in conveying the message "we are at war" by means of displays and threats and stratagems.[28]

The question to be asked after 9/11 should have been whether it was to the advantage of the only superpower to be engaged endlessly in a War on Terror againt a shadowy enemy that doesn't possess armies, negotiators, or rules of engagement. Will the definition of the traumatic situation as "war" help us to diffuse the conflict or will it elevate the enemy in the eyes of the world to the status of a worthy adversary on an equal footing? The assumption that we first must declare a war in order to defeat such an enemy ignores the most basic tenet of unconventional warfare: it can be by its very nature interminable and unwinnable. The Basque ETA is a good example of the great difficulty of ending an armed struggle once you put it in motion—despite its anachronism and irrelevance. A declaration of "war"—between the superpower with a military budget equal to the combined budgets of all other armies on one side and a group of suicidal believers with box cutters on the other—is from the start self-defeating. Unable to find and destroy the elusive enemy, the superpower is likely to find irresistible the temptation to identify as the enemy a more conventional target it can easily defeat, such as the army of a "rogue state," and mistake an act of conventional warfare for the destruction of the terrorist enemy who is engaged an an entirely different type of warfare. This was clearly the case in Iraq, even if no links whatosever to the 9/11 terrorists could be proven. In a classic case of counterterrorism's capacity for self-fulfilling escalation, the superpower has found its nemesis, not in the military capability of the terrorist enemy, but in the blunder of its own blind reaction.

This direct, allegedly eye-for-an-eye, all-out declaration of endless war—war meant literally, with all its political and legal consequences—was the greatest boost for whatever underlies the name al Qaeda, as proven by subsequent events; the greatest challenge for such puny underground groups is for their host societies and the enemy they are fighting against to take their threat seriously. This was also the greatest possible categorical mistake in military terms—it justifies as *reality* the grand fiction of an actual war between a few hundred poorly armed rebels and the greatest military power ever. As the classic literature on terrorism made clear, terrorist violence shuns by definition all organizational and tactical formalities; the goal of military "victory" loses its traditional meaning; the concept of "war" itself is no longer the same—it becomes at best a "proxy war" in which concrete targets and actions are selected primarily because of their symbolic value, and there is no protocol to end the conflict.

Questioned about the ongoing war in Iraq, and the War on Terror in general, the standard reply from public officials is a statement of igno-rance—"there are no good answers." While the authorization of a military adventure costing thousands of lives and hundreds of billions of dollars continues its course, the lawmakers profess not to know how to disengage. What type of ignorance is this?

"There are known knowns, there are things we know we know," Rums-feld mused in Feburary 2002, while readying for the war in Iraq. "We also know there are known unknowns; that is to say, we know there are some things we do not know. But there are also unknown unknowns—the ones we don't know we don't know." Zizek added the fourth term to Rumsfeld's list: there are also *unknown knowns*, namely, "things we don't know that we know—which is precisely the Freudian unconscious." An example of the "unknown known" is the Abu Ghraib scandal, which shows the danger of "the disavowed beliefs, suppositions and obscene practices we pretend not to know about, even though they form the background of our public values."[29]

Counterterrorism abides by the law that we must first ignore—make unknown—that which is known to the various historical fields of knowl-edge and experience established through the arts and sciences, including military science. You must start by ignoring what is known to your own intelligence community.[30] The crucial "known" that the counterterrorist must ignore is ultimately the political sequence that created the terrorist enemy in the first place as well as the self-generating nature of his own counterterrorist crusade.

The overwhelming reality is that counterterrorism has turned into the pivotal political culture of the republic. The ideological and strategic consequences of incorporating self-generating Terror within the central axiom of our political and ethical life have proven to be disastrous. There is a consensus by now, acknowledged even by President Bush's top counterterrorism advisers, that the War on Terror, with its calamitous invasion of Iraq, has made the United States more vulnerable, not less. This is why it is crucial to reveal that we are caught in a historic Catch-22. In the final analysis, if one is not to regress to self-validating magical premodern thinking, the maddening Catch-22 demands a paradigmatic change that will shatter the very premises of counterterrorist culture and allow for new coordinates of the politically possible at this historic moment to emerge.

The Obscene and Its *Double*: *Guernica*'s Shadow

"The photographs *are* us," Susan Sontag reminded an ashamed American public after the Abu Ghraib images were made public.[31] The cause of democracy and liberty in the Middle East, as well as the great crusade against "the axis of evil" worldwide, had ended with the picture of private Lynndie England dragging an Iraqi prisoner about on a dog leash. Naked were not only the tortured Iraqi prisoners (the large majority of them detained randomly on the streets), but also the emperor. He had self-abrogated dictatorial power to select people for indefinite detention without charges, to be held and abused in secret prisons around the world, while making a mockery of the U.S. Constitution and international law. Our values had become the mirror image of the ones attributed to the loathsome enemies. It was no longer the Statue of Liberty that symbolized the United States; now it was the figure of the global terrorist, incarcerated in Abu Ghraib and Guantánamo, dressed in an orange prison suit and walking slowly in shackles . . . this was now the image that condensed the political reality of the United States. The Terrorist had become, by the startling power of the image, the emperor's inverted figure. It visualized for the entire world the unspoken truth: the emperor, too, is a torturer and a tyrant—his own empire is erected on terror.

These images unlock the ideological meaning of the War on Terror's apocalyptic fear and its symbiotic relationship with the suicidal nuclear armaments race. As such, they display the mark of the *politically obscene*—another dimension of the Catch-22 that derives from the passion for ignorance. There is much use of the pornography comparison when defining terrorism ("you know when you see it"), but no mention of the obscene. The reality of obscenity relies also on the subjectivity of the perceiver. The drama of counterterrorism is its blindness to what is obvious to the rest of the world: the excess of obscenity displayed by the images of abuse at Abu Ghraib and Guantánamo. "The obscene, which represents death laughing at itself, has a history. It has to do with the evolution of habits, with the relationship that society maintains with the gaze and the body, with the imaginary and with the colors that are granted by the afterworld."[32] For people who have experienced tyranny and repression, torture has a very definite history—the stigma of such obscenity attached to the United States is hard to overstate. Depriving the *homo sacer* terrorist of his legal and ritual rights, including habeas corpus and the Geneva Conventions, becomes suddenly, in the abjection of the images themselves, the ultimate disgrace on the nation that had done its utmost to liberate the world from fascism and Nazism, and to abolish torture and human rights violations. By bringing to everyone's attention the very *dark side*,[33] the *real* of the emperor's power, suddenly he appears naked in the excess of the obscene intimacy brought about by the images.

Obscenity marks also an intense form of eroticism, as shown by Georges Bataille.[34] The obscene is the darkside, the deadly limit of the erotic. It is by means of the obscene that the torturer can have access to the erotic enjoyment of the alleged terrorist's death drive. But obscenity is "double."[35] It creates its own phantom—the inverse doppelgänger. By looking at the world though the eyes of a cadaver, obscenity projects a counterworld. It recalls winged Icarus who, at the pinnacle of his height and close to the sun, burns out and falls to the ground. Obscenity thus operates an inversion, like Marcel Duchamp making his best-known work of art out of a urinal. In this regard obscenity may become subversive.

Through the images of Guantánamo, the bifacial duality of the obscene extends in the end to the entire dynamics of the War on Terror between the forces of Good (led by the American president) and the forces of Evil (led by bin Laden). Such a *double* may end up, in the eyes of much of the world, in a synthetic image formed by the transmutation and fusion of both enemies. This is how Arundhati Roy formulated it: "What is Osama bin Laden? He's America's family secret. He is the American president's dark *Doppelgänger*. The savage twin of all that purports to be beautiful and civilized. . . . Now that the family secret has been spilled, the twins are blurring into one another and gradually becoming interchangeable."[36]

This is an instance of what Walter Benjamin labeled *dialectical images*—images that bring together contradictory axes, antithetical points that condense at a pivotal moment the intersection of past and present: "It is not that what is past casts its light on what is present, or what is present its light on what is past; rather, image is that wherein what has been comes together in a flash with the now to form a constellation. In other words: image is dialectics at a standstill."[37] If terrorism discourse creates its self-fulfilling cycle by distorting temporality in an endless "waiting for terror," the dialectical image flashes a relation of the present to the past that is not purely temporal and archaic but genuinely historical in that it plays both axes dialectically. This implies that the relation is "not temporal in nature but figural." In such recognizable images, which bear the imprint of the perilous critical moment and which obtain legibility only at a particular time, this moment being a "critical point in the movement of their interior," Benjamin tells us that "truth is charged to the bursting point with time."[38] Images from Abu Ghraib and Guantánamo, as well as the systematically suppressed *absent* images from dead soldiers coming from Iraq, were suddenly charged with a truth that was bursting.

The events of 9/11 had turned into overdetermined dialectical images for those who thought that the third world was merely a "victim" of Western economic and military dominance; they showed that the alleged victim could be as brutal and terroristic as it had been depicted by the counterterrorism. Arguments that "terrorism" was basically a Western discourse became mute when confronted with the horror of 9/11 perpetrated on innocent American civilians. The same could be said of the Madrid attacks of March 11, 2004, by jihadist suicides. But it is Sontag's "the photographs *are* us" after Abu Ghraib that becomes the most compelling for the American and Western public; this is the dialectical image that can awaken us the most to the awareness that we too are torturers and barbarians.

For a society engaged in a War on Terror it is most shocking to be shown photographically the Catch-22 that one is a participant in the very abomination one is crusading against. The devastating power of the images comes from their power of simple *montage*: "I have nothing to say, only to show."[39] Montage critically interrupts the ideological context in which the events have taken place. Nothing will call into question more corrosively the edifice of counterterrorism than seeing that its walls are made up of images of Guantánamo and Abu Ghraib.

In the days before the war in Iraq, there was a moment at the United Nations in which an image became so explosive with historic truth that it had to be veiled. That image was a tapestry reproduction of Pablo Picasso's painting *Guernica*. As Secretary of State Colin Powell was going to appear on February 5, 2003, to argue with false evidence that Iraq posed an imminent threat against the United States, thus granting political legitimacy to the upcoming war, UN officials covered the reproduction of *Guernica* with a curtain. Picasso had turned the painting into the symbol of modern warfare's savagery. The burning to the ground by Hitler's airplanes of the historic Basque town of Gernika had been the first experiment in the fascist doctrine of "Total War"—punishing all of society to enable the armed forces to advance more rapidly. When George Steer broke the news, General Franco's propaganda machine tried to spread the lie that Gernika had been burnt by the Republican forces who were defending the town. The shadow of Gernika at that solemn moment was too much to bear. But the cover-up of the painting could not avoid laying bare for the world at large the cover-up of the truth of another imperial war of choice.

Such jolt or recognition by the dialectical image forces the public into a political *awakening*. Suddenly we realize that, in their obscenity, "the photographs *are* us." As the result of such "telescoping the past through the present" we recognize that the images of the War on Terror do not take place in a historical void but follow a certain dialectics. They demand a "new thinking," one that realizes that "[t]here is a secret agreement between past generations and the present one."[40] The difference between the "old thinking" and the "new thinking," Eric Santner writes, "is that in the new thinking the element of the past that is at issue has the structural status of *trauma*.[41] It is the testimony borne by the traumatic past, by what *Guernica* represents, to which now 9/11 must be added, that in modernity counts as true awakening. "Cheney was traumatized by 9/11. The poor guy became paranoid,"[42] is said of the man widely considered to be a main architect behind the War on Terror. The dialectical images of terrorism and counterterrorism unmask the traumatic core of current international politics—of a past that must be brought to an end once and for all.

Notes

Introduction

1. Joseba Zulaika and William A. Douglass, *Terror and Taboo: The Follies, Fables, and Faces of Terrorism* (New York: Routledge, 1996), 239.

2. Richard Jackson, *Writing the War on Terrorism: Language, Politics and Counter-Terrorism* (Manchester: Manchester University Press, 2005), 179.

3. Philip Shenon, "Leaders of 911 Panel Say Attacks Were Probably Preventable," *New York Times*, April 5, 2004, A16.

4. Robert K. Merton, *Social Theory and Social Structure* (New York: Free Press, 1968), 477.

5. Norbert Wiley, "The Self as Self-Fulfilling Prophecy," *Symbolic Interaction* 26, no. 4 (2003).

6. Merton, *Social Theory*, 475.

7. See Joseph Cirincione, *Bomb Scare: The History and Future of Nuclear Weapons* (New York: Columbia University Press, 2007).

8. Edmund Leach, *Custom, Law, and Terrorist Violence* (Edinburgh: Edinburgh University Press, 1977), 36.

9. See John Mueller, *Overblown: How Politicians and the Terrorism Industry Inflate National Security Threats, and Why We Believe Them* (New York: Free Press, 2006).

10. Cirincione, *Bomb Scare*, 122.

11. Begoña Aretxaga, *States of Terror: Begoña Aretxaga's Essays* (Reno: Center for Basque Studies, University of Nevada, 2005), 229.

12. The Iraqi interior minister in the 1960s, Ali Saleh Sa'adi, quoted in Tim Weiner, *Legacy of Ashes* (New York: Doubleday, 2007), 141.

13. Alenka Zupancic, *The Shortest Shadow: Nietzsche's Philosophy of the Two* (Cambridge: MIT Press, 2003), 19.

14. Zulaika and Douglass, *Terror and Taboo*, 9–10.

15. Zupancic, *The Shortest Shadow*, 12–13.

16. Joseba Zulaika, *Basque Violence: Metaphor and Sacrament* (Reno: University of Nevada Press, 1988).

17. Clifford Geertz, "Anti-anti-relativism," *American Anthropologist* 86 (1984): 275.

18. Quoted in R. Radhakrishnan, "Toward an Effective Intellectual: Foucault or Gramsci?" in *Intellectuals: Aesthetics, Politics, Academics*, ed. Bruce Robbins (Minneapolis: University of Minnesota Press, 1990).

19. Søren Kierkegaard, *Fear and Trembling*, trans. Walter Lowrie (Princeton: Princeton University Press, 1941), 67.

20. See my own reflections on the dilemmas of the ethnographer of political violence in "The Anthropologist as Terrorist," in *Fieldwork under Fire*, ed. Carolyn Nordstrom and Anthony Robben (Berkeley: University of California Press, 1966); "Excessive Witnessing: The Ethical as Temptation," in *Witness and Memory: The Discourse of Trauma*, ed. Ana Douglass and Thomas Vogler (New York: Routledge, 2003).

21. Slavoj Zizek, *Welcome to the Desert of the Real* (New York: Wooster Press, 2001), 46.

22. Quoted in Zizek, *Welcome*, 53.

23. Zizek, *Welcome*, 46–47.

24. Zulaika and Douglass, *Terror and Taboo*, 227–39.

25. Zulaika and Douglass, *Terror and Taboo*, 228.

26. H. R. Trevor-Roper, *The European Witch-Craze of the Sixteenth and Seventeenth Centuries and Other Essays* (New York: Harper and Row, 1969), 90.

27. Eric Lichtblau, "Wall St. Fraud Prosecutions Fall Sharply; New Questions on Lax U.S. Oversight," *New York Times*, December 25, 2008, 1.

Chapter One

1. Joseba Zulaika and William A. Douglass, *Terror and Taboo: The Follies, Fables, and Faces of Terrorism* (New York: Routledge, 1996).

2. This analysis of *tropes* and discursive strategies in culture, and of metaphor in particular, is guided primarily by the enduring influence on my thought of my mentor James W. Fernandez. See his pathbreaking *Persuasions and Performances: The Play of Tropes in Culture* (Bloomington: Indiana University Press, 1986).

3. Hayden White, *Tropics of Discourse: Essays in Cultural Criticism* (Baltimore: John Hopkins University Press, 1978).

4. Some of the authors include Edmund Leach, *Custom, Law, and Terrorist Violence* (Edinburgh: Edinburgh University Press, 1977); Michael Taussig, *Shamanism, Colonialism, and the White Man: A Study in Terror and Healing* (Chicago: University of Chicago Press, 1987); Allen Feldman, *Formations of Violence: The Narrative of the Body and Political Terror in Northern Ireland* (Chicago: University of Chicago

Press); Jeffrey Sluka, *Hearts and Minds, Water and Fish: Support for the IRA and INLA in a Northern Irish Ghetto* (Greenwich, Conn.: JAI Press, 1989); Ehud Sprinzak, *The Ascendancy of Israel's Radical Right* (New York: Oxford University Press, 1991); Carolyn Nordstrom and Joann Martin, eds., *The Paths of Domination, Resistance, and Terror* (Berkeley: University of California Press, 1992); Kay B. Warren, ed. *The Violence Within: Cultural and Political Opposition in Divided Nations* (Boulder: Westview Press, 1993); Cynthia Keppley Mahmood, *Fighting for Faith and Nation: Dialogues with Sikh Militants* (Philadelphia: University of Pennsylvania Press, 1996); Begoña Aretxaga, *Shattering Silence: Women, Nationalism, and Political Subjectivity in Northern Ireland* (Princeton: Princeton University Press, 1997); Richard English, *Armed Struggle: The History of the IRA* (Oxford: Oxford University Press, 2003); Antonius C. G. M. Robben, *Political Violence and Trauma in Argentina* (Philadelphia: University of Pennsylvania Press, 2004); Mark P. Whitaker, *Learning Politics from Sivaram: The Life and Death of a Revolutionary Tamil Journalist in Sri Lanka* (London: Pluto Press, 2007).

5. Quoted in Richard Jackson, *Writing the War on Terrorism: Language, Politics and Counter-Terrorism* (Manchester: Manchester University Press, 2005), 45 and 103.

6. Data from Jackson, *Writing*, 166–67.

7. Jackson, *Writing*, 167.

8. Jackson, *Writing*, 170.

9. Louise Richardson, *What Terrorists Want: Understanding the Enemy, Containing the Threat* (New York: Random House, 2006), 3.

10. Alex Schmid and Albert Jongman, *Political Terrorism: A Research Guide to Concepts, Theories, Data Bases, and Literature* (New Brunswick: Transaction Books, 1988), 8.

11. Andrew Silke, "The Road Less Travelled: Recent Trends in Terrorism Research," in *Research on Terrorism: Trends, Achievements and Failures*, ed. Andrew Silke (London: Frank Cass, 2004), 186, 188, 189, 191, and 194.

12. Silke, "The Road," 207.

13. John Horgan, "The Search for the Terrorist Personality," in *Terrorists, Victims and Society: Psychological Perspectives on Terrorism and Its Consequences*, ed. Andrew Silke (Chichester: Wiley, 2003), 23.

14. Marc Sageman, *Understanding Terror Networks* (Philadelphia: University of Pennsylvania Press, 2004), 96.

15. Silke, "The Road," 208.

16. Silke, "The Road," 208.

17. Richardson, *What Terrorists Want*, 4.

18. Just to mention one obvious case: in a world in which the means of violence, including weapons of mass destruction, are by and large produced and controlled by states, what is the value of a category that excludes states from acts of terror (unless they are "rogue states" such as Iraq or Libya), while accepting as legitimate

just war whatever terroristic violence they might perpetrate against their own external and domestic enemies? This leads to the travesty whereby a given year, 1985, is labeled as the apogee of Middle Eastern terrorism because two Americans were murdered in two separate incidents while other events during the same year, such as the CIA's car bombing in Beirut that killed ninety people and wounded 250, or Israel's bombing of Tunis, killing seventy-five people, are not considered to be international terrorism. Or take the year 1988 when an Iranian airliner with 290 passengers on board was destroyed by the U.S. aircraft carrier *Vincennes* and later that same year Pan Am flight 103 with 259 passengers was downed over Lockerbie: the second case is the paradigm of terrorist atrocity, yet the first one is allegedly an accident that happened by unintentional error and therefore not terroristic; the Pan Am case is the epitome of evil and lawlessness to be met with the full force of international counterterrorism, while the downing of the Iranian airliner is an innocent mistake that deserves no punishment; furthermore, the possibility of any linkage between the first case and the second, widely assumed by the experts, is ruled out by definition.

19. Richardson, *What Terrorists Want*, 10.

20. Richardson, *What Terrorists Want*, 8.

21. Richardson's characterization makes accomplices to terrorism people such as Swedish prime minister Olof Palme who openly collected funds in the streets of Stockholm for ETA insurgents when two members of the organization were executed by Franco.

22. Fawaz A. Gerges, *The Far Enemy: Why Jihad Went Global* (Cambridge: Cambridge University Press, 2005), 35 and 39.

23. See Leonard Weinberg and Ami Pedahzur, *Political Parties and Terrorist Groups* (London: Routledge, 2003).

24. Bruce Hoffman, *Inside Terrorism* (New York: Columbia University Press, 2006).

25. H. R. Trevor-Roper, *The European Witch-Craze of the Sixteenth and Seventeenth Centuries and Other Essays* (New York: Harper and Row, 1969), 154.

26. Biological weapons expert Milton Leitenberg, quoted in John Mueller, *Overblown: How Politicians and the Terrorism Industry Inflate National Security Threats, and Why We Believe Them* (New York: Free Press, 2006), 22.

27. For a larger version of my criticism, see Joseba Zulaika, "Terror, Totem, and Taboo: Reporting on a Report," *Terrorism and Political Violence* 3, no. 1 (1991): 34–49.

28. C. Rose, F. Ferracuti, H. Horchem, P. Janke, and J. Leaute, *Report of the International Commission on Violence in the Basque Country* (Vitoria: Eusko Jaurlaritza, 1986), 9.1.21.

29. Max Weber, *Max Weber and the Methodology of the Social Sciences*, trans. and ed. Edward A. Shils and Henry A. Finch (Glencoe, Ill.: Free Press, 1949).

30. Rose et al., *Report*, 9.1.1.

31. Rose et al., *Report*, 8.18.

32. Gary Sick, *All Fall Down: America's Tragic Encounter with Iran* (New York: Random House, 1985), 171.

33. Don Van Natta Jr., Elaine Sciolino, and Stephen Grey, "In Tapes, Receipts, and a Diary, Details of the British Terror Case," *New York Times*, August 28, 2006, A1.

34. Giorgio Agamben, *Homo Sacer: Sovereign Power and Bare Life* (Stanford: Stanford University Press, 1998), 57.

35. Editorial, "All Things Considered," October 27, 2005.

36. Editorial, "Legalized Torture, Reloaded," *New York Times*, October 26, 2005, A26.

37. Editorial, "The Prison Puzzle," *New York Times*, November 3, 2005, A26.

38. Anthony Lewis, "Making Torture Legal," *New York Review of Books* 51, no. 13 (July 15, 2004), 4.

39. See, among many others, J. Dempsey and D. Cole, *Terrorism and the Constitution: Sacrificing Civil Liberties in the Name of National Security* (New York: New Press, 2002), 152–53.

40. The emergency situation after 9/11 facilitated fundamental changes in law enforcement procedures. It eliminated barriers between law enforcement and intelligence gathering. It gave the CIA the benefit of grand jury powers with none of the criminal justice system's protections against their abuse. It granted the FBI unlimited access to specific categories of information, including surveillance of library, bank, hospital, and university records. In short, it radically transformed the realities of both government authority and accountability. One of the key premises of the Patriot Act is guilt by association. Ethnic profiling has thus been implemented once again. The Bush administration called in eighty thousand foreign nationals from predominantly Arab or Muslim countries for fingerprinting and photographing; the FBI sought out another eight thousand for interviews; and more than five thousand were placed in preventive detention, their hearings held in secret and their names undisclosed, "yet as of September 2007, not one of these people stands convicted of a terrorist crime. The government record . . . is 0 for 93,000" (David Cole and Jules Lobel, "Why We're Losing the War on Terror," *Nation*, September 24, 2007, 14.) Such ethnic profiling is the natural consequence of a counterterrorism culture in which deeply ingrained notions of sin and taboo gain respectability. This is the land of Abu Ghraib, Guantánamo, and the Patriot Act. It is the realm in which government after government invokes terrorism as the irresistible rationale for abrogating the civil liberties of the citizenry.

41. During the administration of George W. Bush, U.S. unilateralism and its unwillingness to join the community of nations regarding key initiatives such as the International Criminal Court and the Kyoto Declaration added to the perception that the only superpower has decided to arrogate to itself the right to an exceptional status. Yet, given its overpowering military capacity, such American exceptionality

is precisely what worries most of the rest of the world's sovereign peoples. Since 9/11 the United States, under the banner of its War on Terror, has imposed a state of exception both at home and in international affairs as well. As the exceptional sovereign among nations, the United States engages in preemptive wars such as the one against Iraq, implementing its conflicts *outside* the community of nations as represented by the United Nations. Such exceptional use of sovereign power is viewed in starkly opposite ways by the United States and the world community: for the United States and its allies Iraq was a necessary use of force related to the War on Terror, while for the majority of the international community it was "illegal."

42. Agamben, *Homo Sacer*, 15.

43. Agamben, *Homo Sacer*, 18.

44. Shosana Felman, "Camus' *The Plague,* or a Monument to Witnessing," in Shoshana Felman and Dori Laub, *Testimony: Crises of Witnessing in Literature, Psychoanalysis, and History* (New York: Routledge, 1992), 93.

45. Felman, "Camus' *The Plague,*" 101.

46. Albert Camus, *The Plague* (New York: Alfred A. Knopf, 1948), 272.

47. Shoshana Felman, "The Betrayal of the Witness: Camus' *The Fall,*" in Felman and Laub, *Testimony*, 171.

48. Quoted in Felman, "The Betrayal," 174.

49. Albert Camus, *The Fall* (New York: Alfred A. Knopf, 1958), 112.

50. Felman, "The Betrayal," 181.

51. Felman, "The Betrayal," 194.

52. Felman, "The Betrayal," 196.

53. Camus, *The Fall*, 110.

54. Albert Camus, *Neither Victims nor Executioners*, trans. Dwight McDonald (Philadelphia: New Society Publishers, 1986), 27–28.

55. See R. Scott Kennedy and Peter Klotz-Chamberlin, "An Ethic Superior to Murder," in Camus, *Neither Victims nor Executioners*, 9.

56. Hannah Arendt made a useful distinction between moral guilt and collective political responsibility. One can be responsible for things in which one has not taken part but one is guilty only of things in which one has actively participated.

57. Quoted in Mariann Vaczi, "From Orange to Red: The Bush Doctrine's Enemy Construction" (MA thesis, School of English and American Studies, Eötvös Loránd University, Budapest, 2006), 44.

Chapter Two

1. Truman Capote, *In Cold Blood* (New York: Vintage, 1994), 240.

2. Capote, *In Cold Blood*, 240.

3. Capote, *In Cold Blood*, 242.

4. Capote, *In Cold Blood*, 243.

5. Capote, *In Cold Blood*, 244.

6. Capote, *In Cold Blood*, 244.

7. Capote, *In Cold Blood*, 245–46.

8. Capote, *In Cold Blood*, 308.

9. Capote, *In Cold Blood*, 290.

10. Capote, *In Cold Blood*, 290–91.

11. Capote, *In Cold Blood*, 291.

12. Capote, *In Cold Blood*, 291.

13. Capote, *In Cold Blood*, 287.

14. Capote, *In Cold Blood*, 288.

15. Capote, In Cold Blood, 266.

16. Capote, *In Cold Blood*, 319.

17. Joseba Zulaika and William A. Douglass, *Terror and Taboo: The Follies, Fables, and Faces of Terrorism* (New York: Routledge, 1996), 187.

18. *The 9/11 Commission Report: Final Report of the National Commission on Terrorist Attacks upon the United States* (New York: W. W. Norton, 2004), xv–xvi.

19. Report, xvii.

20. Report, 66.

21. Hayden White, *Tropics of Discourse: Essays in Cultural Criticism* (Baltimore: John Hopkins University Press, 1978), chap. 5.

22. Report, 254.

23. We are told, for example, that in the year following the 9/11 attacks, "the total number of undergraduate degrees granted in Arabic in all U.S. colleges and universities in 2002 was six." In 1998, when hunting bin Laden and his al Qaeda operatives was the paramount counterterrorist challenge, only eight FBI agents could speak Arabic. In the fall of 2006 it was also reported that, of the one thousand personnel working in the Baghdad American embassy, only six spoke Arabic. If there is such a systematic ignorance of the very language of one's sources, we can safely assume that miscommunication has to be endemic as well.

24. Report, 146.

25. Report, 146.

26. Claire Sterling's *The Terror Network*, a must read for Ronald Reagan and his secretary of state, Alexander Haig, provided in the 1980s a good instance of such hyperbolic conspiratorial thinking when she spoke of "colossal supplies of weapons employed by the terrorists of four Continents in Fright Decade I." To prove her case she described a transaction of fifty revolvers between the IRA and ETA as signaling terrorism's "inexorable advancing enemy." (Claire Sterling, *The Terror Network: The Secret War of International Terrorism* [New York: Holt, Rinehart, and Winston, 1981], 4 and 7). The Report states that bin Laden has "thousands of followers and some degree of approval from millions more" (48). We are told that not until 1988 did bin Laden's al Qaeda undertake a terrorist operation, but by 2001 "a true terrorist global network" had been established. This included a long list of

organizations and nations worldwide. In a single page of the Report we are given an accounting of bin Laden's network with branches in Cyprus, Zagreb, Sarajevo, Baku, Chechnya, Vienna, and Budapest. It had "enlisted groups from Saudi Arabia, Egypt, Jordan, Lebanon, Iraq, Oman, Algeria, Libya, Tunisia, Morocco, Somalia, and Eritrea" and established relationships with extremist groups "from the African states of Chad, Mali, Niger, Nigeria, and Uganda; and from the Southeast Asian states of Burma, Thailand, Malaysia, and Indonesia." It provided training to groups in the Philippines, Indonesia, Malaysia, Singapore, and Kashmir (58). How can we be sure that such a network is in fact operational? Historical events that took place years before al Qaeda existed are also included in the vast network. Had there not been earlier similar world-embracing conspiracies that came to nothing, such emplotting would be far more believable. Conspiratorial thinking relies on terms such as "link," the meaning of which may hide vastly different types of relationships, from organizational to ideological to coincidental.

27. Report, 58.

28. See Robert Friedman, "The CIA's *Jihad*," *New York* (March 27, 1995), 36–47. This point is elaborated in chapter 8.

29. "Anachronistic as it may sound, President Bush revived the old Leninist logic: if you are not with us, you are against us: 'Every nation, in every region, now has a decision to make. Either you are with us, or you are with the terrorists. From this day forward, any nation that continues to harbor or support terrorism will be regarded by the United States as a hostile regime' . . . And indeed, the nations listened" (Vaczi, "From Orange to Red," 48).

30. Why do "they" hate us? The Report's reply: "They say that America had attacked Islam; America is responsible for all conflicts involving Muslims. Thus Americans are blamed when Israelis fight with Palestinians, when Russians fight with Chechens, when Indians fight with Kashmiri Muslims, and when the Philippine government fights ethnic Muslims in its southern islands. America is also held responsible for the governments of Muslim countries, derided by al Qaeda as 'your agents' "(Report, 51). But is this "their" way of thinking, or is it in fact a mirror reflection of the very counterterrorism discourse? The inability of bin Laden's group to strike against the United States after 9/11 seems in line with Sterling's imaginary fancy of a Europe "encircled" by terrorism on the basis of fifty pistols traded between the IRA and ETA—they are good examples of what Richard Hofstadter called "the paranoid style in American politics" (Richard Hofstadter, *The Paranoid Style in American Politics and Other Essays* [New York: Alfred A. Knopf, 1966]).

31. This is a sample of the narrative: "On the morning of September 11, Secretary Rumsfeld was having breakfast at the Pentagon with a group of members of Congress. He then returned to his office for his daily intelligence briefing. The Secretary was informed of the second strike in New York during the briefing: he resumed the briefing while awaiting more information. After the Pentagon was

struck, Secretary Rumsfeld went to the parking lot to assist with rescue efforts" (Report, 37). One imagines Capote describing an outraged Rumsfeld's intense feelings of anger, sadness, defiance. But the Report seems to presume that such feelings depart from objective reporting and analysis; in short, that they are not "facts." For Capote, those feelings would be the determining facts presaging the future events.

32. See Joseba Zulaika and William A. Douglass, "The Terrorist Subject: Terrorism Studies and the Absent Subjectivity," *Critical Terrorism Studies* 1 (April 2008): 23–45.

33. Report, 72.

34. Report, 72–73.

35. Report, xvi.

36. M. Thomas Inge, *Truman Capote: Conversations* (Jackson: University Press of Mississippi, 1987), 131.

37. Lawrence Grobel, *Conversations with Capote* (New York: NAL Books, 1985), 109 and 215.

38. Inge, *Truman Capote*, 66.

39. Inge, *Truman Capote*, 68.

40. Inge, *Truman Capote*, 72.

41. Capote came to regret ever having gone to the site of the crime: "If I had realized then what the future held, I never would have stopped in Garden City. I would have driven straight on. Like a bat out of hell," he told Plimpton in 1966 (Inge, 52). "If I knew or had known when I started it what was going to be involved, I never would have started it, regardless of what the end result would have been," he told Grobel (1985, 123). And to Norden he confided: "If I had ever known what I was going to have to endure over those six years—no matter what has happened since—I never would have started the book. It was too painful. Nothing is worth it" (Inge, 123).

42. Inge, *Truman Capote*, 72; emphasis added.

43. Inge, *Truman Capote*, 119.

44. Inge, *Truman Capote*, 120.

45. Robin Morgan, *The Demon Lover: The Roots of Terrorism* (New York: Washington Square Press, 2001).

46. In the film *Blood Diamonds* the hero, portrayed by Leonardo di Caprio, is a vicious killer in pursuit of diamonds, but in the end he is "saved" while dying by the love of the woman journalist who turns the tragedy into reporting and a denunciation of the illicit diamond trade. Lovable killers are, after all, all too human. It is the killers you should not and can never fall in love with that are the true enigma. These are the terrorists.

47. Inge, *Truman Capote*, 56.

48. Grobel, *Conversations*, 90.

49. Grobel, *Conversations*, 111.

50. Inge, *Truman Capote*, 122.

51. Inge, *Truman Capote*, 64.

52. Inge, *Truman Capote*, 67.

53. Inge, *Truman Capote*, 132.

54. Inge, *Truman Capote*, 81.

55. Gerald Clarke, *Capote: A Biography* (New York: Carroll and Graf, 2005), 352.

56. Clarke, *Capote*, 352.

57. Clarke, *Capote*, 336.

58. Grobel, *Conversations*, 106.

59. Clarke, *Capote*, 341.

60. Clarke, *Capote*, 352.

61. When the executions were scheduled for February, Capote was at a ski resort in Switzerland and he decided not to return to the United States. But the hangings were postponed once again and Capote was frantic over and infuriated by the defense lawyers' contention that Perry and Dick might not only escape death but actually be freed. The hanging were rescheduled for April 14. Perry and Dick begged Capote to be with them and he arrived one or two days before the execution. He was unable to talk, tears rolled down his cheeks, he would not answer Perry's calls to the hotel. Perry telegraphed him; Capote cabled back: "Dear Perry. Unable to visit you today. Because not permitted. Always your friend. Truman." Perry knew Capote was lying. The hope that Capote might perhaps obtain another stay of execution was behind the condemned men's frantic effort to reach him. But nothing was further from Capote's intentions. An hour before he was hung, Perry wrote a note to Capote excusing his absence: "I want you to know that I cannot condemn you for it & understand. . . . I have become very affectionate toward you. . . . Your friend always, Perry." Nevertheless, Capote showed up at the last minute and spoke a few words to each of them. Perry told Truman that he loved him.

62. Clarke, *Capote*, 364.

63. As Charles McAtee, the former Kansas director of penal institutions, told Plimpton: "Truman said he could not finish the book unless he witnessed the execution; he had to personally feel it" (Plimpton, 178). He owed everything to those boys riding the final "Big Swing"—his book, his success, his maturity. They had provided him with a compelling reason to escape himself and project his imagination into another subjectivity, an excuse to focus his artistic skills for years upon a spellbinding subject. In short, he owed them the extraordinary opportunity to "have a second chance" at writing and life. All in exchange for his daring to witness their lives. But that was his part of the deal and the description of the last swing with noose around necks was simply the final act of witnessing. The only problem was that Capote, the gossipy voyeur, famous for his social frivolity, had not anticipated that this was a different type of voyeurism.

64. Quoted in Clarke, *Capote*, 399.

65. Eric L. Santner, *On the Psychotheology of Everyday Life: Reflections on Freud and Rosenzweig* (Chicago: University of Chicago Press, 2001), 9.

66. Slavoj Zizek, *Welcome to the Desert of the Real* (New York: Wooster Press, 2001), 46.

Chapter Three

1. Robin Morgan, *The Demon Lover: The Roots of Terrorism* (New York: Washington Square Press, 2001), 19, 18.

2. Quoted in Morgan, *The Demon Lover*, 232.

3. Morgan, *The Demon Lover*, 33.

4. Morgan, *The Demon Lover*, xvi.

5. Joseba Zulaika, *Basque Violence: Metaphor and Sacrament* (Reno: University of Nevada Press, 1988), 182.

6. Giles Tremlett, "ETA Brings Women Fighters to the Fore," *Guardian*, August 27, 2002, 12.

7. Morgan, *The Demon Lover*, 24.

8. Morgan, *The Demon Lover*, 24.

9. Oriana Fallaci, *A Man*, trans. William Weaver (New York: Simon and Schuster, 1980), 11.

10. Fallaci, *A Man*, 156.

11. Fallaci, *A Man*, 17.

12. Fallaci, *A Man*, 17.

13. Santo L. Aricò, *Oriana Fallaci: The Woman and the Myth* (Carbondale: Southern Illinois University Press, 1998), 178.

14. Aricò, *Oriana Fallaci*, 192.

15. Roland Barthes, *A Lover's Discourse: Fragments* (New York: Farrar, Strauss and Giroux, 1978), 100.

16. Aricò, *Oriana Fallaci*, 184.

17. Fallaci, *A Man*, 55.

18. Fallaci, *A Man*, 126.

19. Aricò, *Oriana Fallaci*, 186.

20. Quoted in many places, including in Margaret Talbot, "The Agitator," *New Yorker*, June 5, 2006.

21. Fallaci, *A Man*, 23.

22. Fallaci, *A Man*, 23.

23. Fallaci, *A Man*, 27.

24. Fallaci, *A Man*, 28.

25. Fallaci, *A Man*, 33.

26. Fallaci, *A Man*, 50.

27. Fallaci, *A Man*, 75.

28. Fallaci, *A Man*, 79.

29. Fallaci, *A Man*, 148.

30. Fallaci, *A Man*, 150.

31. Judy Harris, "Oriana Fallaci—The Enjoyment of Hate," *Znet*, September 17, 2006.

32. Liz McGregor and John Hooper, "Oriana Fallaci: Obituary," *Guardian*, Sept. 16, 2006.

33. Fallaci, *A Man*, 158.

34. See, for instance, Shosana Felman, "After the Apocalypse: Paul de Man and the Fall to Silence," in Felman and Laub, *Testimony*, 151.

35. Jean Genet, *Prisoner of Love*, trans. Barbara Bray, intro. Edmund White (Hanover, N.H.: Wesleyan University Press, 1992).

36. Clifford Geertz, "Genet's Last Stand," *New York Review of Books*, November 1992, 3–5.

37. See Edmund White's introduction to the book.

38. Genet, *Prisoner of Love*, 101.

39. Genet, *Prisoner of Love*, 83.

40. Genet, *Prisoner of Love*, viii.

41. Quoted in Edmund White's introduction to *Prisoner of Love*, ix.

42. Genet, *Prisoner of Love*, 71.

43. Genet, *Prisoner of Love*, 186.

44. Genet, *Prisoner of Love*, 188.

45. Genet, *Prisoner of Love*, 38.

46. Genet, *Prisoner of Love*, 87.

47. Genet, *Prisoner of Love*, 222.

48. Genet, *Prisoner of Love*, 99.

49. Genet, *Prisoner of Love*, 41.

50. Genet, *Prisoner of Love*, 149.

51. Genet, *Prisoner of Love*, 223.

52. Genet, *Prisoner of Love*, 259.

53. Genet, *Prisoner of Love*, 226.

54. White, "Introduction," x.

55. Genet, *Prisoner of Love*, 97.

56. Genet, *Prisoner of Love*, 51.

57. Genet, *Prisoner of Love*, 257.

58. Genet, *Prisoner of Love*, 264.

59. Genet, *Prisoner of Love*, 341.

60. Genet, *Prisoner of Love*, 257.

61. Genet, *Prisoner of Love*, 246.

62. Genet, *Prisoner of Love*, 249.

63. Genet, *Prisoner of Love*, 204.

64. Genet, *Prisoner of Love*, 316.

65. Genet, *Prisoner of Love*, 144.

66. Genet, *Prisoner of Love*, 3.

67. Genet, *Prisoner of Love*, 149.

68. Genet, *Prisoner of Love*, 309.

69. Genet, *Prisoner of Love*, 88.

70. Genet, *Prisoner of Love*, 195.

71. Genet, *Prisoner of Love*, 211.

72. Genet, *Prisoner of Love*, 90.

73. Genet, *Prisoner of Love*, 117.

74. Genet, *Prisoner of Love*, 323.

75. Genet, *Prisoner of Love*, 27.

76. Genet, *Prisoner of Love*, 27.

77. Genet, *Prisoner of Love*, 149–50.

78. Genet, *Prisoner of Love*, 91.

79. Genet, *Prisoner of Love*, 308.

80. Genet, *Prisoner of Love*, 251.

81. Genet, *Prisoner of Love*, 308.

82. Genet, *Prisoner of Love*, 338.

83. Genet, *Prisoner of Love*, 375.

84. Among Basque rebels, too, the day after the death of the first ETA activist, Txabi Etxebarrieta, the sculptor Jorge Oteiza decided to place a Pietà on the frontispiece of the Marian Basilica of Aranzazu, "with the mother screaming to the sky for her dead son."

85. Genet, *Prisoner of Love*, 272.

86. Genet, *Prisoner of Love*, 301.

87. Genet, *Prisoner of Love*, 325–26.

88. Genet, *Prisoner of Love*, 159.

89. Genet, *Prisoner of Love*, 11.

90. Genet, *Prisoner of Love*, 51.

91. Genet, *Prisoner of Love*, 52–53.

92. Genet, *Prisoner of Love*, 247.

93. Zulaika, *Basque Violence*, 159–86.

94. Genet, *Prisoner of Love*, 285.

95. Genet, *Prisoner of Love*, 53.

96. Genet, *Prisoner of Love*, 179.

97. Barthes, *A Lover's Discourse*, 11.

98. Barthes, *A Lover's Discourse*, 39.

99. Barthes, *A Lover's Discourse*, 42–43.

100. M. Thomas Inge, *Truman Capote: Conversations* (Jackson: University Press of Mississippi, 1987), 57–58.

101. Quoted in Morgan, *Demon Lover*, xx.

102. Quoted in *The 9/11 Commission Report: Final Report of the National Commission on Terrorist Attacks upon the United States* (New York: W. W. Norton, 2004), 52.

103. Morgan, *Demon Lover*, xxii.

104. Barthes, *A Lover's Discourse*, 59.

105. Inge, *Truman Capote*, 60.

106. Barthes, *A Lover's Discourse*, 94.

107. Roy Rappaport, *Ecology, Meaning, and Religion* (Richmond, Calif.: North Atlantic Books, 1979). Ritual is performative and therefore nonverbal in substantial aspects. Its action might be reduced to indexical pointing. Language itself is essentially performative in a ritual context. Furthermore, ritual form displays a typically cybernetic "negative character" in the manner of a thermostat switching on and off—it considers alternative possibilities that did *not* occur in a sort of reductio ad absurdum. Such negative form befits the workings of desire, which inscribes itself *negatively* in language. In anthropological thinking, ritual is needed to act out in a performance the structural relations of a culture. In this sense it becomes *the* basic social act that includes the social contract and any sense of morality.

108. Barthes, *A Lover's Discourse*, 100.

109. Joan Copjec, *Read My Desire: Lacan against the Historicists* (Cambridge: MIT Press, 1994), 169–79.

110. Copjec, *Read My Desire*, 171.

111. Copjec, *Read My Desire*, 174.

112. I borrow the expression "playing terrorist" from Begoña Aretxaga. It is an activity she attributed to young Basque street saboteurs as well as to the Spanish state.

113. Copjec, *Read My Desire*, 176.

114. Copjec, *Read My Desire*, 14.

115. Copjec, *Read My Desire*, 178.

Chapter Four

1. Jerome New, ed., *In Memoriam Norman O. Brown* (Santa Cruz: New Pacific Press, 2005), 48.

2. See Paul Ricoeur, *Freud and Philosophy: An Essay on Interpretation*, trans. Denis Savage (New Haven: Yale University Press, 1970).

3. Quoted in Ricoeur, *Freud and Philosophy*, 289.

4. Ricoeur, *Freud and Philosophy*, 292.

5. Ricoeur, *Freud and Philosophy*, 299.

6. Ricoeur, *Freud and Philosophy*, 300.

7. Ricoeur, *Freud and Philosophy*, 301.

8. Morgan, *Demon Lover*, xxii.

9. Joseba Zulaika, *Chivos y soldados: La mili como ritual de iniciación* (San Sebastián: Baroja, 1989), 31–34.

10. Kurt Vonnegut, *Slaughterhouse-Five* (New York: Laurel, 1966), 15.

11. In the words of his biographer Gerald Clarke, after most likely having taken an overdose of pills and having been awakened by Joanne Carson, "given a choice between life and death, he chose death" (*Capote: A Biography* [New York: Carroll and Graf, 2005], 546). Had Capote allowed her to call the paramedics over the three or four morning hours of delay, "Truman's life probably could have been saved." "Just let me go. I know exactly what I am doing," he said to her, while he continued talking, mostly about his mother.

12. Yukio Mishima, *The Way of the Samurai: Yukio Mishima on* Hagakere *in Modern Life*, trans. Kathryn Sparling (New York: Perigee, 1977).

13. Mishima, *The Way of the Samurai*, 5–6.

14. Mishima, *The Way of the Samurai*, 7.

15. Mishima, *The Way of the Samurai*, 28.

16. Mishima, *The Way of the Samurai*, 103.

17. Mishima, *The Way of the Samurai*, 104–5.

18. Teo Uriarte, *Mirando atrás: De las filas de ETA a las listas del PSE* (Barcelona: Ediciones B, 2005), 90.

19. Robert A. Pape, *Dying to Win: The Strategic Logic of Suicide Terrorism* (New York: Random House, 2005), 79; Mia Bloom, *Dying to Kill: The Allure of Suicide Terror* (New York: Columbia University Press, 2005), 91.

20. Etxebarrieta was a twenty-four-year-old economist considered to be the most brilliant student in his class, a writer who had produced four books of poetry, a young man impregnated with the tragic sense of life and the existential philosophy of Bilbao's (his city's) most important author, Miguel de Unamuno, about whom he had written an essay. He was a sentimental lovesick man who at the time of his death carried in his wallet the photo of his love. Yet he was suddenly a murderer. How had it all come to this? Who was he really? Yes, ETA's propaganda had made it plain by then, in a text written by Etxebarrieta himself, that "any day now we will have a dead body on the table," but now it was no longer mere rhetoric. The revolutionary discourse spoke of readiness to sacrifice everything for the country, including one's life. But now the urgent issue for Etxebarrieta was how to face the man on the road murdered by him.

21. Pape, *Dying to Win*.

22. Yoram Schwitzer, ed., *Female Suicide Bombers: Dying for Equality* (Tel Aviv: Tel Aviv University, Jaffee Center for Strategic Studies, 2006).

23. Christopher Reuter, *My Life Is a Weapon: A Modern History of Suicide Bombing*, trans. Helena Ragg-Kirkby (Princeton: Princeton University Press, 2002).

24. Bloom, *Dying to Kill.*

25. See Lawrence Wright, *The Looming Tower: Al-Qaeda and the Road to 9/11* (New York: Alfred A. Knopf, 2006), 219.

26. Quoted in Alenka Zupancic, *The Ethics of the Real* (London: Verso, 2000), 11.

27. N. Hassan, quoted in Andrew Silke, ed., *Terrorists, Victims and Society: Psychological Perspectives on Terrorism and Its Consequences* (Chichester: Wiley, 2003), 97.

28. See the work of Anne Speckhard and Khapta Akhmedova, "Black Widows: The Chechen Female Suicide Terrorists," in *Female Suicide Bombers*, ed. Schwitzer, 63–80.

29. Roland Barthes, *A Lover's Discourse: Fragments* (New York: Farrar, Strauss and Giroux, 1978), 142.

30. Barthes, *A Lover's Discourse*, 218.

31. Pompeius Festus, quoted in Giorgio Agamben, *Homo Sacer: Sovereign Power and Bare Life* (Stanford: Stanford University Press, 1998), 71.

32. See Joseba Zulaika and William A. Douglass, *Terror and Taboo: The Follies, Fables, and Faces of Terrorism* (New York: Routledge, 1996), chapter 6.

33. One only has to recall the reports in January 2007 regarding the legal defense of the Guantánamo prisoners. The senior Pentagon official in charge of military detainees suspected of terrorism, Charles D. Stimson, was simply "dismayed" that lawyers at many of America's top law firms were representing the prisoners; he asked them point blank to sever their ties with Guantánamo clients. He characterized the five hundred lawyers from about 120 law firms who volunteered to represent the prisoners as having to "choose between representing terrorists or representing reputable firms," thereby intentionally linking them to terrorism in the eyes of corporate America. Leaving aside the well-proven fact that a great many of the Guantánamo detainees do not deserve imprisonment, only the figure of the loathsome Terrorist could justify a public official's open dismissal of the fundamental American value that even the most heinous villain has a right to legal counsel. Fortunately, in three cases the U.S. Supreme Court upheld the legal rights of the detainees.

34. Agamben, *Homo Sacer*, 82.

35. This was most dramatically revealed in the Stalker affair in Great Britain. John Stalker was the police officer in charge of investigating the killing of six unarmed Irish youths by the Ulster police; he was relieved of his post when he was on the verge of uncovering that a shoot-to-kill policy was in place. See John Stalker, *Stalker: Ireland, "Shoot to Kill" and the "Affair"* (Harmondsworth, U.K.: Penguin, 1988).

36. Agamben, *Homo Sacer*, 114.

37. Ariel Merari, Statement before the Special Oversight Panel on Terrorism,

Terrorism and Threats to US Interests in the Middle East (Washington, D.C.: U.S. Congress, 2000), 10.

38. Marc Sageman, *Understanding Terror Networks* (Philadelphia: University of Pennsylvania Press, 2004), 184.

39. A classical study of ritual sacrifice in which the role of drawing lots is examined is René Girard, *Violence and the Sacred*, trans. Patrick Gregory (Baltimore: Johns Hopkins University Press, 1977).

40. Jacques Derrida, *Donner la mort* (Paris: Transition, 1992).

41. See William A. Douglass and Joseba Zulaika, "On the Interpretation of Terrorist Violence: ETA and the Basque Political Process," *Comparative Studies in Society and History* 32 (April 1990): 238–57.

42. Sageman, *Understanding Terror Networks*, 172.

43. In a seminal paper that preceded the development of cybernetics, Arturo Rosenblueth, Norbert Wiener, and Julian Bigelow stated that "purposefulness . . . is quite independent of causality, initial or final" and that they considered it "a concept necessary for the understanding of certain modes of behavior" ("Behavior, Purpose, and Teleology," *Philosophy of Science* 10 [1943]: 19). In general the structure of the terrorist act implies a triangular relationship among perpetrator, victim, and target audience. The counterterrorism literature distinguishes between the victim who is the "target of violence" and the wider group that is the "target of terror." There is an "externality" to the chance logic of terrorism from the viewpoint of the victims; the hostages cannot influence the behavior of the skyjackers whose ultimate target of terror lies beyond what is happening on the plane. On the basis of the subdivision of purposeful behavior's aspects as teleological ("feedback") and nonteleological ("non-feedback"), the terrorists have created a purposeful but nonteleological system without recourse to imma-nent feedback and purpose.

44. Rosenblueth et al., "Behavior," 19.

45. Norman O. Brown, *Life Against Death: The Psychoanalytical Meaning of History* (Middletown: Wesleyan University Press, 1959), 83.

46. Brown, *Life Against Death*, 80.

47. Herbert Marcuse, *Eros and Civilization: A Philosophical Inquiry into Freud* (Boston: Beacon Press, 1955), 8.

48. David Greenham, *The Resurrection of the Body: The Work of Norman O. Brown* (Lanham, Md.: Lexington Books, 2006), 57.

49. Ricoeur, *Freud and Philosophy*, 319.

50. Brown, *Life Against Death*, 16.

51. Brown, *Life Against Death*, 17.

52. Brown, *Life Against Death*, 99.

53. Quoted in Wright, *The Looming Tower*, 4.

54. Ricoeur, *Freud and Philosophy*, 308–9.

Chapter Five

1. Albert Camus, *The Rebel* (New York: Alfred A. Knopf), 53.

2. Slavoj Zizek, "What Some Would Call...: A Response to Yannis Stavrakakis," *Umbra* (2003), 133.

3. Begoña Aretxaga, "The Death of Yoyes: Cultural Discourses of Gender and Politics in the Basque Country," in Begoña Aretxaga, *States of Terror: Begoña Aretxaga's Essays* (Reno: Center for Basque Studies, University of Nevada, 2005), 158.

4. Aretxaga, "The Death of Yoyes," 161.

5. Aretxaga's writing about Yoyes is an exemplary intellectual engagement. Aretxaga herself had been involved in Basque politics and could identify with Yoyes's commitment to activism, followed by disappointment and refuge in writing. Later, when she came to the United States to study anthropology, she described her position as one "characterized by a displacement from militancy by academic writing and a displacement from academic writing by past militancy" (*States of Terror*, 134). The essay on Yoyes was a difficult one to write; it was intellectual witnessing as a tug-of-war, almost exorcism, to elucidate and transform the meaning of Yoyes's and her own life experience shared by Basques involved in radical nationalist politics. Aretxaga was once again risking her own subjectivity by writing in a testimonial manner about Yoyes, thereby documenting the disturbing events and violent transformations experienced by her generation.

6. Elixabete Garmendia et al., *Yoyes desde su ventana* (Pamplona: Garrasi, 1987), 57.

7. Garmendia, *Yoyes*, 72.

8. Garmendia, *Yoyes*, 52.

9. Garmendia, *Yoyes*, 62–63.

10. Cameron Watson points out that that the influence of *The Second Sex* on Yoyes was fundamental in two respects: the existentialist doctrine that defines a person by her or his capacity for *action*, and the feminism that postulates a female subject beyond any reciprocal dependency upon the male ("The Tragedy of Yoyes," in *Amatxi, Amuma, Amona: Writings in Honor of Basque Women*, ed. Linda White and Cameron Watson [Reno: Center for Basque Studies, 2003], 137.)

11. Garmendia, *Yoyes*, 212.

12. Garmendia, *Yoyes*, 72.

13. Garmendia, *Yoyes*, 65.

14. Garmendia, *Yoyes*, 88.

15. Garmendia, *Yoyes*, 218.

16. Garmendia, *Yoyes*, 217.

17. Garmendia, *Yoyes*, 116.

18. Garmendia, *Yoyes*, 40.

19. Garmendia, *Yoyes*, 57.

20. Garmendia, *Yoyes*, 57.

21. Garmendia, *Yoyes*, 173.

22. Garmendia, *Yoyes*, 9.

23. Garmendia, *Yoyes*, 203.

24. Garmendia, *Yoyes*, 67.

25. Garmendia, *Yoyes*, 68.

26. Garmendia, *Yoyes*, 80–81.

27. Garmendia, *Yoyes*, 37.

28. Garmendia, *Yoyes*, 130.

29. Garmendia, *Yoyes*, 130–31.

30. Garmendia, *Yoyes*, 137.

31. Garmendia, *Yoyes*, 148.

32. Garmendia, *Yoyes*, 162.

33. Garmendia, *Yoyes*, 128.

34. Quoted in Garmendia, *Yoyes*, 143.

35. Garmendia, *Yoyes*, 166.

36. Garmendia, *Yoyes*, 194.

37. Garmendia, *Yoyes*, 196.

38. Garmendia, *Yoyes*, 206.

39. Garmendia, *Yoyes*, 184–85.

40. Garmendia, *Yoyes*, 206.

41. Garmendia, *Yoyes*, 191–92.

42. Garmendia, *Yoyes*, 206.

43. Garmendia, *Yoyes*, 163.

44. Garmendia, *Yoyes*, 206.

45. Garmendia, *Yoyes*, 68.

46. Joan Copjec, "The Tomb of Perseverance: On Antigone," in *Giving Ground: The Politics of Propinquity*, ed. Joan Copjec and Michael Sorkin (London: Verso, 1999), 258.

47. Copjec, "The Tomb," 262.

48. Copjec, "The Tomb," 237.

49. Judith Butler, *Antigone's Claim: Kinship between Life and Death* (New York: Columbia University Press, 2000), 2.

50. Alain Badiou, *Metapolitics*, trans. Jason Barker (London: Verso, 2005), 141–45.

51. Garmendia, *Yoyes*, 207.

52. Butler, *Antigone's Claim*, 5.

53. Butler, *Antigone's Claim*, 10.

54. Butler, *Antigone's Claim*, 11.

55. Garmendia, *Yoyes*, 187–88.

56. Garmendia, *Yoyes*, 186–87.

57. Garmendia, *Yoyes*, 27.

58. Butler, *Antigone's Claim*, 27.

59. María Zambrano, *La tumba de Antígona* (Madrid: Siglo XXI, 1967), 26–27.

60. Zambrano, *La tumba*, 21–22.

61. Garmendia, *Yoyes*, 111.

62. Garmendia, *Yoyes*, 110.

63. Butler, *Antigone's Claim*, 46.

64. Butler, *Antigone's Claim*, 47.

65. Zambrano, *La tumba*, 30.

66. Slavoj Zizek, *The Ticklish Subject: The Absent Center of Political Ontology* (London: Verso, 2000), 264.

67. Zizek, "What Some Would Call," 133.

68. Zambrano, *La tumba*, 20–21.

69. Corinthians 1:15.

70. Alain Badiou, *Saint Paul: The Foundation of Universalism*, trans. Ray Brassier (Stanford: Stanford University Press, 2003). Badiou radically secularizes the mythical core of Christian resurrection to counterpose, in the field of thought and the subject, "the invention of life" against "the invention of death."

71. The Spanish government of the socialist José Luis Rodriguez Zapatero and Herri Batasuna, ETA's political wing, after having held secret conversations for four years, did clearly signal that an end to the violence was at hand when ETA observed a cease-fire from March 2006 and throughout 2007. Yet key state apparatuses (in particular the judiciary, largely selected by the former government of José María Aznar, and a significant sector of the media), as well as irredentists in ETA itself, were opposed to a settlement that the overwhelming majority of Basques demand.

Chapter Six

1. George Rudé, *Robespierre* (Englewood Cliffs, N.J.: Prentice-Hall, 1967), 76.

2. Slavoj Zizek, "Robespierre, or, The 'Divine Violence' of Terror," introduction to Maximilien Robespierre, *Virtue and Terror* (London: Verso, 2007), xvii.

3. Tim Weiner, *Legacy of Ashes* (New York: Doubleday, 2007), 42–43.

4. Weiner, *Legacy*, 47.

5. Weiner, *Legacy*, 54.

6. Weiner, *Legacy*, 54.

7. Peter Sichel, quoted in Weiner, *Legacy*, 54.

8. Allen Dulles, quoted in Thomas Powers, *The Man Who Kept the Secrets: Richard Helms and the CIA* (New York: Alfred A. Knopf, 1979), 46.

9. Quoted in Powers, *The Man*, 59.

10. Quoted in Weiner, *Legacy*, 378.

11. Steve Coll, *Ghost Wars: The Secret History of the CIA, Afghanistan, and*

bin Laden, from the Soviet Invasion to September 10, 2001 (New York: Penguin, 2004), 92.

12. Frances Stonor Saunders, *The Cultural Cold War: The CIA and the World of Arts and Letters* (New York: New Press, 1999), 248.

13. Quoted in Saunders, *Cultural Cold War*, 249.

14. Quoted in Saunders, *Cultural Cold War*, 38.

15. Saunders, *Cultural Cold War*, 83.

16. Saunders, *Cultural Cold War*, 83.

17. Quoted in Saunders, *Cultural Cold War*, 97.

18. Saunders, *Cultural Cold War*, 259.

19. Kennan interview for CNN, 1996, National Security Archive transcript, http://www.cnn.com/SPECIALS/cold.war/episodes/01/interviews/kennan.

20. Kennan interview for CNN.

21. Weiner, *Legacy*, 27.

22. Quoted in Weiner, *Legacy*, 73.

23. Weiner, *Legacy*, 92.

24. Quoted in Weiner, *Legacy*, 141.

25. The best-known case is the overthrow of Guatemala's socialist-leaning Jacobo Arbenz who passed a land reform program in a country of impoverished farmers in which 2% of the population controlled 72% of the land, of which only 12% was being farmed. The 2% of upper-class landowners and American corporate interests resented the reform. The CIA had no spies in Guatemala and knew nothing about the political situation or of the support enjoyed by Arbenz, but it deemed this should be one more battleground in the war against communism. Toppling Arbenz would require the help of friends such as Nicaraguan dictator Anastasio Somoza, an arms embargo imposed by the United States, the threat of an American invasion, the usual campaign of propaganda lies and bribery, formulation of a list of fifty-eight Guatemalans marked and approved by the CIA for assassination, as well as a blockade by U.S. Navy warships and submarines—in short, in the words of the CIA's E. Howard Hunt, "what we wanted to do was to have a terror campaign" (Wiener, *Legacy*, 99). But it was not enough; in the end the CIA convinced Eisenhower to send planes to bomb military positions in Guatemala City. Forty years of military repression, death squads, and tens of thousands of dead were awaiting Guatemala.

26. Weiner, *Legacy*, 142.

27. The man who captured and sent Lumumba to his death was Mobutu Sese Seko, the man picked up by the CIA to be the Congo's dictator and the guarantor of American interests on the continent for the next thirty years. Another dictator who had held power for thirty years with the help of the U.S. government was Gen. Rafael Trujillo of the Dominican Republic, a brutal man who would hang his enemies from meat hooks and who had become an international embarrassment. Thus, the CIA, with Kennedy's approval, dispatched in the American diplomatic

pouch the pistols that would be used by Dominican conspirators to assassinate Trujillo.

28. Weiner, *Legacy*, 190.

29. Weiner, *Legacy*, 192–93.

30. Weiner, *Legacy*, 279.

31. With Kennedy's and Johnson's approval, the CIA had already subverted the 1964 elections by infusing about a dollar per Chilean vote through the Catholic Church and the trade unions on behalf of pro-American Eduardo Frei. As the 1970 elections were approaching, Kissinger was worried about Allende and started feeding cash for political warfare against him: "I don't see why we have to let a country go Marxist just because its people are irresponsible" (quoted in Weiner, 307), he declared. What began as a campaign to buy votes ended up sending automatic weapons for military conspirators and would-be assassins. The CIA spent millions to create political and economic chaos. The September 11, 1973, coup led to Gen. Augusto Pinochet's murder of more than thirty-two hundred people and the jailing and torturing of tens of thousands. The head of the Chilean intelligence service, Manuel Contreras, went so far as to assassinate Allende's ambassador, Orlando Letelier, in Washington with a car bomb on the premise that he could get away with it by threatening to blackmail the United States by airing his secret deals with the CIA.

32. Powers, *The Man*, 9.

33. See Robert M. Gates, *From the Shadows: The Ultimate Insider's Story of Five Presidents and How They Won the Cold War* (New York: Simon and Schuster, 1996), 143–49.

34. Chalmers Johnson, *Nemesis: The Last Days of the American Republic* (New York: Macmillan, 2007), 110.

35. Quoted in Johnson, *Nemesis*, 110.

36. See Noam Chomsky, *The Culture of Terrorism* (Boston: South End Press, 1988).

37. Leonard Weinberg and William Eubank, "Political Terrorism and Political Development," in *Terrorism and Political Violence: Limits and Possibilities of Legal Control*, ed. H. Han (New York: Oceania, 1993), 32.

38. George F. Kennan, *Around the Cragged Hill: A Personal and Political Philosophy* (New York: W. W. Norton, 1993), 115 and 182.

39. Kennan, *Around the Cragged Hill*, 183.

40. Milt Bearden, quoted in Weiner, *Legacy*, 431.

41. Brian Jenkins, "Future Trends in International Terrorism," in *Current Perspectives on International Terrorism*, ed. R. Slater and M. Stohl (New York: St. Martin's, 1988), 246–66.

42. According to the annual *Patterns of Global Terrorism* reports, there was no single terrorist fatality in the United States during the years 1986–92. The

numbers for Americans killed and wounded worldwide during those years were: in 1986, 12 killed and 100 wounded; in 1987, 7 killed and 47 wounded; in 1988, 192 killed (189 in the Pan Am Flight 103) and 40 wounded; in 1989, 16 killed and 19 wounded; in 1990, 10 killed and 19 wounded; in 1991, 7 killed; in 1992, 2 killed and 1 wounded.

43. Ronald Hinkley, "American Opinion toward Terrorism: The Reagan Years," *Terrorism* 12 (1989): 388.

44. Martin Schulz, quoted in Alan Cowell, "Possible German Role in Russian Plutonium Deal Is Investigated," *New York Times*, May 18, 1995, A4.

45. Arthur Miller, *Timebends* (New York: Grove Press, 1987), 160.

46. Saunders, *The Cultural Cold War*.

47. Johnson, *Nemesis*, 277.

48. Johnson, *Nemesis*, 271.

49. Gore Vidal, *Perpetual War for Perpetual Peace: How We Got to Be So Hated* (New York: Nation Books, 2002), 22–40.

50. Quoted in Richard Jackson, *Writing the War on Terrorism: Language, Politics and Counter-Terrorism* (Manchester: Manchester University Press, 2005), 67.

51. Slavoj Zizek, *The Parallax View* (Cambridge: MIT Press, 2006), 152.

52. Alain Badiou, *Ethics: An Essay on the Understanding of Evil*, trans. Peter Hallward (London: Verso, 2001), 61.

53. For a provocative summary of the notion of evil in the history of philosophy, see Javier Echeverria, *La ciencia del bien y del mal* (Barcelona: Herder, 2007).

54. Thomas E. Ricks, *Fiasco: The American Military Adventure in Iraq* (New York: Penguin, 2006), 16.

55. Ricks, *Fiasco*, 30.

56. James Fallows, "The Fifty-first State," *Atlantic Monthly*, November 2002.

57. Amos Oz, quoted in Avishai Margalit, "The Uses of the Holocaust," *New York Review of Books*, February 17, 1994, 1, 4, 10.

58. Quoted in Peter Kornbluh, "CIA Outrages in Chile," *Nation*, October 16, 2000.

59. Quoted in Weiner, *Legacy*, 105.

60. Powers. *The Man*, 119.

61. Powers, *The Man*, 120.

62. Weiner, *Legacy*, 184.

63. General Andrew Goodpaster, quoted in Weiner, *Legacy*, 157–58.

64. Powers, *The Man*, 129.

65. Quoted in Weiner, *Legacy*, 338 and 339.

66. Weiner, *Legacy*, 78.

67. Quoted in Weiner, *Legacy*, 198.

68. Quoted in Weiner, *Legacy*, 276.

69. Weiner, *Legacy*, 450.

70. Duane Clarridge (head of CIA operations in Latin America during the 1980s, where he was involved in the contra end of the Iran-contra affair), quoted in Weiner, *Legacy*, 414.

71. Quoted in Weiner, *Legacy*, 336.

72. Rodney Needham, "Dual Sovereignty," in Rodney Needham, *Reconnaissances* (Toronto: University of Toronto Press, 1980), 65.

73. Edward E. Evans-Pritchard, *The Divine Kingship of the Shilluk of the Nilotic Sudan* (Cambridge: At the University Press, 1948).

Chapter Seven

1. John Mueller, *Overblown: How Politicians and the Terrorism Industry Inflate National Security Threats, and Why We Believe Them* (New York: Free Press, 2006), 2, 13.

2. Mueller, *Overblown*, 15-24.

3. For a history of this radical change in nuclear nonproliferation policy, see Joseph Cirincione, *Bomb Scare: The History and Future of Nuclear Weapons* (New York: Columbia University Press, 2007).

4. For a critical assessment of Walzer's perspective, see Talal Asad, *On Suicide Bombing* (New York: Columbia University Press, 2007).

5. The epistemological rupture consists in that, without ETA, the possibilities of obtaining the maximum levels of Basque self-government are currently more real than ever, whereas with ETA they are nil. This does not invalidate the opposite argument that, without ETA, most probably the current levels of Basque self-government could not have obtained. The traumatic excess of ETA implies the radical fracture not only among the various political identities living in Basque society but within the Basque nationalist community as well. In short, there is the irony that ETA's "return" is also the denial of ETA's project of a separate Basque nation. Such a paradox leads to situations that are closer to "madness" than to a viable political project. Any semblance of practical reality is ignored in order to espouse the utopian "independence" of an idealized nation that is nowhere on the horizon. The increasingly polarized and foreclosed political domain leads thus to a maddening situation. That is, "the paradox that this form of *willing* the nation into being appears to be destroying it" (Begoña Aretxaga, *States of Terror: Begoña Aretxaga's Essays* [Reno: Center for Basque Studies, University of Nevada, 2005], 247).

6. Quoted in Aretxaga, *States of Terror*, 248.

7. Michel Foucault, *Madness and Civilization: A History of Insanity in the Age of Reason*, trans. Richard Howard (New York: Random House, 1988), x.

8. Foucault, *Madness and Civilization*, 22-23.

9. Foucault, *Madness and Civilization*, 16.

10. Foucault, *Madness and Civilization*, 57.

11. Foucault, *Madness and* Civilization, 38.

12. Foucault, *Madness and Civilization*, 39.

13. Shoshana Felman, *Writing and Madness (Literature/Philosophy/Psychoanalysis)*, trans. Martha Noel Evans and Shoshana Felman (Ithaca: Cornell University Press, 1985), 36.

14. Felman, *Writing and Madness*, 52.

15. Felman, *Writing and Madness*, 55.

16. Paul Wilkinson, *Terrorism and the Liberal State* (New York: New York University Press, 1986).

17. Aretxaga, *States of Terror*, 253.

18. Aretxaga, *States of Terror*, 256.

19. Michael Taussig, *The Magic of the State* (New York: Routledge, 1997).

20. Aretxaga, *States of Terror*, 266.

21. The crisis of the European Union, after the failure of France, Ireland, and the Netherlands to ratify its constitution in referendums in 2005, underscores the reluctance of the citizenry to accept integration into a supranational state. In short, while the sharing of some sovereignty in economic, environmental, and security matters by the European states is irreversible, at the same time those very entities are asserting themselves as the basic components of such a super-state network.

22. Spain, for example, has succeeded in keeping Catalonia and the Basque Country under military and political control, but the project of Spain as a true nation-state has failed to fully impose its language upon all of the citizenry or to abolish Catalan and Basque identities. In the "state of autonomous communities" that emerged in post-Franco Spain, both Catalonia and the Basque Country, despite their long historical record as distinctive countries with strong linguistic and cultural identities, were treated as two more "autonomies" equal to other provinces and regions that have no comparable nationalist history nor similar aspirations to greater self-government. Presently, after twenty-five years of autonomy, both Catalonia and the Basque Country are involved in the difficult political process of reconfiguring their Statutes of Autonomy. Their requests for more self-government are met with suspicion by the rest of Spain's autonomous communities, not to mention the central government. In the case of the Basques, their president proposed in 2002 a new statute that included, ominously for some, "the right of the Basques to decide their future." In theory it can be said that democracy affirms the right of a political community to decide its destiny. In practice, the Spanish Constitution does not recognize the right of self-determination of any of its historical nationalities, and it assumes in unambiguous terms that sovereignty is the prerogative of the Spanish state alone.

23. As an instance of the extent to which the potentialities intrinsic to the constitution are a matter of political interpretation, there is the debate on the reform of the Catalan Statute of Autonomy that took place in November 2005.

The conservative Popular Party argued acrimoniously that the proposed reform was unconstitutional, whereas other parties found it well within constitutional purview.

24. See Joxerramon Bengoetxea, *La Europa Peter Pan: El constitucionalismo europeo en la encrucijada* (Oñate: IVAP, 2005), chapter 4.

25. Not surprisingly, the very structure of the Spanish state of autonomies is central to the debate. As Juan Luis Cebrián, the first director of the most influential Spanish newspaper, *El País*, wrote on the occasion of the first anniversary of Socialist prime minister José Luis Rodriguez Zapatero's post-Aznar Spain, "The great unfinished business of Rodriguez Zapatero . . . is the reorganization of what is called the territorial question and that makes reference rather to the reform of the structure of the State" ("Estado de la nación y Estado federal," *El País*, May 11, 2005). And he went on to propose without hesitation a federal Spain:

> [T]he increasing weakness of the nation-state, overwhelmed by globalization, has led to expansion the political spaces, a phenomenon whose most obvious example is the European Union. Inside it live side-by-side great and small states, poor and rich ones, with sometimes immense differences among themselves. The citizens of all those countries enjoy, in principle, the same individual liberties. But their identities, and their needs, are different. The only way to solve the apparent contradiction between the freedom they are entitled to as citizens and the recognition of the right to self-government they claim as countries resides in the most successful experiment among those carried out by the political practice throughout history: the federal method.

The application of a comparable model to Europe—whose increasing federalism Cebrián sees as unavoidable—and to Spain's multinational reality appears to be the logical solution to the present Catalan and Basque conundrums. Scotland, Belgium, Northern Ireland, and Sri Lanka provide similar cases. But "logic" is the least of concerns when the state perceives any of its tentacular powers to be at stake.

Cebrián's article was preceded by a series of reports by *El País* about "the waning State." Contrary to the perception of those who view the state as a giant, except for Social Security funds the Spanish state's treasury administers only 19% of public revenues, the rest falling under the control of the autonomous governments. Between 1995 and 1999 alone, the Spanish state lost 60% of its employees, while the autonomous administrations have increased their personnel by about 68%. The number of workers employed by the central state is comparable to the number found in an autonomous government such as that of the region of Andalucia. Since Franco's regime was known for its centralization, now anything in the opposite direction is considered to be more democratic and efficient. This has raised the alarm as to how to stop such a centrifugal dynamic. The insatiable demand for transferring more and more governmental responsibilities coming from the peripheral nationalities has brought accusations from the centrists of permanent blackmail. The fact is that the central state still has the opportunity to politically maneuver and please the "friendly" autonomies—thus Andalucia, governed by the Socialists, had to wait until Aznar left office and the Socialist Zapatero took power in order to receive the 3.7 billion euros it was due from the central government. Such hard bargaining between the state and the autonomies is becoming one more aspect of the autonomous puzzle, giving rise to fears that the very survival of the State of Autonomies engineered by the post-Franco Spanish democracy is in question.

26. Jacques Derrida, "A Dialogue with Jacques Derrida," in G. Borradori, *Philosophy in a Time of Terror: Dialogues with Jurgen Habermas and Jacques Derrida* (Chicago: University of Chicago Press, 2003), 94. See also Jacques Derrida, *Rogues: Two Essays on Reason* (Stanford: Stanford University Press, 2005), 157.

27. Derrida, "A Dialogue," 187–88.

28. Derrida, "A Dialogue," 113.

29. Cirincione, *Bomb Scare.*

30. Cirincione, *Bomb Scare*, 106.

31. Jason Epstein, "Hurry Up Please It's Time," *New York Review of Books*, March 15, 2007, 4.

32. Epstein, "Hurry Up," 4.

33. Cirincione, *Bomb Scare*, 117.

34. Hannah Arendt, *On Violence* (New York: Harcourt, Brace and World, 1969), 14.

Chapter Eight

1. Neil MacFarquhar, "In Bombing, a Deluge of Details," *New York Times*, March 19, 1995, A9.

2. Editorial, "The Trial of Omar Abdel Rahman," *New York Times*, October 3, 1995, A14.

3. John Miller and Michael Stone, *The Cell: Inside the 9/11 Plot and Why the FBI and CIA Failed to Spot It* (New York: Hyperion, 2002), 148.

4. Lawrence Wright, *The Looming Tower: Al-Qaeda and the Road to 9/11* (New York: Alfred A. Knopf, 2006), 6.

5. Joseba Zulaika and William A. Douglass, *Terror and Taboo: The Follies, Fables, and Faces of Terrorism* (New York: Routledge, 1996), 228, 232–33.

6. Dipak K. Gupta, *Understanding Terrorism and Political Violence: The Life Cycle of Birth, Growth, Transformation, and Demise* (London: Routledge, 2008), 140.

7. Steve Coll, *Ghost Wars: The Secret History of the CIA, Afghanistan, and bin Laden, from the Soviet Invasion to September 10, 2001* (London: Penguin, 2004), 50.

8. Coll, *Ghost Wars*, 86.

9. Coll, *Ghost Wars*, 88.

10. Coll, *Ghost Wars*, 89.

11. Quoted in Coll, *Ghost Wars*, 104.

12. Coll, *Ghost Wars*, 93.

13. Quoted in Coll, *Ghost Wars*, 105.

14. Milton Bearden, the CIA station chief in Islamabad from 1986 to 1989 who had been in charge of funding and training the Afghan anti-Soviet guerrillas, quoted in Coll, *Ghost Wars*, 147.

15. Quoted in Coll, *Ghost Wars*, 129.

16. Coll, *Ghost Wars*, 168.

17. Coll, *Ghost Wars*, 204.

18. Coll, *Ghost Wars*, 209.

19. Coll, *Ghost Wars*, 211.

20. Coll, *Ghost Wars*, 238.

21. An Afghan exile quoted in Coll, *Ghost Wars*, 182.

22. Quoted in Coll, *Ghost Wars*, 465.

23. Quoted in Coll, *Ghost Wars*, 484.

24. Quoted in Coll, *Ghost Wars*, 9.

25. Coll, *Ghost Wars*, 9.

26. Andrew C. McCarthy, *Willful Blindness: A Memoir of the Jihad* (New York: Encounter Books, 2008), 120–121.

27. Robert Friedman, "The CIA's *Jihad*," *New Yorker*, March 27, 1995, 46–47.

28. Miller and Stone, *The Cell*.

29. Miller and Stone, *The Cell*, 74. El Sayyid Nosair had been arrested for the New York murder of Meir Kahane, the right-wing Israeli who advocated expelling non-Jews from Israel.

30. Miller and Stone, *The Cell*, 74.

31. Miller and Stone, *The Cell*, 88.

32. Miller and Stone, *The Cell*, 87.

33. Miller and Stone, *The Cell*, 114; emphasis added.

34. Quoted in Peter L. Bergen, *The Osama bin Laden I Know: An Oral History of al Qaeda's Leader* (New York: Free Press, 2006), 204–5. The date the fatwa was issued is not known.

35. Bergen, *Osama bin Laden I Know*, 204.

36. Bergen, *Osama bin Laden I Know*, 208.

37. Quoted in Bergen, *Osama bin Laden I Know*, 196.

38. Quoted in Bergen, *Osama bin Laden I Know*, 200.

39. Quoted in Bergen, *Osama bin Laden I Know*, 205.

40. Quoted in Bergen, *Osama bin Laden I Know*, 207.

41. Quotes in Bergen, *Osama bin Laden I Know*, 207.

42. Quoted in Bergen, *Osama bin Laden I Know*, 206.

43. Quoted in Bergen, *Osama bin Laden I Know*, 170.

44. Quoted in Bergen, *Osama bin Laden I Know*, 183–84.

45. Quoted in Bergen, *Osama bin Laden I Know*, 195.

46. Wright, *Looming Tower*, 280.

47. Anonymous [Michael Scheuer], *Imperial Hubris: Why the West Is Losing the War on Terror* (Washington, D.C.: Brassey's, 2004), 17.

48. Anonymous, *Imperial Hubris*, 19 and 168.

49. Quoted in Bergen, *Osama bin Laden I Know*, 182.

50. Quoted in Bergen, *Osama bin Laden I Know*, 203.

51. Quoted in Bergen, *Osama bin Laden I Know*, 216.

52. Quoted in Bergen, *Osama bin Laden I Know*, 207.

53. Quoted in Bergen, *Osama bin Laden I Know*, 208.

54. Miller and Stone, *The Cell*, 159.

55. Miller and Stone, *The Cell*, 191.

56. Miller and Stone, *The Cell*, 282.

57. Miller and Stone, *The Cell*, 297.

58. *The 9/11 Commission Report: Final Report of the National Commission on Terrorist Attacks upon the United States* (New York: W. W. Norton, 2004), 345.

59. Report, 345.

60. For a detailed account, see Wright, *Looming Tower*, 310–44.

61. Report, 272.

62. See Michael Isikoff and Daniel Klaidman, "The Hijackers We Let Escape," *Newsweek*, June 10, 2002, 20–28.

63. Mark Mazzetti, "C.I.A. Details Errors It Made before Sept.11," *New York Times*, August 22, 2007, A1.

64. Report, 272.

65. Report, 274.

66. Report, 275.

67. Report, 275.

68. Report, 276.

69. Gary Sick, *All Fall Down: America's Tragic Encounter with Iran* (New York: Random House, 1985), 42.

70. Wright, *Looming Tower*, 342.

71. Miller and Stone, *The Cell*, 74.

72. David Johnston and Eric Schmitt, "Uneven Response Seen to Terror Risk in Summer '01," *New York Times*, April 4, 2004, 22.

73. Richard Clarke, *Against All Enemies: Inside America's War on Terror* (New York: Free Press, 2004).

74. Philip Shenon, "Leaders of 9/11 Panel Say Attacks Were Probably Preventable," *New York Times*, April 5, 2004, A16.

75. In the case of the CIA, see Thomas Powers, *The Man Who Kept the Secrets: Richard Helms and the CIA* (New York: Alfred A. Knopf, 1979), 66.

76. John Mueller, *Overblown: How Politicians and the Terrorism Industry Inflate National Security Threats, and Why We Believe Them* (New York: Free Press, 2006), 1.

77. Marc Sageman, *Understanding Terror Networks* (Philadelphia: University of Pennsylvania Press, 2004), 56.

78. Friedman, "The CIA's *Jihad*," 38.

79. Fawaz A. Gerges, *The Far Enemy: Why Jihad Went Global* (Cambridge: Cambridge University Press, 2005), 178.

80. See Copjec, *Read My Desire*.

81. Chalmers A. Johnson, *Nemesis: The Last Days of the American Republic* (New York: Macmillan, 2007), 9.

82. Thomas E. Ricks, *Fiasco: The American Military Adventure in Iraq* (New York: Penguin, 2006), 22.

83. Ricks, *Fiasco*, 13.

84. Quoted in Ricks, *Fiasco*, 88.

85. Ricks, *Fiasco*, 30.

86. Ricks, *Fiasco*, 31; emphasis added.

87. Ricks, *Fiasco*, 128.

88. Quoted in Ricks, *Fiasco*, 87.

89. Ricks, *Fiasco*, 92.

90. See Zulaika and Douglass, *Terror and Taboo*, 54.

91. Frances Stonor Saunders, *The Cultural Cold War: The CIA and the World of Arts and Letters* (New York: New Press, 1999), 11.

92. Quoted in Ricks, *Fiasco*, 158.

93. Quoted in Ricks, *Fiasco*, 267.

94. Quoted in Ricks, *Fiasco*, 181.

95. Linda Robinson, *Tell Me How This Ends: General David Petraeus and the Search for a Way Out of Iraq* (New York: PublicAffairs, 2008), 70.

96. John Nagl, *Learning to Eat Soup with a Knife: Counterinsurgency Lessons from Malaya and Vietnam* (Chicago: University of Chicago Press, 2005).

97. Robinson, *Tell Me How This Ends*, 78.

98. Robinson, *Tell Me How This Ends*, 79.

99. Robinson, *Tell Me How This Ends*, 79.

100. David H. Petraeus, "Learning Counterinsurgency: Observations from Soldiering in Iraq," *Military Review* (January–February 2006): 1–14.

101. Petraeus, "Learning," 3.

102. Petraeus, "Learning," 8; emphasis added.

103. Robinson, *Tell Me How It Ends*, 177.

104. Robinson, *Tell Me How It Ends*, 233.

105. Robinson, *Tell Me How It Ends*, 252.

106. Frank Rich, *The Greatest Story Ever Sold: The Decline and Fall of Truth; From 9/11 to Katrina* (New York: Penguin, 2006), 4.

107. Peter Winch, "Understanding a Primitive Society," in *Rationality*, ed. Bryan R. Wilson (Oxford: Basil Blackwell, 1977), 88.

108. Tim Weiner, *Legacy of Ashes* (New York: Doubleday, 2007), 159; emphasis added.

109. Edward E. Evans-Pritchard, *Witchcraft, Oracles and Magic among the Azande* (Oxford: Clarendon Press, 1937), 12.

110. Evans-Pritchard, *Witchcraft*, 475.

111. Some of these reasons are that action of a mystical type that transcends experience cannot be contradicted by experience; it is a coherent system whose various aspects explain and reinforce each other; contradictory beliefs are not noticed because they are not brought together simultaneously into opposition; and beliefs are vaguely formulated.

112. Evans-Pritchard, *Witchcraft*, 319.

113. Evans-Pritchard, *Witchcraft*, 72; emphasis in original.

114. In James Frazer's monumental *Golden Bough*, he established the existence of two types of sympathetic magic based on the two great associative principles of similarity and contiguity, namely, homeopathic or imitative magic and contagious magic. The first type assumes that things that resemble each other are the same; the second type assumes that things that are once in contact will always be in contact. Both types of magic tend to work together. Evans-Pritchard investigated the temporal axis of magical action at a distance by concentrating on the oracle, "one of the most important institutions of social life," and its methods of "revealing what is hidden" (*Witchcraft*, 261, 258). His pathbreaking study held that, among the Azande, witchcraft, oracles, and magic were "like three sides to a triangle. Oracles and magic are two different types of combating witchcraft. . . . [O]racles determine who has injured or who is about to injure another by witchcraft, and whether witchcraft looms ahead" (*Witchcraft*, 387). In order to enter the realm of "mystical" powers characteristic of witchcraft and magic, the time and space coordinates of ordinary experience must be overcome. As a result, everything appears to be causally linked to everything else. This is the terrain in which "conspiracy theories" and domino effects flourish. The counterinsurgency chief James Angleton, for example, "a man of loose and disjointed thinking" (Weiner, 276), came to believe that there was a "master plot" run by Moscow that had taken over the CIA.

115. Begoña Aretxaga, "Terror as Thrill: First Thoughts on the 'War on Terrorism,'" *Anthropological Quarterly* 75 (2001): 141.

Epilogue

1. Joseph Heller, *Catch-22* (New York: Simon and Schuster, 1961).

2. Gregory Bateson, *Steps to an Ecology of Mind* (New York: Chandler Publishing, 1972).

3. Jan Solomon, "The Structure of Joseph Heller's *Catch-22*," in *Critical Essays on Catch-22*, ed. James Nagel (Encino, Calif.: Dickenson Publishing, 1972), 79.

4. Jane Mayer, *The Dark Side: The Inside Story of How the War on Terror Turned into a War on American Ideals* (New York: Doubleday, 2008), 58.

5. See Alenka Zupancic, *The Shortest Shadow: Nietzsche's Philosophy of the Two* (Cambridge: MIT Press, 2003), 12–13.

6. Amos Oz quoted in Avishai Margalit, "The Uses of the Holocaust." *New York Review of Books*, 1994, 1, 4, p. 10.

7. Quoted in Tim Weiner, *Legacy of Ashes* (New York: Doubleday, 2007), 9.

8. Weiner, *Legacy*, 7.

9. Weiner, *Legacy*, 514.

10. "Intelligence is a sacred cow. . . . The CIA isn't worth a damn," raged Nixon after one such failure. "Get rid of the clowns," he ordered his new CIA director, James Schlesinger, after he won reelection in 1972. "What use are they? They've got 40,000 people over there reading newspapers" (quoted in Weiner, *Legacy*, 315 and 322.) It was certainly an antipodal view of the popular perception of the CIA as an all-knowing, omnipotent organization.

11. Quoted in Weiner, *Legacy*, 244.

12. The debate about what Moscow was up to during the middle 1970s is a case in point: convinced that the CIA was underestimating Soviet nuclear strength, members of the Foreign Intelligence Advisory Board pressed President Ford to let an outside group make the estimate. It came up with a report that dramatically overstated the Soviet military buildup and led to a vast increase in American military spending. "We were going to be second-rate; the Soviets were going to be Number One," President Ford commented on the alleged Soviet advantage during his presidency (quoted in Weiner, *Legacy*, 191). They were 180 degrees wrong. Like the "bomber gap" of the late 1950s and the "missile gap" exploited by Kennedy (the false claim that the Soviets had five hundred intercontinental ballistic missiles ready to strike at the United States when it actually had four), it was all wrong and all based on the alleged veracity of secret intelligence. It also was conducive to justifying further U.S. militarization. Intelligence had been corrupted and blatantly politicized. The consequences of such ignorance could be dire, as during the Cuban missile crisis, when Kennedy realized how little he understood the Soviet leader's strategy. At one point, Kennedy complained that what Khrushchev was doing was akin to the United States putting medium-range ballistic missiles in Turkey and that would be "goddamn dangerous." He was ignorant that the United States had actually done just that.

13. Quoted in Weiner, *Legacy*, 380.

14. Quoted in Weiner, *Legacy*, 381–82.

15. Richard Helms, quoted in Thomas Powers, *The Man Who Kept the Secrets: Richard Helms and the CIA* (New York: Alfred A. Knopf, 1979), 144.

16. Powers, *The Man*, 153.

17. Carl Ford, quoted in Weiner, *Legacy*, 502.

18. Chantal Hunt and John Hunt, quoted in Frances Stonor Saunders, *The Cultural Cold War: The CIA and the World of Arts and Letters* (New York: New Press, 1999), 395.

19. Quoted in Weiner, *Legacy*, 411.

20. William Webster, quoted in Weiner, *Legacy*, 422.

21. Amis's conversation with Weiner, quoted in Weiner, *Legacy*, 449.

22. See a particularly chilling case in Thomas Powers, *Intelligence Wars: American Secret History from Hitler to al-Qaeda* (New York: New York Review Books, 2002), 337–40.

23. Richard Clarke, *Against All Enemies: Inside America's War on Terror* (New York: Free Press, 2004), 24.

24. See, for example, Martin Bright, "Guantánamo Has 'Failed to Prevent Terror Attacks,'" *Guardian*, October 3, 2004.

25. H. R. Trevor-Roper, *The European Witch-Craze of the Sixteenth and Seventeenth Centuries and Other Essays* (New York: Harper and Row, 1969), 119.

26. Adam Liptak, "Suspected Leader of Attacks on 9/11 Is Said to Confess," *New York Times*, March 15, 2007, A1.

27. Lawrence Wright, *The Looming Tower: Al-Qaeda and the Road to 9/11* (New York: Alfred A. Knopf, 2006), 52.

28. For a further development of this view, see Joseba Zulaika and William A. Douglass, *Terror and Taboo: The Follies, Fables, and Faces of Terrorism* (New York: Routledge, 1996), 78–83.

29. Slavoj Zizek, "The Empty Wheelbarrow," *Guardian*, February 19, 2005, 17.

30. Thus Michael Scheuer, a senior U.S. intelligence officer with almost two decades of experience and credited with knowing bin Laden more than any other American, wrote that bin Laden is "a combination of Robin Hood and St. Francis of Assisi," adding: "Bin Laden and most militant Islamists, therefore, can be said to be motivated by their love for Allah and their hatred for a few, specific U.S. policies and actions they believe are damaging—and threatening to destroy—the things they love. Theirs is a specific target for specific, limited purposes." These are some of the "knowns" to the U.S. intelligence community that must be made unknown for the War on Terror to work (Anonymous, *Imperial Hubris: Why the West Is Losing the War on Terror* [Washington: Brassey's, 2004], 19 and 17).

31. Susan Sontag, "Regarding the Torture of Others," *New York Times Magazine*, May 23, 2004, 24–29, 42.

32. Corinne Maier, *Lo obsceno* (Buenos Aires: Ediciones Nueva Visión, 2005), 25.

33. See Mayer, *The Dark Side*.

34. Georges Bataille, *The Accursed Share: An Essay on General Economy*, vol. 2, *The History of Eroticism* (New York: Zone Books, 1991).

35. Maier, *Lo obsceno*, 39.

36. Arundhati Roy, "The Algebra of Infinite Justice," *Guardian*, September 27, 2001. Quoted in Johnson, *Nemesis*, 2.

37. Walter Benjamin, *The Arcades Project*, trans. Howard Eiland and Kevin McLaughlin (Cambridge: Harvard University Press, 1999), 463. Quoted in Eric Santner, *On the Psychotheology of Everyday Life: Reflections on Freud and Rosenzweig* (Chicago: University of Chicago Press), 87–88.

38. Benjamin, *The Arcades Project*, 463.

39. Quoted in Susan Buck-Morss, *The Dialectics of Seeing: Walter Benjamin and the Arcades Project* (Cambridge: MIT Press, 1989), 73.

40. Walter Benjamin, *Illuminations* (New York: Harcourt, Brace and World), 253.

41. Santner, *On the Psychotheology*, 126.

42. Lawrence Wilkerson, the chief of staff of former secretary of state Colin Powell, quoted in Mayer, *The Dark Side*, 6.

Index